THE PROMISE OF WHOLENESS

THE PROMISE OF WHOLENESS

Cultivating Inner Peace, Mindfulness, and Love in a Divided World

Eric Ehrke

ROWMAN & LITTLEFIELD
Lanham • Boulder • New York • London

Published by Rowman & Littlefield
An imprint of The Rowman & Littlefield Publishing Group, Inc.
4501 Forbes Boulevard, Suite 200, Lanham, Maryland 20706
www.rowman.com

Unit A, Whitacre Mews, 26-34 Stannary Street, London SE11 4AB

British Library Cataloguing in Publication Information Available

Library of Congress Cataloging-in-Publication Data

Names: Ehrke, Eric, 1951– author.
Title: The promise of wholeness : cultivating inner peace, mindfulness, and love in a divided world
      / Eric Ehrke.
Description: Lanham : Rowman & Littlefield, 2019. | Includes bibliographical references and
      index.
Identifiers: LCCN 2018029444 (print) | LCCN 2018031050 (ebook) | ISBN 9781538119822 (elec-
      tronic) | ISBN 9781538119815 (cloth : alk. paper)
Subjects: LCSH: Mind and body. | Inner peace. | Mindfulness (Psychology)
Classification: LCC BF161 (ebook) | LCC BF161 .E385 2019 (print) | DDC 128/.2—dc23
LC record available at https://lccn.loc.gov/2018029444

∞ ™ The paper used in this publication meets the minimum requirements of
American National Standard for Information Sciences Permanence of Paper
for Printed Library Materials, ANSI/NISO Z39.48-1992.

Printed in the United States of America

May this book bring inner
peace, love and harmony to all
those people who spend
sleepless nights wondering why
things are the way they are and
want so much more.

CONTENTS

PROLOGUE

For this feeling of wonder shows that you are a philosopher, since
wonder is only the beginning of philosophy.—Plato[1]

Cultivating inner peace, mindfulness, and love in every area of our life
often feels like three bridges too far. To most of us, the odds of accomplishing these three milestones seem as likely as winning the lottery.
The Promise of Wholeness provides the ancient philosophical foundation and effective strategies to develop inner peace, mindfulness, and
loving relationships. Embodying immortal principles and developing
effective practices to experience our divine origins in the midst of the
divisiveness of everyday life are worthy goals. Reconciling our daily
challenges and merging into mystical union with the divine makes humans feel whole. *The Promise of Wholeness* is a guidebook about love,
mindfulness, and reunification and how to get there from wherever you
are.

Philosophers in ancient Greece used the word *henosis*, which means
unity, oneness, and union, to describe this process of overcoming division (duality) and illusion, which get in the way of this union. Western
and Eastern philosophers considered unity a universal phenomenon
and spiritual connection an eternal aspiration. Since henosis is the actual word used by the immortal philosophers quoted in this book, henosis
will be substituted for the promise of wholeness going forward.

Our world is instantaneous, and this has become the new normal.
The length of time between imagination and actualization is disappearing. Love, however, is eternal but remains an enigma like the purpose

of illusion. Love and illusion represent opposite ends of a very confusing continuum, so enduring wisdom from ancient philosophers is quoted throughout the book for your consideration. The principles and values it takes to be happy and whole endure, but makeovers are needed to modernize the message. Literature, clinical examples from my psychotherapy practice, and personal stories from courageous individuals are significant contributors throughout the book.

With that in mind, I have always wondered why people are cruel and hurt one another, when love seemed so simple and felt spectacular. As a child with a significant stuttering problem, I experienced bullies and cruelty firsthand. My church said God loved me, but most of the time I noticed priests and nuns obsessing about sin and confession—not love. Even as a child, those observations made me wonder about the meaning of life, why humans suffer and whether enduring love truly exists. In adulthood, my questions and thoughts led me to a Greek word for unity, henosis, which describes the journey of the soul and its reunification goal with the divine. Some call enlightenment the experience of "our divinity" while in a physical body. Merging the necessary philosophy, psychology, and practices to experience henosis, or heaven on earth, is complicated and requires unlocking the mysteries of being human. Thus unlocking paradox and the promise of wholeness also became part of my quest.

Discussions about life's purpose always fascinated me, but mostly, I watched people. Enduring love and true happiness proved to be elusive quarries, and I noted when something worked or missed the mark. Resolving life's paradoxes and the mysteries confronting people in their day-to-day lives became my profession, but what philosophy, literature, and psychology teach us about love, happiness, and suffering became my true passion. The often-divergent perspectives on these three potent topics matter and affect billions of lives every day. This book is a culmination of my discoveries, working observations, and practical suggestions gleaned through my lifetime of wonder.

As a psychiatric social worker, clinical psychotherapist, and transformational teacher for more than forty years, I have witnessed both love and human angst on a daily basis. While working with individuals, families, and groups, I learned how humans are deeply affected by larger systems. This book results from clinical experiences, personal observations, and my own awakenings. As a psychiatric social worker, for example, early in my career I noticed when parents and families learned to work together, the symptom bearer within that family almost always immediately got better. I still marvel at how quickly families improve when parents rekindle their marriage and speak in one voice. Families function as one entity with many moving parts. If one member is off, the whole group dynamic is affected. The parenting and relationship classes I led taught partnering skills to support unity in couples, through healthy communication, emotional bonding, and conflict resolution. Every theory and modality was worth studying if it produced positive results for every individual in the larger system.

Because the resiliency of the human spirit inspired me, I studied under many traditional and transformational spiritual teachers. Initially, I trained in classic family systems theory and eclectic modalities such as Gestalt, Jungian, and Ericksonian hypnosis therapies. Merging psychology and spirituality with both Western and Eastern classical philosophies felt natural to me. My perspective is that every philosophy and psychological theory is worth studying if it reveals what love is and what it's not. Psychotherapy is a potent force for good because it helps people heal, release trauma, and become more productive in their lives. The meditative modalities, transcendent philosophies, and complementary healing strategies I gleaned from spiritual teachers were subsequently taught to my clients and helped them not only to survive but more importantly *thrive*.

As a practitioner of family systems theory, I educate families, couples, and bonded groups about intimacy and how to reach their full potential as a unified entity. Emotions and personal reactions get entangled and are interconnected, and I teach people about unconscious empathy and how poor energetic boundaries affect their moods. To help build awareness of how emotional material migrates within groups of people, I explain the Somatic Empathy Theory (see chapter 8), which describes how the surrounding emotional milieu may enter our body and how, at a subconscious level, we will process those emotions as our own. Some of my clients and my daughter have graciously shared their own important discoveries about empathy and emotional contagions that stick like Velcro in this book. In chapter 9, I introduce the Theory of Incorruptibility and how it relates to our soul's reunification goal. The word "incorruptibility" is used generously throughout the book, and my hope is that by the time you finish reading, you will have a new understanding of this word.

Historically, we have relied on storytellers to craft relatable characters so readers could be entertained by the antics of someone similar to us struggling with epic dramas, similar to our own life. When readers experience the story as an observer rather than a participant, the salient issue or why a character makes choices is easier to understand. A storyteller accomplishes this task by constructing compelling, timeless parables and fairy tales filled with heroes we love and empathize with versus villains we love to hate. I have included many hidden gems of wisdom contained within several well-loved examples from philosophers, literature, and motion pictures. By comparing the experiences and emotions of the heroes and villains with the philosophical and psychological concepts addressed in *The Promise of Wholeness*, we can freely explore difficult subjects. Fairy tales thankfully are free from "truth," which allows us to objectively explore their immortal wisdom and empathize with how a character's struggle relates to our own experiences. Many great philosophical masters choose fiction as a method to educate for similar reasons.

History is full of examples of scientific theory and religious dogma that promote accepted truths until future evidence and new discoveries change our paradigm. Pope Urban VIII and the Roman Catholic Inquisition, for example, placed Galileo on house arrest in 1633 until his death for publishing his heliocentric theory suggesting that the earth revolved around the sun because he opposed the accepted opinion. However, I have hope because even in repressive environments flickers of light occasionally pierce the night of accepted dogma. Philosophers accept the noble endeavor of being branded dimwits by their contemporaries and, if lucky, lauded as geniuses posthumously. Sometimes sharing a hard-won perspective and suggesting a novel solution to ease suffering is that important.

If tracked historically, we find that new discoveries activate primal fears and childlike stress responses because change triggers pushback. Convinced that the absolute truth has been captured already, a sedentary mind instinctively grasps a previously accepted theory for security. This is how our reptilian mind (chapter 7) seems to be programmed. Noticing how insecurity and intellectual complacency stifle earnest objectivity, philosophy became a refuge of rationality for many seekers, including myself. The giants of philosophy, who dared to ask the tough questions, built a worthy sanctuary for original thinking a long time ago.

Philosophy is an ancient art form that asks questions, makes observations, and seeks truth by comparing, contrasting, and removing preconceived notions. Truth is relative and rarely stationary, for it is a perception that varies widely depending on our personal experiences. The goal of innovation is to challenge status quos and accepted truths that, by necessity, must evolve to accommodate new discoveries. For example, for more than a century, scientists have believed that our human brain could not produce new neurons, but evidence today has proven that "fact" to be inaccurate. Bold questions open doors and pave the way to new discoveries. Perceptions about how the universe works need to grow as science matures when more vantage points come into focus. As of the writing of this book, quantum theory provides an example of how modern scientific discoveries are exciting not only to physicists, but also to philosophers and theologians, who feel empowered when the ontology they intuitively sensed is proven accurate by current scientific theory.[2]

Philosophers synthesize divergent opinions, seek common denominators, and define universal principles to help humanity transcend suffering, find purpose, and give the life they are leading noble meaning. Psychotherapists ask questions, make observations, and help people transform suffering, resolve problems, and give the life they are leading noble meaning. This transcendence of suffering is accomplished when we recognize illusion and incorporate loving solutions. Philosophers seek the macro meaning and psychotherapists the micro, with both aspiring to reach the same goals—liberate us from suffering, access love, and attempt to resolve the paradoxes of being human. The Greeks referred to their method of reasoning through rational examination of contradictory hypotheses leading to discovery and conclusion as *dialectic*. Plato's famous discussions with Socrates popularized the term and cemented its immortality. A renowned philosopher and former professor of divinity at Cambridge University, Dr. William Ralph Inge (1860–1954) eloquently described the dialectic process:

> Dialectic literally means the art of discussion . . . and does away with the hypotheses, which belong to some sciences and not to others. Such particular hypotheses are only postulates, and we desire to find the non-hypothetical first principle. Dialectic, thus understood, is

the art of discovering affinities of forms or ideas and kinds of catego-
ries with each other. Dialectic is especially concerned with the relationships between Being, Change and Permanence.

It's a science that enables us to reason about each thing, to say
what it is and how it differs from others, what it has in common with
them, where it is, whether it exists, to determine how many real
beings there are, and where not-being is to be found instead of true
meaning. It treats good and evil, of all that is subordinated to the
Good (divine) and its contrary, of the nature of that which is eternal
and of that which is not. It also speaks of all things scientifically and
not according to simple opinion. . . . It traverses the whole domain of
the spiritual, and then by analysis returns to its starting point. Then it
rests, in contemplation of the One (divine), and hands over disquisi-
tions to another art, subordinate to itself.

Dialectic receives clear principles from Spirit, which furnishes
Soul with what it can receive. In possession of these principles, it
combines and distinguishes its material, till it comes to pure spiritual
knowledge. Dialectic is the most precious part of philosophy; all
existing things are "Matter for it"; it approaches them methodically,
possessing things and thoughts in combination. Dialectic, then, is the
study of first principles, which leads to intuitive wisdom. It passes
through logic, and at last rises above it.[3]

In *The Promise of Wholeness*, the term "dialectic discovery" is used
to describe the method and forum for discussing mental, physical, and
spiritual discoveries unburdened by double-blind scientific studies.
Quantum theory has proven that observation and intention do influence
outcomes. We are subjective creatures, so interpretations of a similar
event often vary widely due to individual perspectives and frames of
reference. Even Einstein's theory of relativity states that everything is
moving at a relative speed to everything else. Scientific method requires
a double-blind study with a neutral control group to counter bias and
provide objective results to validate a theory, all of which is not relevant
to dialectic discovery. Intention has power, and a control group with
mixed intentions predictably will produce divergent results.

Our perception of what we believe is real informs our future experiences. The recollection of the resulting belief system and releasing the
emotional sludge that recycles suffering—whether true or false—is a
powerful practice. Reimaging and sculpting an empowering memory
creates sovereignty. Dialectic discovery observes the data, remains

malleable, and only accepts what retains value in future experiences. Standing strong amid the slings and arrows of life takes a significant amount of courage. Staying put, lying down, and remaining small merely recycles it all.

Dr. Inge wrote thirty-five books about ancient philosophy and the dialectic arts. He synthesized the brilliant ideas of many humble philosophers who changed the course of human history. Many claimed that they could see a little further because they "stood on the shoulders of giants," as Isaac Newton famously wrote in 1676. Newton never claimed he was the original author of this quote because it was already five hundred years old and came from Bernard of Chartres, who in 1159 wrote, "We are like dwarfs on the shoulders of giants, so that we can see more than they, and things at a greater distance, not by virtue of any sharpness of sight on our part, or any physical distinction, but because we are carried high and raised up by their giant size."

I believe that one of the giants that Chartres referenced was a Greek philosopher who taught in Rome in the third century. At that time, the Roman Empire, which previously had been a melting pot of cultural and religious diversity, was starting to unravel. Tolerance for ethnic, moral, and religious differences allowed an easier transition for a conquered civilization to assimilate into the Roman society. An unforeseen outcome evolved because disparate religious notions and divergent philosophies merged together into a colossal mishmash of mythology, astrology, and conflicting cosmology throughout the empire. Citizens began to pick and choose the most interesting concepts that spoke to their heart, like patchwork spirituality quilts. Zealots closed ranks to retain religious purity, while the majority of the citizens mixed and matched philosophies. Does this practice sound familiar today?

Philosophers seek similarity within diversity, and many ancient Romans respected the musings of a brilliant Greek philosopher named Plotinus, who stood up and taught about oneness and unity in Rome in 244 CE. During a time in history tragically barren of greatness, this giant was "the greatest metaphysician of antiquity" according to many authors and "one of the most vigorous thinkers that humanity ever produced." Both men and women gathered to hear Plotinus discuss the purpose of life, the nature of the soul, and the divine (which he called The One). Discussing such wisdom with women was uncommon and controversial in ancient times, but this man followed the lead of the philosopher Plato on the topic of teaching women. The records show that at least four of his students were women; one of them was Salonina, the wife of the Roman Emperor Gallienus.

> Nothing can be more absurd than the practice that prevails in our country of men and women not following the same pursuits with all their strengths and with one mind, for thus, the state instead of being whole is reduced to half.—Plato[4]

The great philosophers attempted to understand the angst, suffering, indifference, and depression that have proliferated throughout the ages and show us that we are one and that what we believe creates our paradigm of experience. Yet, even today, a parent in the midst of struggling with the tragic loss of a child might ask, "Why would I create this version of hell?" Others may wonder, "If we are all one and everything is supposed to be so lovey-dovey, why is my partner or boss so clueless? I don't want to be *one* with an idiot!"

In my forty years as a psychotherapist and seeker on the spiritual path, I never imagined that the father of the modern mind/body/spirit self-help movement popular today had walked on this earth about two millennia ago. I was astounded when I discovered that current metaphysical researchers, theosophical authors, and quantum physics theorists are, either intentionally or by "accident," recycling an obscure Greek philosopher's spiritual ontology of the universe.

The forgotten Greek philosopher Plotinus bravely interpreted Plato's writings, added his own insights, and unified these theories by including the perspectives of the most prominent philosophers of his own time. He offered a rationale about the nature of time, illusion, and the universe based upon his own mystical experiences that remains relevant today. At a time when previous Greek philosophers emphasized logic over experience, Plotinus taught in ancient Rome about the human soul, unity consciousness, and how to access oneness.

I was elated to find that the current metaphysical literature isn't "new" but actually revitalized ancient wisdom. This father of the new age worldview completely validated my awareness and the lifetime of clinical experiences I'd gathered. In reality, this man was a giant in his own right and provided the foundation for our current metaphysical understandings as well as universal insights into the purpose of existence. If he were alive today, I would have traveled any distance to listen with my own ears to this man.

A flood of contemporary authors, cinematographers, and spiritual teachers are adding their perspective on why "bad" things happen and offering valuable models about how to escape from our personal and collective hells. One might say that our authors, cinematographers, and teachers today are simply doing as philosophers have always done. So whether that wisdom makes sense or seems trite, contemporary contributions are important. I reference many of these contemporary messages as they provide modern examples of applied philosophical wisdom. Since ancient texts are frequently difficult to comprehend due to outdated language, I will present a brief summary of several sources and translate that inspired wisdom into understandable concepts, everyday language, and practical examples that coincide with my clinical experience as a psychotherapist and healer.

Here, on the pages of *The Promise of Wholeness*, I will continue the tradition of the great philosophers and add my perspectives and experiences as a spiritual explorer and modern clinical psychotherapist to these innovative philosophies in an attempt to present an accurate summary of my own dialectic discoveries about how humans can remain loving and steadfast in a wide range of circumstances.

The Platonic tradition invites students into discussions to expand ideas based on personal insights; so too will I weave my insights throughout the book. And the term "henosis" combines philosophies of the past, present, and future and then offers an opportunity for us to choose the methodology appropriate for our situations that leads us to reunification, or oneness with all that is.

The Promise of Wholeness explores universal questions and the ineffable enigmas of the unifying principles binding humanity together that enchant philosophers. We will quest to find the original, recycled, and/or eternal concepts driving our drama and perplexing paradoxes—the things that defy logic about what it means to be human. Examining what we can do invites experimentation, exploration, and eventually the transmutation of the root of our suffering. Heartfelt passion adds power to our questioning, which in turn determines the depth, quality, and deliciousness of our responses.

Most books give answers, but I believe you will find *The Promise of Wholeness* different. Intelligence is not measured by how much we know, but by the quality of our questions and the courage we dedicate to find accurate answers. I hope reading *The Promise of Wholeness* will help you ask more spectacular questions.

ACKNOWLEDGMENTS

It is said that wisdom and pain are our primary teachers, and like most of us, I am a slow learner. This book would not have been possible without the motivation provided by pain and suffering. My heartfelt gratitude goes out to every illusion that kicked my butt and gave me insomnia. Adversity, bullies, and blamers provided countless all-nighters until newfound solutions soothed my confusion.

To the thousands of clients and patients that walked into my office in the midst of suffering, I honor you, with special thanks to those who consented to have their stories told in this book. Brave souls lighten loads with courageous hearts, and I deeply appreciate our walk together. To my many partners at the Ommani Center and Therapies East Associates over the past thirty-plus years, thank you for your collective wisdom, caring consultations, and mutual dedication to the field of psychology. I want to thank Ragani Buegel, a brilliant acupuncturist/ kirtan artist who worked with our mutual clients suffering from fibromyalgia. Our work together not only benefited Ruth, whose story is included in chapter 8, but also helped inspire the Somatic Empathy Theory. Solving mysteries and their underlying causes lie at the heart of lasting peace and well-being. Working with you has been a pleasure.

My gratitude also extends to my spiritual teachers, who include Consuela Newton, Aleta St. James, and Virginia Fidel, who taught me invaluable information about healing, meditation, and conscious living. The twelve years I spent as a student and faculty of the Inner Focus School of Soul Directed Advanced Energy Healing provided the foundations of my spiritual training. I'm deeply appreciative of the visionary talents of AlixSandra Parness DD and the enlightened faculty that included Laurel Mamet, Marcy Wolter, Paul Ditscheit, and Sheilana Massey DD. To my good friends Gabrielle Laden and Dr. Cynthia Smith, your friendship and wisdom have been inspiring.

Writers need muses, and Kara Catrelle whispered encouragement in my ear during crucial times in my life and I am grateful for her friendship. I'm also appreciative of Jennifer Hawthorne, my initial editor who taught me writing basics during the first incarnation of this book. When Ja-lene Clark entered my life, she immediately recognized the importance of a book combining psychological wisdom, eternal principles, and practical applications. Through four years of developmental editing, mentoring, and multiple revisions, a close friendship was forged. This book would not have been possible without Ja-lene's guidance and her patience and encouragement. With deep appreciation, I want to thank Joanne Sprott for her copy and line editing, which added invaluable, insightful, and necessary refinements. I am grateful to Jo Ann Deck for editing the author's edition of this book and presenting this manuscript to publishers. Jo Ann, you have been a godsend.

It's my honor and joy to acknowledge my wife, Nancy, and my daughters, Elizabeth and Allison, for their help with this book. Nancy's loving and practical nature has been a blessing throughout our marriage, and our adult daughters are cut from the same cloth. Nancy graciously gave me the space I needed to complete the book, and without complaint she handled many life tasks I couldn't due to my writing activities. Nancy and my daughters have consistently challenged me to defend or define my theories whenever they struggled with my perspective, which helped me refine my thoughts. Thank you all for your loving support, intellectual integrity, and emotional honesty, which have enriched our family and made this book grounded and practical. Allison, I deeply appreciate your invaluable additions to this project with your website design and personal story in chapter 8.

And lastly, I want to extend my deep admiration to the brilliant Greek metaphysician Plotinus, who for his multicultural Roman world revitalized the work of Plato; to Plato, whose many insights offer a pathway for modern life; to L. Frank Baum, whose stories often illustrate practical application of classical teachings; and to all the brilliant psychologists and souls mentioned in this book. Together they remind us of the eternal principles and inspired wisdom that create inner peace, mindfulness, and love.

Part I

In part I of *The Promise of Wholeness*, the nature of love and the forms of cherish, grace, and equanimity have their own chapters after Plotinus, an extraordinary Greek philosopher, is introduced in the first chapter.

The principles and values that create inner peace, mindfulness, and love in our lives enable us to transform what no longer serves. Love and illusion lie on a continuum, and accepting why light/dark exists is as important today as any time in history.

Part I explores the love/illusion continuum, the victim/perpetrator paradigm, and the paradox of oneness in diversity, among other topics. The many challenges and philosophical considerations associated with the initial five forms will be presented before part II offers practical strategies and solutions.

I

ANCIENT PERSPECTIVES
ABOUT WHOLENESS

A philosopher questions what is, wonders why not, and aspires to perceive creation through the eyes of the creator. A psychotherapist asks questions to discover why what is "is" and empathizes with the perceptions of his or her clients. A storyteller crafts stories with various characters with strengths, imperfections, and vulnerabilities to teach us about life through the paradoxes and mysteries of human drama. Essentially, all three are doing the same thing—seeing life through the point of view of another person or deity. Similarly, each of these three perspectives will be used throughout this book.

The quest to discover the meaning of life, transcend illusion, and unravel the mysteries of enduring love and happiness perplexes people today, as it has throughout history. Many earnest philosophers have contributed to this honorable endeavor, from Laozi to the Sufi mystic Rumi and from the storyteller-philosopher creators of *The Matrix* films to Frank Baum, the author of *The Wonderful Wizard of Oz*.[1] In fact, every philosopher, psychotherapist, or thoughtful author at one point or another wonders about the purpose of life and the promise of wholeness. No matter what method or medium is chosen—be it fiction or nonfiction—masterful writers and philosophers have aspired, since antiquity, to liberate mankind from pain and suffering by identifying the universal principles that truly enrich us.

Philosophy is embedded in the roots of virtually every pursuit. Wondering why we are here is a noble endeavor, a timeless puzzle many of the Greek philosophers explored. Plato and Aristotle, for example, introduced ancient man to a benevolent universe, transcendent Goodness (the Divine), and unity in Athens, Greece, from 427 to 322 BCE. Later Plotinus (204/5–270 CE) emerged as the preeminent scholar on Greek philosophy in Rome. *Henosis* was the word Plotinus used to define the organizing principle of oneness within the universe; a term that loosely translates to the word *unity* today. Plotinus believed that the sole purpose of being human was for the soul to experience dualism (separateness) and then reunification with The One (divine) while in a physical body. Throughout his life and for approximately twenty years in Rome, this Greek philosopher taught about the spiritual path (darkness to light) and mankind's basic goodness and unity, which he considered the most compelling forces in the universe. His lectures about the nature of evil and time, for example, predated and matched the best information I have ever encountered and are as relevant today as they were in antiquity. Plotinus contemplated (meditated) regularly to deepen his personal experience with The One and described a loving divine presence whose center is everywhere and circumference nowhere.

The two hundred years following the death of Jesus Christ were tumultuous times. The ancient Roman and Greek mythologies were dying, while multiple competing ontologies about the nature of being were birthing. Plotinus is considered the last great Greek philosopher and lived in Rome as its preeminent scholar. He openly disagreed with the early Christian hierarchy about the purpose of life and the nature of the divine. However, two generations after Plotinus's death, Emperor Constantine united a divided Roman Empire and attempted to dismantle his valuable philosophical insights. Fortunately, aspects of Constantine's censorship failed and we can read about Plotinus and his wisdom today.

Like Plotinus and the other philosophers before and after him, the meaning of life has intrigued me. My hope with *The Promise of Wholeness* is to offer practical solutions and successful strategies gleaned from my forty-plus years of clinical experience. The subsequent chapters will reveal how timeless philosophy has merged with current science, spirituality, and psychology. When diversity coalesces into a unity—seekers soon realize, as others have throughout history—then immortal and modern wisdom become indistinguishable. Before we tackle the current problems facing us today, we will go more deeply into our ancestors' understandings.

MERGING THE GREAT PHILOSOPHERS INTO CHRISTIANITY

During the sixth century BCE, the fathers of Greek philosophy explored the complexities of the rational mind, unity, democracy, the love of wisdom, and universal principles like harmony. Many of these philosophical concepts (like mankind's basic goodness, ethics, metaphysics, ontology, and social policies) survived from 600 BCE through the moment Constantine united the Roman Empire and converted it from a hodgepodge of conflicting beliefs to Christianity in 325 CE. The religious hierarchy Constantine established mixed and matched Roman, Gnostic, and Greek philosophy with Christianity to create yet another new theology. During the rule of Constantine, the Council of Nicaea convened to reconcile philosophical differences, establish the divinity of Jesus Christ, and organize Christian thoughts into what the Council believed was most familiar, appropriate, and attractive—therefore acceptable to its citizens.

When the Council concluded that Jesus Christ was the Son of God and equal to God the Father, Constantine immediately had a problem to resolve. Plotinus had a large following and had taught in Rome just seventy years before Constantine ruled. Plotinus was well respected by the people and taught similar beliefs about the soul, but some of his views about human nature conflicted with this new version of Christian theology. Apparently, the three centuries of religious persecution the Christians suffered did not provide Emperor Constantine and his successors with reasons to accommodate divergent opinions. Sopater, the prominent Greek philosopher in Constantine's court, was executed. Many scholars were labeled "pagans," then killed or exiled during this tumultuous time of transition to Christianity as state religion. Temples, libraries, and academies were razed in an attempt to erase incongruent teachings so that the people would eventually forget them. The memory of Plotinus, who had taught in Rome only a couple of generations earlier, needed to be eradicated. Constantine's Christianity repackaged Greek teachings about monotheism, divine forms, and the soul into a hybrid that contained familiar elements of Greek ontology and Christian theology. Constantine understood the importance of creating a new theology to unify the Roman Empire and aid its transition to Christianity. While reading *The Promise of Wholeness*, it is important to understand the possible motivations and benefits to Rome if Plotinus disappeared.

Branding Plotinus and Greek philosophy as "pagan" in ancient, and again in medieval, times allowed Christian spin-doctors to marginalize many important spiritual contributions to Western civilization. Over the centuries, the word "pagan" eventually evolved into a pejorative term that became synonymous with self-indulgent, materialistic, unsophisticated earth-worshipping nonsense. Because of the validity of the elements of that pagan wisdom, no historian today would call Socrates, Plato, or Aristotle heathens or hedonistic; nevertheless the label stuck and diminished their message. Thankfully the writings survived, and those messages are so universal that they align with the basic tenets of most religions.

MONOTHEISM AND THE PHILOSOPHY OF PLOTINUS

Plotinus introduces his thoughts about our divine origins in the following quote. His loyal student Porphyry preserved his lectures, and this quote is taken from Porphyry's book *The Enneads*.

> The material body is made up of parts, each holding its own place, some in mutual opposition and others variously interdependent; the soul is in no such condition; it is not whittled down so that life tells of a part of the soul and springs where some such separate portion impinges; each separate life lives by the soul entire, omnipresent in the likeness of the engendering father, entire in unity and entire in diffused variety.[2]

Plotinus was born in Egypt and spent many years in Alexandria studying, debating, questioning, and then interpreting Plato's writings. Interested in Persian and Indian philosophy, in 243 CE he joined the Roman Emperor Gordian's ill-fated excursion into Persia. After the emperor's assassination by his own soldiers, Plotinus returned to Rome and became the preeminent scholar of the Roman Emperor Gallienus until 268 CE, when illness forced him to retire.

The Western and Near-Eastern civilized world was greatly influenced by Plotinus, knowingly or unknowingly. His spiritual ontology about The One (goodness and the divine), intellect (all known knowledge), and the soul (our divine nature and human purpose on earth) has provided inspiration for countless people since his birth about two hundred years after Christ. The Roman Emperor Constantine and the early Christian religious hierarchy included many of Plotinus's ideas about the nature of the soul into the Christian canon even though they tried to erase its author from history. Near-Eastern scholars also incorporated the philosophy from Plotinus about virtue, rational mysticism, and divine emanation into Islamic and Hindu literature because his perspectives were universal.

Any current philosophical discussion about the nature of the human soul will explore concepts that Plotinus presented to the brightest students of the Roman Empire from 244 to 268 CE. Some historians rate his philosophical contributions alongside Socrates, Plato, and Aristotle. Dr. William Ralph Inge described his admiration for Plotinus as follows:

> I was naturally brought to pay special attention to the great thinker who must be, for all time, the classical representative of mystical philosophy. No other guide even approaches Plotinus in power and insight and profound spiritual penetration. . . . There is no Greek philosopher who did not intend to be an ethical teacher and in Plotinus the fusion of religion, ethics, and metaphysics is almost complete.[3]

So why isn't the name Plotinus on the tip of everyone's tongue? His teachings about the spiritual path (darkness to light), the basic goodness of mankind, and the preeminence of unity/wholeness as the most compelling force in the universe are just as relevant for everyone today as they were in antiquity. I was astounded to discover that his ideas about the nature of evil and time, for example, predated and matched the best information I ever encountered, philosophically or psychologically. He described a loving divine presence whose center is *everywhere* and circumference *nowhere*. Plotinus contemplated (meditated) regularly to deepen his personal experience with The One.

But survival, power, and control preoccupied the mind of ancient man and still dominate the worldview of many cultures today. Roman leaders persecuted religious minorities like the early Christians. Unfortunately, politicians and religious leaders couldn't conceive of a deity absent of total power and control like rulers require on earth. The ideas that The One emanated love throughout creation and was an embodiment of goodness were confusing and perhaps too idealistic. Constantine needed to consolidate a recently conquered empire, and the Christians wanted to control their destiny with an organized religion. I believe the work of Plotinus was thrown into the abyss because he was so forward-thinking.

In my research, I found that Plotinus was a practical man with impeccable ethics. Due to his virtuous and generous nature, acquaintances often appointed Plotinus as their children's guardian. Gentle, brilliant, and otherworldly, he was loved by everyone who met this humble servant of humanity. His devoted pupil Porphyry reported that Plotinus contemplated or meditated regularly and achieved "mystical union with the One" on four separate occasions but was terribly disorganized, like an absent-minded professor.

The foundation and grandest expression of Plotinus's philosophy revolves around his description of divinity or The One. In his ontology, The One emanates forms of itself (e.g., pure love, grace, and the ability to cherish), which serve as divine models for humanity to approximate in the physical world. The One permeates everything throughout the universe and is both unknowable and unfathomable; any attempt to describe The One diminishes its true nature. Plotinus believed that a soul separates from The One to experience life on earth, yet even while our body experiences suffering and happiness, the soul retains its inherent goodness and never loses its divine connection. People are spiritual beings having a human experience, rather than human beings having a spiritual experience. Plotinus contemplated and then provided his own explanation as to why unity and the nature of the soul fascinated him throughout his lifetime.

> Many times it has happened: Lifted out of the body into myself; becoming external to all other things and self-encentered; beholding a marvelous beauty; then, more than ever, assured of community with the loftiest order; enacting the noblest life, acquiring identity with the divine; stationing within It by having attained that activity;

poised above whatsoever within the Intellectual is less than the Supreme: yet, there comes the moment of descent from intellection to reasoning, and after that sojourn in the divine, I ask myself how it happens that I can now be descending, and how did the soul ever enter into my body, the soul which, even within the body, is the high thing it has shown itself to be.[4]

Plotinus encouraged people to contemplate The One to access all knowable knowledge, which the Greeks called intellect. Embodying goodness and healthy principles reminds us of our spiritual essence or soul. Focusing only upon pleasure and/or physical sensations keeps us separate from our soul and its desire to experience mystical union with The One while in a human body. I was fascinated to find out that Plotinus concludes, through deductive reasoning, questioning, dialectic discovery, and his own mystical union with The One, that the characteristic common throughout the universe is unity. He observed that everyone and everything depends on unity; thus unity/wholeness is the universal goal of life. Reunification or enlightenment with the divine is the purpose of our soul's existence.

THE ANCIENT ORIGIN OF THE WORD *HENOSIS*

Our soul rejoices when we express our divine nature and align with the basic goodness of The One. According to Plotinus, a good life entails an internal journey where we move away from solely addressing our physical needs and want to express virtue and the higher forms and embody the wisdom gleaned in contemplation with The One. *Henosis* was the word Plotinus used to describe the soul's journey to reunification with the divine while on earth. "Unity" and "oneness" are wonderful words but, like "love," so overused we need clarification. "Henosis" is an underused Greek term, which bypasses contemporary mindsets, preconceived notions, or previous baggage associated with familiar words that become cliché. Nowadays bookshelves are filled to capacity with buzzwords like "higher consciousness," "oneness," "unity consciousness," "enlightenment," and more. I wanted an accurate term free from contemporary beliefs, and from Plotinus, I found a timeless, underused term. "Henosis" has stood the test of time without being bastardized from its original definition.

The original Greek definition merges two words:

- The translation of "en" or "hen" means one singularity, the realm of oneness or the Ultimate Source that created us all.
- The literal meaning of "osis" indicates a condition or state of being. Many medical conditions end in this suffix due to these shared origins.

When the words "hen" and "osis" are combined, the literal translation means "the state of being one" or "the condition of unity" or—I would add—"the promise of wholeness." Henosis is a *condition* of unity, and this book describes what assists or prevents us from achieving enduring happiness. Here is an insight from Plotinus on unity:

> The integral omnipresence of a unity numerically identical is in fact universally received; for all men instinctively affirm the God in each of us to be one, the same in all. It would be taken as certain if no one asked How or sought to bring the conviction to the test of reasoning; with this effective in their thought, men would be at rest, finding their stay in that oneness and identity, so that nothing would wrench them from this unity. This principle, indeed, is the most solidly established of all, proclaimed by our very souls; we do not piece it up item by item, but find it within beforehand; it precedes even the principle by which we affirm unquestionably that all things seek their good; for this universal quest of good depends on the fact that all aim at unity and possess unity and that universally effort is towards unity.[5]

Plotinus believed we are born with a blank slate (*tabula rasa*) and create our own experiences. The human goal is to become one with our soul and experience henosis. This insight from Plotinus is profound and thought provoking even to this day. To Plotinus, darkness is similar to mud that occasionally splashes on the face of a stainless statue. Wisdom washes away the muck and love restores humans to our natural divine state. Every productive healing modality I encounter today uses the same formula. When love is mirrored to humans, illusions release and people return to wholeness. According to Plotinus, the meaning of life entailed the migration of the inherent goodness of the soul to primordial oneness, while living within a human.

Astonishingly, nearly two thousand years ago, Roman citizens were being taught about unity and that each human, at his or her core, was an aspect of The One (divine). Nothing could wrench us from this unity. Evil and/or the illusions of earth were like mud that washes off a stainless statue, to Plotinus. To modernize his concept, we ascribe meaning to our experiences and the mind categorizes our perceptions as good or bad (mud) based on previous programming. Both good and bad were aspects of The One according to Plotinus. He considered suffering a harsh element of mortal life, an aspect of a purification process revealing illusions that block awareness of our soul and eventually henosis. Plotinus disagreed with the religious leaders and philosophers who thought humanity needed redemption or salvation to experience unity after our lifetime. He taught his students to lead a virtuous life to master the illusions of the physical world. By communing directly with their soul, they could access all known wisdom (called *intellect* in ancient Greece) without a priest or holy man intervening or programming minds on their behalf. The more I studied, the more I realized that Plotinus was amazingly accurate and matched contemporary wisdom. Contemplation, internal reflection, personal experience, and deductive reasoning are essential keys for accessing eternal wisdom and mystical union.

Plato named the ultimate creative principle in nature, which unifies everything in the universe, *goodness*. A hundred years previously, however, a Chinese philosopher named Laozi wrote his timeless masterpiece, the *Tao Te Ching*, about the harmony that exists everywhere in nature. His wisdom about how to lead a virtuous life became known as Tao or The Way. Both men eschewed deities, dogma, and devotion commonly accorded to the ancient gods. Plotinus and Laozi described a transcendent presence that is the peace, love, and harmony flowing throughout the universe and within each of us. Unaware of Laozi and his similar ontology on the other side of the world, Plotinus studied Plato, then named this creative principle *The One* and showed others *the way* to enduring love and happiness, which he called *henosis*. Laozi and Plotinus seem to have traveled similar paths to the same destination.

The Greeks and the Chinese interpreted the wisdom offered by these great men in unique ways appropriate to their cultures. The Greeks struggled with the concepts of *being* and *becoming* due to con-

ceptual limitations of their alphabetic language, whereas conceptual
Chinese characters allowed more room for interpretation. Conflict was
tolerated and debate encouraged by the Greeks, while the Chinese
preferred a consensual model. Athenian politicians were not inclined to
take council from their philosophers and even executed Socrates, while
many Chinese rulers regularly consulted with philosophers to mold
their society. Both ontologies promoted differing reunification strategies but arrived at similar definitions of enduring happiness.

RESURRECTING GOODNESS

Plotinus was a source of inspiration for his contemporaries, but he became a formidable rival of ancient orthodox Christians and a number of
Gnostic scholars. Even though he did believe in one God, Plotinus
disagreed openly with the conservative Christian hierarchy promoting
the original concept of the Holy Trinity (the Father, the Son Jesus
Christ, and the Holy Spirit) that eventually won the approval of Emper-
or Constantine and the Council of Nicaea.

Additionally, Plotinus believed that the human soul is inherently
good since he considered it an aspect of the divine. The Council of
Nicaea chose to continue the concept of a sinful origin for humans
based on the Genesis story of Adam and Eve, which early Christian
writers used to justify the need for a savior/redeemer. One could argue
that the concept of sin gives a religious hierarchy job security—if man is
flawed, he requires a redeemer and an intermediary to save his soul
from eternal fire. Fear of eternal damnation is a powerful tool to motivate and control citizens. The arguments from Plotinus that humanity
didn't need salvation or redemption were diametrically opposed to early
Christian ideology.

What we call self-empowerment today and the inherent goodness of
man didn't fit Gnostic philosophy or an official Christian doctrine that
wanted to create a religious hierarchy or support an emperor intent
upon consolidating control over his empire. So, fifty-five years after the
death of Plotinus, Constantine and those organizing canon law rejected
his philosophy on monotheism and mankind's inherent goodness. Perhaps Constantine and his successors feared that the scholars devoted to

Plotinus would undermine the fledgling Christian state religion; therefore, extermination of all records was necessary.

Constantine and his successors exiled Greek philosophers and attempted to erase any memory of Plotinus. The previous imperial effort to eradicate the Christian movement may have been a factor. Destroying temples and teaching academies with opposing philosophies unwelcomed by leaders was a common practice in ancient times. I believe this is the reason every school that taught Greek philosophy in the Roman Empire was razed and its teachers were either killed or exiled. The Council of Nicaea and subsequent religious authors incorporated the ideas of Plotinus supporting the new Christian theology.

Thankfully, Porphyry, a loyal student of Plotinus, documented his lectures and timeless philosophy in his book *The Enneads*. Intolerant leaders have burned books, killed or exiled the messengers, and quieted dissidents throughout history but without total success. I could happily speculate how much spiritual and political freedom would have flourished around the world if the metaphysical concepts embedded in Greek philosophy explored in this book were embodied worldwide. Humanity could not tolerate concepts promoting a self-actualized citizenry, equality, and universal unity during the Roman Empire. Political and religious leaders still struggle to implement these concepts today. I believe that now is the time to fully resurrect the timeless wisdom Plotinus expressed and put it to good use.

Now that Plotinus has been introduced, we can explore his concept of henosis. Later, using this foundation, we will also explore spiritual insights, literature, and practical methods to create more enduring forms of happiness and access henosis.

THE PLOT IN US

You cannot conceive the many without the one. And at first he would most easily discern the shadows and, after that, the likeness or reflections in water of men and other things, and later, the things themselves, and from these he would go on to contemplate the appearances in the heavens and heaven itself. Until philosophers are kings, or the kings and princes of this world have the spirit and power of philosophy, and political greatness and wisdom meet in one, and those commoner natures who pursue either to the exclusion of the

other are compelled to stand aside, cities will never rest from their
evils—no, nor the human race, as I believe—and then only will this
our State have a possibility of life and behold the light of day.

—Plato[6]

If you spoke with Plotinus, he would tell you that he had happily spent
his life as a traditional philosopher, nobly clarifying Plato's writings and
integrating the prominent philosophers of his time into his work. Philosophers are pathfinders, those who take the time to observe humanity
without regard to social norms—the status quo—and instead explore
the paradoxes and mysteries of being human from the perspective of
the creator. A psychotherapist does not *create* the angst of the client; he
or she asks questions, observes, and offers suggestions to help clients
create more love and happiness by examining what plotlines recycle
suffering.

We all have a *plot in us*, and that plot resembles a sapling growing
under a fence. The twists and turns the sapling takes to grow around
and through the fence to mature into a tree are obvious as long as the
fence remains in place. When the fence is removed, the reason for our
contortions is not so obvious. Family dynamics provide freedom and
obstacles that will either build character or stunt our growth—just like a
gnarly tree curled around a fence. Once we leave our family and the
fence fades away, the adaptations we adopted as a result often appear
distorted or look bizarre to an uninformed eye. Contorted delusions and
stunted emotion can prevent us from recognizing that we are all stainless statues and treasured saplings at our core. Saplings seek light and
survive by twisting and turning around the paradoxical puzzles and obstacles that life provides. Philosophers, therapists, and internal wisdom
invite us to look inside to find the "answer" or the *plot in us*. My desire
is to provide you with what I believe is a coherent map and accurate
directions for growing your soul around that gnarled, convoluted fence
of human drama.

In 1150 Saint Bernard of Clairvaux wrote, "Hell is full of good
wishes and desires," which evolved into the famous proverb, "The road
to hell is paved with good intentions." Intention is the primordial creative impulse that initiates our motivation to grow beyond our family
dynamics, fences, and those confounding paradoxes. I believe that every human endeavor, regardless of its ultimate outcome, originates with
a noble intention. The plots in the human drama are endless, but ulti-

mately there is only one core storyline. *People start with good intentions and either hit or miss the mark.* For example, the hero and the terrorist are at opposite ends of the same plot. Heroes want to help victims but may perpetrate terror depending on what they do to their adversaries. History is replete with heroes liberating victims and succumbing to intoxicating illusions. Power can corrupt and seduce humans to terrorize others to preserve control . . . even heroes with noble intentions.

Human nature at our divine core is the essence of goodness, while the hell we experience comes from our choices due to inexperience, ignorance, or immaturity. (Remember, mud washes off a stainless statue.) Pain and suffering motivate people to grow and contort around obstacles like any young sapling. The salient task is to remember and/or recognize the initial core *need, want, or desire* seeding our original inspiration. Separating this original positive intention from ill-conceived problem-solving strategies is an important activity. We are not indelibly flawed for missing the mark, so after missing it, revisit the positive intention and create another plan to meet the core need, want, or desire until success is experienced.

It is easy to polarize, demonize, and revictimize others and ourselves while we suffer. Perhaps the most difficult challenge for people to comprehend is that both *pleasure and pain* are personal trainers leading us to henosis. Illusion, however, has many guises, so building a good BS detector is advised to create more love and happiness in our lives.

The original symbol depicting the confounding concept of heaven (eternal pleasure) versus hell (eternal pain) is represented in the circle of life, which originated from an ancient image of a snake eating its own tail (*ouroboros*). The snake image evolved from the circle into a figure eight/infinity shape. Think about it; two opposite ends (human and soul) become one (divine) and morph into the infinite (oneness). That very poetic image of the concept of infinity is repeated in many cultures, for example, traditionally both the snake in the West and the dragon in the East represent transcendence. Additionally a popular belief today is that a powerful spiritual energy, called kundalini, located at our sacrum and *coiled like a serpent*, travels up our spine as our illusions clear.

In the eighteenth century, historians revived Plotinus, categorizing his expanded explanations of Plato's teachings as the Neo-Platonic school of philosophy. Porphyry, his devoted pupil, summed up his life in these words:

He left the orb of light solely for the benefit of mankind. He came as a guide to the few who are born with a divine destiny and are struggling to gain the lost region of light, but know not how to break the fetters by which they are detained; who are impatient to leave the obscure cavern of sense, where all is delusion and shadow, and to ascend to the realms of intellect, where all is substance and reality.[7]

I find Porphyry's statement profound, liberating, and hopeful. In today's language, Porphyry's use of the word *sense* refers to our physical/animal lower nature mired in delusion.[8] Plato, and later Plotinus, called the highest attributes—virtues and qualities humans possess—divine *forms*. Before I introduce you to the specific forms that will appear in future chapters, a synopsis of Plato's and Plotinus's original definition of a form is needed.

A PRIMER ON FORMS

Plato and Plotinus believed the physical world was created from the union of being and not being, same and different, the one and the many. Plato's Theory of Forms states, in essence, that the ideal properties of a virtue, principle, or value necessary to reunite with the divine are transcendent and timeless. A form is considered a perfect template of actualized wisdom and/or the complete realization of an ideal principle or quality for humans to emulate. Incorporating a form into daily practice is the ultimate challenge to become whole.

Unbounded by space and time, a form energizes and inspires self-realization, which I believe is why Plato considered forms more important than physical objects in the tangible world. The eight form meditations and related materials are presented in subsequent chapters in the following order: Illusion, Love, Cherish, Grace, Equanimity, Empathy, Incorruptibility, and Wholeness.

In ancient Greece, matter was an object with unrealized potential that humanity could experience, sense, and/or activate. A divine form, or realized wisdom, could fully energize physical matter to achieve spiritual unity. Matter possessed potential, while a form provided humans the possibility for its full physical expression. The future and the past were considered mental distractions, because The One, the soul, and the physical body existed in the infinite present from Plotinus's perspective. He believed that The One energizes the soul and a soul motivates a human being to learn how to become incorruptible. Forms help humans realize their potential, and each soul aspires to embody the divine forms on earth. Only through the highest realms of reason, intuition, and contemplation could humans tap into what Plotinus considered all known wisdom and access their divinity.

The following quote from Plotinus speaks to the purpose of a form from his perspective:

> Newly awakened it is all too feeble to bear the ultimate splendor. Therefore the Soul must be trained—to the habit of remarking, first, all noble pursuits, then the works of beauty produced not by the labor of the arts but by the virtue of men known for their goodness: lastly, you must search the souls of those that have shaped these beautiful forms.
>
> But how are you to see into a virtuous soul and know its loveliness?
>
> Withdraw into yourself and look. And if you do not find yourself beautiful yet, act as does the creator of a statue that is to be made beautiful: he cuts away here, he smooths there, he makes this line lighter, this other purer, until a lovely face has grown upon his work. So do you also: cut away all that is excessive, straighten all that is crooked, bring light to all that is overcast, labor to make all one glow of beauty and never cease chiseling your statue, until there shall shine out on you from it the godlike splendor of virtue, until you shall see the perfect goodness surely established in the stainless shrine.
>
> When you know that you have become this perfect work, when you are self-gathered in the purity of your being, nothing now remaining that can shatter that inner unity, nothing from without clinging to the authentic man, when you find yourself wholly true to your essential nature, wholly that only veritable Light which is not measured by space, not narrowed to any circumscribed Form nor again diffused as a thing void of term, but ever immeasurable as something greater than all measure and more than all quantity when you perceive that you have grown to this, you are now become very vision: now call up all your confidence, strike forward yet a step—you need a guide no longer—strain, and see. [9]

Plotinus reminds us that illusions, such as power, control, and unworthiness, are just splatters of mud on a stainless statue. Plato and

Plotinus believed the purpose of education was not only to gain wisdom, but also to learn how to consistently incorporate the principles and values within the forms. Mud was a metaphor Plotinus used to describe the form of illusion. Forms were considered a living entity of conscious awareness, and washing off what diminished beauty was a loving act. The form of love, for example, guides us to our stainless, soul-like qualities and the unlimited potential for enduring happiness.

The forms are simple in themselves but complicated by our personal perceptions, triumphs, and struggles. Incorporating the forms into a daily practice enhances mindfulness and soulfulness. By the time you finish reading *The Promise of Wholeness*, my hope is that you will have experiential understandings of the form meditations and become comfortable with the methods and techniques in the addendum I recommend for incorporating these principles in your everyday life.

MANKIND ENSLAVED BY SHADOWS

As we become incorruptible to illusion and embody more of the forms, we liberate ourselves from suffering. Thousands of years ago, an Eleusinian Mystery[10] called *metempsychosis* (or transmigration of the soul) created many shackles binding humanity to the concept of divine rewards and retribution. Metempsychosis is an ancient Hellenic concept originating from the Orphic religion. This tradition believes that after our death, the soul transmigrates into a human being or possibly an animal based upon the qualities a person exhibits during life. A deity sits in judgment and either punishes or rewards the soul. Penance or indulgences mitigate the punishment in a subsequent life, while grace and redemption from the gods secure higher status in future incarnations. Self-purification and virtue produce favor and a higher form of reincarnation.

During Eleusinian Mystery ceremonies commemorating metempsychosis, a follower would enter a dark cave, contemplate with Hades, eat the raw flesh of a bull, and drink wine to absorb the essence of Dionysus to aid them on their journey upward toward the heavens. Dionysus was the Greek god associated with a religious ecstasy called *enthousiamos* (enthusiasm), which meant "to be inspired by a god." Those who drank from the river of *Lethe* (forgetfulness) would remain lost as an indication that they had forgotten their divine nature. Those who consumed the waters from the river *Mnemosyne* (memory) were allowed access to the upper chamber of the cave. Brilliant light, sacred artifacts, and omniscient experiences revealing the unity of god awaited them in the abode of the blessed.

Thus divine judgment, dualism (body as evil and the soul divine), and codes of conduct entered Hellenistic thought. Being a human in the Orphic tradition required purification. Images of what we now call hell, purgatory, and heaven may have been seeded in these and other ancient ceremonies. Many religions have similar mysteries about atonement, hope, mystical union, and redemption embedded within similar philosophical bedrock. The Council of Nicaea may have modified the concept of metempsychosis when Christian law was canonized into concepts such as heaven and hell.

Plato rejected most of the Orphic teachings but did accept the opposing nature of our body and soul that we commonly associate with dualism. He also thought humanity was rewarded or punished upon death, while Plotinus rejected this notion. Some Greek philosophy scholars wonder whether the Eleusinian Mystery ceremony honoring the Orphic principle of metempsychosis just described inspired Plato to write his "Allegory of the Cave." Decide if you agree or disagree after reading my summary of his allegory.

INTERPRETING PLATO'S ALLEGORY OF THE CAVE

The following "Allegory of the Cave" summary and interpretations are my own. Plato's depiction of what I call our primary love templates, the form of illusion, and our human quest to ascend to henosis together form a timeless depiction of the paradox of being human.

A group of prisoners are chained together to the floor of a cave since birth, unable to move their heads from side to side; therefore the prisoners only have the capacity to see what is in front of them. The prisoners feel emotions but can't see that a fire burns brightly behind them and beyond their view. Between the roaring flames and behind their backs is a walkway.

Flickering shadows and reflections dance on the wall in front of the prisoners. Since birth they have been enchanted by those images and, for entertainment, make predictions. The distorted reflections generated are their primary template of what reality is because this is all they have ever known. They predict what the shadows will do next, compete with their friends, and rejoice when they accurately anticipate the movements of the reflections. What the prisoners do not see is that people are making gestures and placing cutout symbols or forms near the fire to create fantastic, convoluted, gnarled images on the imperfect surfaces of the cave wall.

One day, a prisoner breaks free from his shackles and realizes he is in a dark cave and explores what else exists. As he makes his departure, he turns around to see the people holding the cutouts before the fire that created the shadowy figures on the wall he mistook for reality. He realizes that what he thought was real was only a form of illusion that was created by people he never knew existed. He leaves the cave, confused by his realization. When he exits, he is blinded initially due to the bright sunlight outside but loves the warmth of the sun—so different from the fire.

Seeing his own reflection for the first time in the river nearby is a revelation, and gradually, the prisoner's eyes adjust to his new world. Like every good philosopher, he begins basing his decisions upon his observations and personal perceptions. Freedom from the cave of illusions provided an opportunity to experience henosis.

In summary: Humans are chained from birth to illusions based on our perceptions, which create suffering. We, the prisoners, see reflections that we mistake for reality and then create primary templates and personal paradigms to make our experiences more predictable (e.g., Lovers always leave me. I did (blank) therefore I am not worthy. Love always hurts.). These primary templates about the nature of love originate from the form of illusion and are modeled by our families.

> Be empty of worrying. Think of who created thought! Why do you
> stay in prison, when the door is so wide open?—Rumi[11]

If we possess the courage to exit the cave, the freedom to choose how to interact with the physical world and the other prisoners is our decision as Rumi suggests. How we interpret the nature of reality, our divinity, and goodness/henosis is based upon our own perception. Plato taught that accepting new "forms" of reality requires the practical knowledge that comes from one's own observation and private inspiration.

I believe that Plato created this allegory to make the following observation: Everyone is imprisoned at birth with primary love templates, belief systems, and personal paradigms based upon ancestral, societal, and religious models. Enlightenment occurs when we unshackle our minds from the illusions attempting to organize prisoners into herds. If we remain solely concerned with safety and security and never have an independent thought, we risk becoming imprisoned by illusion and therefore suffering. Plato suggests that passivity and a lack of curiosity imprison us in illusion and shadow. Our divinity and goodness must be perceived through our own senses and actual experience.

Plato and Plotinus thought that practical wisdom came from direct observation and personal experience. This maturation process involves our mind, body, and spirit embodying the essential principles, values, and forms into the fabric of our being. Maturity occurs when we find the courage to peek behind our "story" and unlock the plotline of our lifetime of experiences—that continuously create shadows and distort our perception. The courage it takes to crawl out of our cave of illusions propels humans to self-actualize, transform delusion, and eventually learn how to become incorruptible.

In the motion picture *The Wizard of Oz* (1939), the film shifted from black and white to Technicolor when a Kansas twister deposited Dorothy Gale into a new paradigm, just like an escaped prisoner from Plato's cave. Dorothy Gale needed time to adjust to her new circumstances, and Glinda the Good arrived in a ball of light and gave her permission to explore Oz unshackled. When Plato's prisoner wised up to the illusions shackling his peers, he developed a new relationship with sunlight, goodness, and his soul through personal experience. Similarly in Oz, Dorothy released her remaining shackles when she realized she always had the power to return home.

Humans learn how to become incorruptible through trials by fire, like Dorothy eventually does in *The Wizard of Oz* by maintaining her principles when nothing seems to be working. This process allows us to turn our heads to see the spiritual reality and the people behind the scenes holding up the confusing cutouts creating our templates and paradoxical shadows. Incorporating the purest attributes and embodying the values within each form provide a reliable method to return to Kansas (or henosis).

Socrates and Glaucon ended their cave dialogue by exploring what happens to people after the experience of an a-ha moment. In summary, the dialogue shows that people are usually dragged kicking and screaming to face their templates/paradigms before they can release and feel the incorruptible wisdom that shines from within.

> I must go beyond the dark world of sense information to the clear brilliance of the sunlight of the outside world. Once done, it becomes my duty to go back to the cave in order to illuminate the minds of those imprisoned in the "darkness" of sensory knowledge.—Plato[12]

Plato thought that, once awakened, an ex-prisoner like Socrates would be compelled to share what they learned because sharing wisdom was preferable to silence. The sad fact is that most cave dwellers are sedentary creatures, believe what is familiar, and may even want to kill people for sharing the wisdom that rattles what is believed to be comforting truth. In fact, Socrates concluded it was his duty to teach others what he had learned and was executed for his beliefs in 399 BCE. He said, "I would not yield even to one man against the just because of a fear of death, even if I were to perish by refusing to yield."[13]

The award-winning films *The Matrix* (1999), *The Matrix Reloaded* (2003), and *The Matrix Revolutions* (2003) were written by the Wachowski siblings and used Plato's Allegory of the Cave and Theory of Forms as two of their inspirational resources. This modern science-fiction thriller portrayed that a truer reality existed beyond the illusions of modern man, who was imprisoned in a virtual-reality dream state. Many philosophy professors use video clips from these films to illustrate Plato's relevancy today.

THE QUEST FOR UNIFICATION

When a piece of literature remains relevant for a thousand years, ancient wisdom and timeless philosophy are brilliantly woven into the fabric of the story. A legendary poem written between 1181 and 1191 CE by the French poet Chretien de Troyes, *Perceval, the Story of the Grail* is such a tale. The original poem describes a young man's struggle with duty, honor, and the nature of true happiness as he matures into knighthood, serves his king, and quests to find the Holy Grail.

At least three subsequent authors added to the poem that eventually evolved over time into the famous story of King Arthur and the Knights of the Round Table. Historians love to debate whether King Arthur actually existed while romantics relish the love triangle between King Arthur, Sir Lancelot, and Guinevere. Some say this medieval allegorical tale was inspired by spiritual practices used by the Templar Knights. When a king, queen, knight, and/or wizard in a fable struggle with similar flaws bewitching us all, the morals within the story gain universal appeal. Paradoxical illusions and perplexing problems must be resolved before the quest to return to henosis is complete.

Chretien de Troyes wrote his metaphorical poem as a parable about alchemy, where a base metal, in this case a human boy, transmutes himself into gold (self-healing, then reunification/enlightenment). Through the transformative spiritual initiations described in the poem, a knight can possess the Holy Grail. The grail has been described as an ark, a bowl, a chalice, or a salver—a tray composed of precious metal. Its original spelling was *graal*, which some associated with a woman or *sangraal*—royal bloodline. Perhaps it was intentionally named to confuse the uninitiated in ancient times and to avoid religious persecution from Rome or heresy charges, all of which inevitably led to the Templar Knights' demise in 1312.

The noble principles and values explored in the Holy Grail fable continue the conversation about the universal qualities necessary to return to henosis. This legendary tale about the challenges put before Perceval, the Fisher King, and eventually King Arthur provides metaphors about what it takes to master the forms. Keys to unlocking shackles and resolving the paradox of being human are woven within the story because examples about how one becomes incorruptible are invaluable. Chivalrous, Perceval and King Arthur rejected others' illusions, perceived the world with their own eyes, and served a greater noble cause. On this subject, Dr. Inge writes:

> The Soul is "deceived" and "bewitched" by the charm of sensuous things, which bear an illusory resemblance to the world of Spirit.
> It beholds itself in the mirror of Matter, and, like Narcissus, falls in love with the image, and plunges in after it. The whole duty and happiness of a spiritual being is to remember that "its source must be also its end." [14]

In the original poem, *Perceval, the Story of the Grail*, the Fisher King's unsuccessful attempts to heal his wounds in the temporal world mirror the universal struggle of man to navigate earthly illusion without possessing a strong spiritual/soul connection. The perpetual agony of the king represents humanity's cycles of suffering due to its failure to unify our human and divine natures. This story was modernized into an award-winning movie entitled *The Fisher King* (1991) about a long-suffering woman who agonized about what to do with her emotionally disconnected partner who didn't understand her needs and had his own illusions about happiness or his life's purpose. Peace, love, and harmony descend upon Perceval, the Fisher King, and other characters within this story as they mature and become whole.

Perceval's mythological quest to find the Holy Grail, which some imagine Jesus may have drunk from during the Last Supper, is another appealing or enjoyable aspect about the story. But I believe the story captivates and powerfully endures because it provides an accurate metaphor that describes humanity's collective mythical journey to find the meaning of life and resolve the eternal mystery around the actual nature of enduring love and inner peace. For me, the Holy Grail symbolizes humanity's quest to unify its physical and spiritual nature to reach enlightenment and/or henosis. The heroes and heroines in these stories face many fearsome dragons and inner demons. Maintaining their principles, facing illusion head on, and releasing their private delusions made them truly incorruptible.

Stories like these offer heartwarming strategies to escape the allegorical cave of shadows that Plato presented to humanity. "Coming of age" epics provide enduring navigational maps toward the forms that reflect our basic human desire to discover our very own "Holy Grail." Our true spiritual nature is pure joy, love, and happiness. Feats of accomplishment like fulfilling a quest, falling in love, or healing our "Fisher King" wounds provide a profound joy and heartfelt satisfaction reminiscent of our divine birthright. When experiencing success or the transcendent, it's so powerful that it does feel like we just *crawled* out of a cave or *arose* out of a deep slumber. Once aware, no one forgets or wants to become lost again. The recurring theme in the retellings of this parable reminds the reader that those who drink from the cup of everlasting life (leave the cave) will rise from the dead (resolve their dysfunctional templates and paradigms) and find henosis (sun).

In their objective aspect Body, Soul and Spirit [divine] are respectively, the world as perceived by the senses; the world perceived by the mind as spatial and temporal order; and the spiritual world. The organs which perceive the world under these three aspects are bodily senses, discursive thought and spiritual perception or intuitive knowledge. Of these, the last alone perceives the world as it really is, sub specie aeternitatis [universal perception]. It is only when we exercise this highest faculty of our nature, "a power which all possess but few use" that we ourselves are completely real and in contact with reality. This reality is neither an independently existing external universe, nor a subjective construction thrown off by the mind. It is constituted by the unity in duality of the spiritual faculty and the spiritual world, which it "beholds" in exercising self-consciousness.

—William Ralph Inge[15]

NOW THAT YOU HAVE BEEN INTRODUCED TO HENOSIS, WHAT'S NEXT?

When Paramahansa Yogananda introduced ancient Indian practices, the philosophy of yoga, and its rich meditative tradition to Americans in 1920, passion for Eastern philosophy and its rich traditions exploded throughout the Western hemisphere. Eastern philosophy's popularity has continued to expand around the world while interest in Greek and ancient philosophy has greatly diminished. Passion for philosophy waxes and wanes, but few people realize that Plotinus mastered all the Greek traditions, was a brilliant teacher recognized throughout the Roman Empire, and inspired countless Western and Middle Eastern philosophers. Plotinus didn't just introduce henosis (unity) to the world, *he helped create it*. In his book *Studies in Comparative Philosophy*, Swami Krishnananda described the universal appeal of Plotinus in the following manner: "Plotinus, the celebrated mystic, comes nearest in his views to the Vedanta philosophy, and is practically in full agreement with the Eastern sages, both in his theory and his methodology."[16]

The Wachowski siblings turned the timeless wisdom of the Greek philosophers into a brilliant cutting-edge science-fiction motion picture trilogy in the *Matrix* series. These productions are visual treasures depicting how quantum physics and philosophical concepts create our world in graphic detail. *The Wonderful Wizard of Oz*, which depicts

Dorothy's return home to Kansas, is a fairy tale metaphor for the yellow brick road to henosis. Practical examples and analogies from literature/ films, like those just referenced, will continue to be provided in future chapters to show how ancient wisdom has been woven into contemporary examples to improve our understanding.

Every one of us has an opportunity to objectively review our illusions and create henosis individually and collectively. My fondest hope is that the eight forms explored in this book will release your cave shackles and become your yellow brick road to henosis. Complex concepts anchor more securely with successful experiences, so I include suggestions and recommended courses of action throughout *The Promise of Wholeness*. From my personal and professional experiences, intention, passion, and action when unified are powerful tools able to transcend and transform any situation. A practical Camel Wave Meditation designed to help you incorporate the forms of illusion, love, cherish, grace, equanimity, empathy, incorruptibility, and henosis into your daily lives is located in appendix A.

The upcoming chapters will provide philosophical insights, literary examples, and psychological wisdom to lay a sound foundation for henosis. We will explore the purpose and paradoxes of being human, including the nature of love, suffering, anger, and what I call the victim/ perpetrator paradigm. The polarizing topic of terrorism and the challenge to develop an incorruptible human solution will be approached in depth from multiple angles. Contemporary discoveries about the brain and exercises from my clinical experience as a psychotherapist and transformational teacher will be provided so readers can take what I share and apply it to their own research or personal pursuits.

Over the years I have noticed many emotionally sensitive individuals, myself included, who were completely unaware of how emotional energy moves between people. Self-critical of my mood swings and unaware of the need for energetic boundaries, I developed somatic-related empathy problems. Chapter 8 includes the Somatic Empathy Theory and assessment tools for self-diagnosis, practical remedies, and clinical examples, so that sensitive individuals can turn this ability into an asset.

The ability to remain incorruptible to illusion, especially when nothing we do seems to be working, is a massively important skill to master the closer we get to henosis. When a theory and my clinical experience have repeatedly aligned and provided consistent results, I include the supporting indigenous wisdom, quantum theory, psychology, and ancient philosophy to consider. While this is a lot of information to consider, all of these topics are included in *The Promise of Wholeness* to provide a more complete foundation to both the casual reader and the professional.

It is said that the level of love we attain during our lifetime is all we take with us when we die. The path of our soul is an arduous journey into the perplexities of a paradoxical world of light and illusion. Shared human dramas provide us with the motivation to return to our divine origins. Even though the roots of Plotinus's philosophy were cast aside many years ago, I believe it endures and remains as relevant today as it was two thousand years ago.

2

ILLUSION AND THE PARADOX OF BEING HUMAN

THE FORM(S) OF ILLUSION

Illusion provides opportunities for humans to explore what love is not. Pain is a precious tool, prying our hearts open and pointing us toward our destiny. Childhood trauma and/or the absence of love foster illusions of separateness, abandonment, and/or isolation and are quite difficult to overcome. Suffering can either cause us to recycle our illusions or speed up our emotional maturation process. Becoming aware of our primary love templates and victim/perpetrator paradigms will liberate us from suffering and help us discover what love is.

Basic human nature categorizes things as good or bad, right or wrong, positive or negative. Love is considered a noble, sweet, or sublime experience, while pain—which may actually be the catalyst that initiates events that ultimately expand our ability to love—is judged to be problematic, a curse, a punishment, or at least something to be avoided. If someone said to you, "There, there. . . . Don't worry, your pain and suffering have good purpose! Just find your positive intention and learn your lesson, and you'll understand why this hurts and learn from the experience," would you feel comforted by such a response? To say that there is a "good" purpose for pain sounds hollow when our heart is breaking.

People recoil from suffering, yet pain has a destiny. As much as we may desire to ignore it or hide it, pain illuminates our illusions hidden in the shadows. Illusion is the creative force motivating us to create love from its opposition. Once we recognize that the form of illusion serves a good purpose by pointing out poor coping strategies and mistaken belief systems, we can sort out the source of our suffering. Real change takes time, however; as Aristotle observed, "For as it is not one swallow or one fine day that makes spring, so it is not one day or a short time that makes a man blessed and happy."[1]

To Aristotle, happiness was an ongoing stable dynamic that, using our terminology today, occurs during the maturing process of *self-realization*. Paramahansa Yogananda (1893–1952) moved from India to the United States and founded the Self-Realization Fellowship in 1920, which introduced meditation, yoga, and the art of balancing one's body, mind, and soul, or self-realization, to the West. Believing in the unity of all religions, Yogananda defined self-realization as follows: "the knowing—in body, mind, and soul—that we are one with the omnipresence of God; that we do not have to pray that it come to us, that we are not merely near it at all times, but that God's omnipresence is our omnipresence; that we are just as much a part of Him now as we ever will be. All we have to do is improve our knowing."[2] From a Western perspective, self-realization is the fulfillment of one's own potential (talents and abilities), but the Eastern definition includes an incorruptible knowledge of our true self (our divinity) beyond delusions of paradox and duality. By cherishing ourselves in every circumstance and accepting our divinity, we can experience the enduring happiness related to self-realization.

Suffering and illness provide opportunities for us to discern love from illusion. Bookshelves today are filled with books about manifesting principles and how like attracts like. These books say all we have to do is focus on positive intentions and desired outcomes. If we just visualize what we want coming to us, we'll heal, be happier, love more, get that great job, become amazingly wealthy, or find the perfect mate. Just ignore the bad stuff and it will go away. Envision success and it will be yours. Positive thinking is beneficial, but this strategy fails to take into account that we were designed to experience duality. The most primal part of our brain is designed to alert us about what may cause harm or kill us to ensure survival.

Duality is a paradox, suspended in the tension created by its opposition; its true nature is fluid and complex. Suffering creates desire, and inspired actions create love. Like does attract like, but unified polarities have purpose. For example, we have a pleasure/pain continuum, a unity/indifference continuum, a love/hate continuum, and so forth. Points within a continuum are perceived as separate entities, but these divisions are aspects of a singular continuous divine whole designed to teach us about reciprocity. Complications arise when we desire to experience a preferred point within a continuum without acknowledging the purpose of contrast, opposition, and the multiplicity within unity. This dynamic is confusing and paradoxical to most of us—and the definition of a paradox is a situation, person, or thing that combines contradictory features or qualities. Physical experience has tension and opposition in contrast to the actuality of our soul constantly residing in oneness. Our human challenge revolves around understanding why the divine created so much diversity within divinity. The protagonist and antagonist oppose one another, but both are necessary parts of a reciprocal relationship within a greater story about wholeness.

PROTAGONISTS AND ANTAGONISTS

> For there is no Form of Evil. . . . But the nature which is opposed to
> all form is privation.[3]

Plato and Plotinus did not consider people "evil" due to negative behaviors and offered humanity a gentle but revolutionary perspective about punishment compared to Hammurabi's (c. 1810 BCE–1750 BCE) an eye-for-an-eye philosophy. When the Greek philosophers modernized that idea, those considered evil were lost in illusion and played the role of antagonist leading us, the protagonist, to our destiny. The protagonist and antagonist play reciprocal roles on opposing ends of the same continuum representing differing perspectives within a greater story. The antagonist pokes, prods, and tortures the protagonist until a choice is made. In other words, illusion lets us experience negative circumstances in order to encourage us to seek enlightened responses and eventually become incorruptible. Plotinus believed that all of our experiences are very real to us on the physical plane but are illusionary spiritually. Therefore it was likely that "the evil one" was a soul playing a vital role as an actor wearing an ill-fitting human body as an appropriate costume. In his ontology, the soul separates from The One, which causes a nagging spiritual itch needing to be scratched until we achieve reunification. Our challenge is to wake up from the seduction of illusion and unite our heart and soul while still wearing that human costume of the body. Plotinus's perspective on this topic follows: "For it is the part of the soul that is in the body that sleeps; but the true awakening is a true getting up from the body, not with the body. Getting up with the body is only getting out of one sleep into another, like getting out of one bed into another; but the true rising is a rising altogether away from bodies."[4] Some of us think we have achieved transcendence and then really struggle if our suffering returns. Yes, good times are wonderful and love is our preferred state, but it is important to realize that suffering has a starring role at the other end of our reciprocity continuum. Suffering will relentlessly point us, and not in a gentle way, to our destiny. Images from media of human exploitation, poverty, and war remind us of the abundance of agony. When we are inundated with these images of terrorism or homicide daily, it's difficult to focus only on loving, optimistic thoughts. When we are suffering and barely surviving, grace and enlightened outcomes seem inaccessible. While mourning the death of family members after a terrorist attack, the idea of cherishing our enemies seems ridiculous. When tragedy strikes, it doesn't take long before one wonders, "Where is this love that people speak about? Do we have an absentee deity? Why am I in this mess?"

Punishment, fighting back, and/or demanding retribution are unsustainable solutions because punitive acts create polarity and an us-versus-them circle of trauma. To punish an antagonist or adversary, we must become a judge and executioner, which may keep us in the mindset of victim and/or perpetrator merely recycling pain. Unresolved suffering is often buried deep within each participant. Many antagonists were victimized and unwittingly become perpetrators by pushing pain onto others due to unexamined suffering. Forty years plus of clinical experience working with both perpetrators and victims have convinced me of this fact. Predators need to be held accountable and society protected, but punitive actions without the necessary wisdom gained from reconciling trauma and accepting responsibility can recycle generational trauma and deepen victim/perpetrator paradigms. When the hearts of both the protagonist and antagonist heal, a pathway for feeling worthy of love reopens. Dr. Seuss addresses this dynamic in *How the*

Grinch Stole Christmas, when the Grinch makes the transition from being wounded and stealing the Whos' Christmas to opening his heart:

> And what happened then? Well, in Whoville they say
> That the Grinch's small heart grew three sizes that day!
> And then the true meaning of Christmas came through,
> And the Grinch found the strength of ten Grinches, plus two!
> And now that his heart didn't feel quite so tight,
> He whizzed with his load through the bright morning light
> With a smile to his soul, he descended Mount Crumpet
> Cheerily blowing "Who! Who!" on his trumpet.[5]

Love grew in the Grinch's wounded heart, his strength returned, and his soul smiled. Love is the most powerful force in the universe. Gentleness, tolerance, and compassion are choices we can choose over recycling pain. The Grinch demonstrated how the antagonist can flip-flop roles to become a protagonist. Healing victim and perpetrator behavior requires a tedious journey back to reconcile with the source of our wounding. Everyone gets lost in illusion, recycles suffering, and wonders if the wrongs plaguing humanity will ever heal. Apocalyptic predictions abound, and feeling small compared to a worldwide issue like terrorism is common. A popular belief today claims that we "create our reality." So if recycling the shadows we mistake for reality and fighting off the "Grinches" within humanity are our only choices, then what's the point? There is a lot of information out there to sort through and many people claim to know the answer. Yet those answers can seem placating and taking responsibility for global unrest feels overwhelming. What could be worth all this trouble? All this suffering dividing us must have a purpose. Everything has a purpose.

Religions have borrowed their definitions about the purpose of pain from many sources, including the Greek concept of *transmigration*, which described deities sitting in judgment and doling out punishment to motivate humans to become more civilized. Religions with punishing deities have reinforced the notion of retaliation, retribution, and righteous indignation, which have historically led to inquisitions, atrocities, and genocides. Now, the reflex to punish others and/or yourself is a misunderstood thought seed buried deep in the mind of humanity. In the mid-1300s, for example, men used self-flagellation to ward off the Black Death, believing if they suffered like Christ, loved ones would stop dying.[6] Sadly, self-punishment as a strategy to achieve goodness failed to create good and punishment by incarceration has not eradicated crime. War has not eliminated war. Punishment does not prevent or stop crime; it just seems to create more of it. What can we do? I suggest we ask better questions, like: how do we develop the principles and discipline to remain incorruptible while we suffer *and* while we are happy? The first key to resolving a *macro* problem like the philosophy of a punishing deity is in exploring our initial experiences with illusion within the *micro*cosm of the family.

THE PRIMARY LOVE TEMPLATE

When the soul comes to earth, we put on human glasses and stop seeing with divine perception. Enchanted by our newfound family, we start viewing the world through the veils of human illusion. Our human heart, of course, feels the byproducts of its unfolding dramas: I am rich; I am poor; I am unlovable; I am irresistible; I am stupid; I am a genius; I am beautiful or ugly. On and on we go on a scary roller coaster ride taking us up, down, right, and left. While our brain evaluates our experiences and makes decisions about the nature of life, we pick which role we will play in it. Based upon others' and our perceptions, each script informs our primary conclusions and mental prescriptions until we re-evaluate them as an adult. These decisions become neural circuits, which function as a safe-threat detection and defense system. Life scripts reflect our accumulated wisdom and level of emotional maturity and can be rewritten as we evolve.

In the 1990s, neuroscientists monitored the prefrontal cortex of a monkey as the monkey viewed a researcher eat a nut the monkey desired. The researchers noticed that particular cells in the monkey's brain acted in an identical fashion *as if the monkey had eaten the nut himself.*[7] This led to the exciting new discovery termed *mirror neurons.* Theories about how empathy, human bonding, and social attachment possibly are hardwired in our frontal cortex by the mirroring effect of neurons immediately flourished. The role mirror neurons play within people is currently being studied by neuropsychologists and enthusiastically debated by brain researchers around the world. Studying the brain with MRI scans, scientists have discovered that humans possess mirror neuron systems that may be associated with social development, self-awareness, emotional connection such as empathy, and intention. This research is in its infancy so I will skip the ongoing debate. But I wonder if this is the mechanism an infant uses to develop what I term a primary love template.

Families provide loving models as well as painful ones, which activate corresponding mirroring neurons. For the purposes of this book, I will focus on the negative templates and offer solutions for those tainted by familial illusions because a significant source of human suffering originates from our primary templates based upon illusion. Our soul has a goal of leading us to wholeness even if we are blind (sans our divine eyesight). Everyone suffers and experiences love in paradoxical forms during their lifetime.

As babies, our happy presence is charming and extremely appealing. The thing that separates a human from the pure nature of its soul is almost transparent in a giggly infant. Babies enchant us with infectious enthusiasm, joy, and wonder and this cute, chubby, uncorrupted, innocent "Buddha" nature. But as we mature, we accumulate love but also suffering. A human seeks attachment and loving connections but also preoccupies itself with survival and wants any physical and emotional pain to stop.

Discerning love from illusion is a dicey proposition for a child. Children *instinctively* accept *all* the positive and negative behaviors witnessed growing up as *normal*. Parents present offspring the interesting dichotomy of "do as I say and not what I do." But children actually copy what parents do and not what parents say. Assumptions, conclusions, and life scripts are made, which become primary love templates based on these early experiences. The normal process of individuation occurs when a child begins to follow his or her own instincts and refuses to follow the expectations of authority figures.

Autonomy is the primary developmental milestone of adolescence. Young men and women resist familial patterns and cultural traditions. Hypocritical parental behavior infuriates adolescents and invites rebellion. Teens instinctually point out the inconsistencies of an offending authority figure but may engage in the same offense or mimic the same hypocrisy, if they lack self-awareness and remain unconscious. By developing the determination and courage to individuate from parents, adolescents can mature into responsible, sovereign adults. Recognizing primary love templates is a crucial milestone toward maturity.

Unfortunately some adolescents never mature beyond saying "no" and fail to develop philosophical principles or discover honorable purposes for their existence, which is, I believe, essential for enduring love and happiness. Reactivity and resistance as developmental strategies will inadvertently replicate familial models and similar responses from the world. Like attracts like, so judgment and resistance will pull more of what we judge to be painful onto us. Opposition on its own never teaches us how to move or grow beyond parental and ancestral prescriptions. Revising an entrenched family prescriptive template requires the young adult to go beyond idealism and pushback.

Every family has entrained patterns, which I call templates, that deserve celebration and others . . . reexamination. Without self-reflection, we are likely to replay the same scenarios witnessed in our youth. For example, this is how some of us think perfectionism creates love or how we become very self-critical if parents modeled and rewarded similar behavior. Whether we engage in those activities consciously or subconsciously, a primary love template will recycle until we realize what is occurring. Family tradition and/or primary love templates can inspire unshakable optimism or crushing pessimism. Simply said, consistent behaviors modeled by our parents and caregivers create primary templates and illusions about love that can create success or failure.

Primary love templates become protagonists and/or antagonists in our human drama and move us toward our destiny to discover what love is and what love is not. Idealistically, as adults we know what we want, have principles, and pursue our dreams from a foundation of focused intention, heartfelt passion, and disciplined behavior. Whether positive or negative, life provides mirrors that help us see our reflection, discover our purpose, and liberate us from recycling dysfunctional life scripts and ancestral templates.

Emotional suffering and physical pain are confusing forms of communication. Our mind gravitates toward its unconscious illusions, and our body tells us when something we are doing hurts. As adults, our intimate relationships provide mirrors to help us see our reflection. Persistent pain, self-sabotage, or a lack of success may force us to choose to *reject* behavioral patterns that fail to serve our needs. But if a healthy choice is such an obvious choice, a "no-brainer" as this idea suggests, why is there so much suffering in the world? Why would we choose to suffer and fail to love ourselves again and again? Why do we recycle familial mirrors and addictive patterns that promise pleasure but produce pain? Why do we continue to endure abusive relationships when we really want to be loved? To find our own answer, we can explore how our primary love template informs our relationship dynamics in the following ways:

1. Positive and negative childhood experiences create primary love templates.
2. Modeled forms of success/suffering become prescriptions.
3. Mirror neurons respond to how we were treated and our corresponding template models.
4. In relationship dynamics, we treat others as we internally treat ourselves.

When a toddler imitates parents, we may proudly proclaim, "He's a chip off the old block." This acknowledgment reinforces the ongoing mimicking behavior of the mirror neurons but also encourages children to encode parental behavior patterns as a survival strategy. All the positive or negative sensations we experience during our formative years are encrypted in neural circuits as forms of love. Similarly to the gravitational force on earth, mental patterns and the expectation of love are very compelling. We treat ourselves this way internally and externally treat others similarly from this first love template until we have a reason to reexamine it. The primary love template has two phases of self-awareness.

The initial phase of the primary love template occurs when:

1. Children accept the entire positive and negative milieu witnessed while growing up as normal, which becomes the primary love template.
2. Every behavioral pattern, emotional reaction, and mental belief system our parents/caregivers model is encoded into neural circuits and mirrored patterns and is then recycled internally and/or externally. This is why abused youth often link love with pain or believe negative self-talk is normal while maturing. Self-

actualized parents model optimism and opportunity to children this same way.

3. Children pass through the "second phase of awareness" as the models are hardwired into life scripts; they then proceed to *treat themselves* in similar ways.

The crucial points of the second phase of the primary love template include:

- Parental models become prescriptive templates that children recycle internally. As adults, they treat themselves in similar ways throughout life until they realize that they reproduced these templates within themselves.
- Children internalize and/or replicate both the spectacular and dysfunctional familial neural circuits in this manner externally until they realize what they are doing.
- As adults, they then attract people, places, and especially lovers that will mirror every spectacular and dysfunctional template buried within until they see their reflection, reach a resolution, and address each delusion.

The second phase of self-awareness reminds us to appreciate our spectacular and dysfunctional scripts that were originally encrypted in our primary love template. Unraveling our own riddles and the illusions provided by others is daunting. Even though we inadvertently recycle parental/caregiver patterns of neglect, abuse, and even success, what happens in our life and the challenges we experience are ours to resolve. Reviewing any productive and unproductive reoccurring patterns we have experienced throughout our life enables conscious choices. If we notice that we have recycled a primary love template based on other people's shadows, perhaps it may be too daunting for us to deal with on our own. We may need assistance because brutal self-knowledge is critical to untangling dysfunctional templates.

ENCHANTED BY THE VICTIM/PERPETRATOR PARADIGM

Victimization heals with love and compassion. When retaliation and revenge become our primary motivation, a victim/perpetrator paradigm can develop. In this reciprocal relationship, victims can be compared to a catcher behind the plate in baseball, while perpetrators are pitchers. Each is convinced he or she is engaging in a solitary activity, but the catcher fails to realize how he throws the ball back to the pitcher to continue the game. This timeless dynamic allows the tragic drama of pitch and catch to endlessly recycle. Self-soothing pity-parties of helplessness, finger-pointing hopelessness, and rage-filled retaliatory fantasies are the types of things keeping the ball in play. Victims tend to believe compensation is due for the pain endured. Society trains many of us to want retribution, feel it is our privilege to retaliate, and believe we are entitled to do so because we have endured so much suffering. The seduction deepens when people take comfort in the pain and sympathy their story garners. Trouble occurs when we embrace our suffering to soothe our internal wounds. This gives us permission to disassociate from violent urges to retaliate against the perpetrator without examining our self-sabotaging behavior.

Under stress, a blamer blames others for what occurs in his or her life. The blamer lacks self-awareness or necessary self-discipline to self-examine. This failure to become self-responsible combined with a dysfunctional primary love template of internalized pain and/or dissociated rage can lead to a victim/perpetrator paradigm. Those claiming victim status and perpetrators hold opposite sides of a reciprocal pole within the victim/perpetrator paradigm, since both struggle with personal responsibility and internal emotional honesty. Perpetrators and victims victimize themselves and each another while claiming innocence and blaming the other, which recycles the victim/perpetrator paradigm.

Pain provides information about our internal malfunction and reveals imbalances in our body, heart, and mind. Others mirror these malfunctions to us so we can see the reflection of our conscious and unconscious primary love templates. If a bully decides to be cruel to another child, for example, the form of illusion provides the idea and the opportunity for a perpetrator to experience cruel impulses and the possible enjoyment or internal relief from watching someone suffer. The pain that the bully imposes on his victim is a mirror for both the bully and victim. The bully may feel a twisted form of empowerment momentarily by copying a perpetrator that victimized them. A victim may imagine retribution will right wrongs by dreaming that bullies "get what they deserve" later. *At the core, the bully and the victim are*

exactly the same—both dream of power. The victim/perpetrator paradigm provides opportunities for everyone to see their reflection in the
mirrors of illusion. Whether in that moment we are the bully or the
victim, mirrors are provided with the strength and power necessary to
get our attention so that we can see our twisted dream or cruel reflection and eventually find where love exists.

Here are some additional considerations within the victim/perpetra-
tor paradigm:

- Perpetrators frequently were victims of violence and/or emotional
  or physical neglect.
- Perpetrators seek victims and victims feel victimized and then
  flip-flop roles.
- Anger/rage and helplessness/passivity are different reactions to
  the suffering continuum, but both methods dissociate from personal trauma.
- Dissociation cuts off the ability to feel our own pain, but seeing
  another suffer can provide a twisted sense of relief.
- When emotional indifference and/or violence are modeled, the
  victim can encode a sense of unworthiness or invisibility as a primary love template survival strategy.
- Violence projects internal rage onto another and is another primary love template survival strategy that masks vulnerable emotions within the perpetrator.

The victim/perpetrator paradigm occurs because perpetrators are
usually disconnected from internal wounds within their own hearts,
which makes any objective form of self-examination extremely difficult.
Sometimes narcissism and entitlement primary love templates develop
to mask emotional wounds, which blind us from realizing the harm we
cause others. Unfortunately, on a bigger scale, recycled rage and love
linked to pain are also the reason why the victim/perpetrator paradigm
persists. Throughout human history, bullies, predators, and abusers terrorize, while martyrs, saboteurs, and those using other passive forms of
rage tend to self-victimize. Children raised in these environments frequently link love with pain and abandon (self-sabotage or victimize)
themselves in similar "invisible" ways just like the models witnessed
from parents or abusers. This phenomenon is how cycles of abuse,

victimization, and self-sabotage have proliferated and perpetuated themselves in both families and the larger society alike. Healing and releasing a dysfunctional primary love template that evolves into the victim/perpetrator paradigm requires passionate dedication.

A perpetrator parent, for example, will, as twisted as it may sound, get a sense of relief from witnessing a child's experience of pain. The complexity of the victim/perpetrator paradigm is that the parent is usually disassociated from his or her own pain but experiences a sense of relief when someone else is suffering. When an individual or parent is emotionally cut off from their pain, that person often purges their unconscious rage through periodic violent episodes . . . frequently focused on loved ones. The result of unconscious rage within the family unit is that the emotional needs of the child are in effect "invisible" to the perpetrator/parent. Children will tend to re-victimize self or perpetrate against others if their unconscious primary love template persists.

Primary love templates recycle until we become conscious and create a new path. Twisted over the millennia, this paradigm has mutated into the insidious virus we commonly call terrorism. Terrorism, in all of its forms, is a pandemic problem that we have yet to develop an appropriate response to; it will be reviewed in chapter 9.

When Albert Einstein said that energy cannot be created or destroyed but only changed from one form to another,[8] he probably knew that his brilliant observation also applied to emotion. Thus, emotional trauma can be transformed into love in a productive manner or a pernicious victim/perpetrator paradigm. Paradoxically, I have come to realize the baffling truth, through the examples of my clients, that untreated internal rage actually calms down when an unconscious individual witnesses someone else suffer. Maybe the Romans created the gladiator games for this reason. Deriving satisfaction from the suffering of another has been part of every culture throughout the world since the beginning of time. Who hasn't felt compelled to watch another's tragedy? As long as humans remain unconscious to primary love templates that link love to pain, repetitive cycles of violence, bullying, murder, or abuse will occur and reoccur in families and society.

Our encrypted primary love templates and the victim/perpetrator paradigms of neglect or abuse we inadvertently recycle are our responsibility to resolve. Reviewing and addressing every dysfunctional pattern recycling our suffering is a good practice and requires self-realization. It can be daunting to deal with victim and perpetrator tendencies on our own. Please seek assistance if you run into trouble because brutal self-knowledge is critical to untangling dysfunctional patterns and templates. Facing negative patterns on your own can be overwhelming.

USING RESTRAINT

In 1974, my first job with my brand new undergraduate degree in psychology paid two dollars and ninety cents per hour to supervise juvenile delinquents at a residential treatment center. I was a naïve twenty-three-year-old white kid from the suburbs who knew nothing about chronic poverty, generational abuse, and predatory violence. I figured I'd be teaching young men necessary survival skills; little did I know that I was about to get the education of my life. Book smart and street dumb, my education started the first day when a coworker called me out while laughing loudly as she corrected my inept attempt to make a conduct-disordered youth feel guilty.

This private facility was the end of the line for emotionally disturbed young men aged ten to seventeen, who had been kicked out of other institutions before the state locked them up for good. Many of the staff served as soldiers in Vietnam and endured similar adversities and disadvantages that these angry, violent young men experienced. The residents followed my coworkers' rules for the most part but would curse and call me out in front of everyone.

Bullies had picked on me for stuttering in my youth, but these guys were masters. Being a nice guy was a detriment, and copying what other staff said in similar situations just brought cascades of laughter. A coworker from the Bronx pulled me aside one day and said, "They smell your fear like animals in the jungle. . . . They're ripping you up. You better handle this right quick or they'll eat you alive."

Awash with anxiety, stuttering aside, I was struggling to keep my job. Two months later, the lead supervisor I respected the most took me into his office and told me that I should probably find another line of work. Failure was foreign to me; my success as a high school and collegiate All-American swimmer didn't hold water here. Sleepless nights ensued, and I had to sink or swim.

Steeling my courage, I decided to face my tormentors. Driving to work, I prepared myself to confront violence head on, the way I'd approached athletic competition. In those days, the protocol for restraining guys who acted out meant wrestling with the adolescent man-to-man. While providing external control, staff required the young men to talk about their rage rationally before we released our brute-force restraint. This was a one-on-one procedure that took hours of intensive interaction, not to mention many scrapes and bruises.

Our institution in Ohio didn't have quiet rooms or leather restraints that psychiatric hospitals typically use nowadays. By restraining every guy who was out of control, I tried to become a valued staff member worthy of respect. Little did I know that these angry young men would teach me profound truths about trauma, abreactions (the expression of repressed emotion), and how dissociated pain heals. Nothing I have learned in my academic and professional life since then was more powerful than this experience.

One day, after a major rule infraction, restraining the offender turned out to be the best course of action. While he was screaming obscenities, scratching to draw blood, and spitting in my face, something strange occurred. He stopped fighting. In the next moment, deep, gut-wrenching sobs from the bowels of some inner torment suddenly escaped the young man and filled the room. Relaxing my grip and inches from his face, I gently whispered, "What's happening?" Regressed into a violent memory from his childhood, he told his story as I tenderly held him. As we talked, our hearts touched, tears flowed, and love filled the void where rage and his victim/perpetrator paradigm previously ruled.

In those moments, we both understood the healing powers of love, presence, and henosis. Having released my fear of violence associated with my primary love template, I helped the young man access and heal the untouched terror associated with his. As a privately enraged, sensitive, stuttering male, my fears mirrored his unaddressed trauma. This activated his primal rage, which he in turn directed at me just as others had done to him. On this occasion, we both expressed our primary love template differently and discovered an enlightened solution.

Pain pushed us into our trauma, and the healing power of human connection and resonating hearts changed our lives. A friendship was forged in steel that day and never diminished during his stay. We both became more whole, and an important secret about human nature was revealed, which I used to help others throughout my career. What I learned through dialectic discovery by helping this young man heal an aspect of his primary love template helped me treat many others down the road. As my career progressed, I found that hypnosis, guided imagery, and transcendence techniques provided similar results without the scrapes and bruises.

Along the way, I also discovered how anger always has a core sensitive emotion and a want/need/desire underneath it, which anger tries to protect. Like the great and powerful persona the wizard created in *The Wizard of Oz*, anger can get very loud, fiery, and scary, just the way Dorothy and her companions initially experienced it. When Toto pulled open the curtain, he revealed a frightened humbug magician pulling levers to create the illusion of the Great and Powerful Oz. Anger is an energizing emotion, but learning how to find the core sensitive emotion behind anger's curtain was crucial in my professional development. I gained respect over the months from my peers after similar successes added to my knowledge about trauma . . . others' and mine.

Predators prey off the emotional energy of the weak, and vulnerability means death to children raised in violent households. In 1974, psychologists knew little about posttraumatic stress disorder (PTSD was added to the DSM-III in 1980), and dissociation was never discussed during my undergraduate psychology degree. When I began studying, modern psychotherapy was in its infancy.

Bad exists so we can experience our goodness. We were locked up together for a good purpose—everyone learned something critical about the *essential mystery* within each of us. Laozi wisely reminded us long ago that our heroic journey includes self-responsibility: "The good man is the teacher of the bad, and the bad is the material from which the good may learn. He who does not value the teacher, or greatly care for the material, is greatly deluded although he may be learned. Such is the essential mystery."[9]

MIRROR REFLECTIONS

Those boys taught me many crucial lessons I never learned in my formal education, for truly embodying emotional resonance and presence requires an experiential education. Fear of stuttering involved my fear about failure; fear in the ward was directly related to my experience of cruelty, violence, and the victim/perpetrator paradigm, which the residents shared with me. Fear activates knee-jerk judgments and defensiveness toward a perceived antagonist until we acknowledge our disowned trauma. The mirrors of illusion are very efficient; the residents of the residential treatment center bullied me until I faced my fear and dormant anger. My fragility was judged, and this activated the young man's internal rage until I was able to face my fear of anger.

As reflecting mirrors, we expressed the same pain differently and eventually addressed our shared fragility. My illusion was thinking those young men were fundamentally different than me. The first alligator that I had to literally wrestle and master was my own fear/anger before anyone would allow me to crawl into the swamp to help someone with his or her alligator.

The delusions related to the victim/perpetrator paradigm and the need to punish a perpetrator for recycling trauma are extremely difficult to unravel. When innocence is lost through perpetuating the cycle of punishment, victimization, and unrelenting perpetration, people usually pick from the following four choices:

1. Bury the pain, blame, and recycle the event by pushing responsibility onto others (perpetrator behavior).
2. Bury the pain, blame ourselves, and recycle the event by deciding that we deserve it (victim behavior).
3. Bury the pain through dissociation and addictive behaviors until it resurfaces (avoidant behavior).
4. Heal the pain and developing incorruptible solutions (described in chapter 9) (mature behavior).

I restrained the young men on a regular basis during the next four months, and similar patterns of emotional release and bonding frequently occurred. The bullies and blamers learned about expressing vulnerable feeling, while those with depressive and self-destructive tendencies due to internalized trauma took more emotional responsibility. Since I carried similar seedlings of pain as the residents, the shared experience of working through our issues in such an intimate fashion deepened our bonds in productive ways. Each needed, myself included, a different approach to find the pain underneath human rage and fear.

We all have been mistreated and neglected in one way or another. Unfortunately for the young men at the center, many had more than their share. One had witnessed his mother's murder, for example. Another young man, who was dipped in boiling oil, had bones broken, and was intentionally shot with a rifle by his mother, taught me an important lesson on how pain links with love. Whenever we complimented him, he would defecate on the floor in a misguided attempt to turn things around because pain was a safer sensation to him than love. We taught each other about rage, facing our fears, and how the pain buried within our hearts will drive us until we become liberated. Everyone was richer from the process of heartfelt connection within a healing community.

After facing my fears of violence with these young men, I stopped worrying if they respected me or followed my instructions. Confident that those under my care would do what they were supposed to do one way or another, I relaxed. When I healed my fears, the mirrors of laughter and disregard stopped overnight. Fifty young men started to treat me with respect, and I became a valued staff member.

Failure was a force pushing me to go where I never would have gone on my own. Fighting through my mistakes gave me the confidence to look illusion in the eye with just a promise and a mind full of fear. Lessons learned in the crucible of pain endure and create wisdom discernable only by initially surviving the experience. Thriving comes later by developing sovereignty and eventually incorruptibility, but first and foremost, we need to discover how pain heals. Emotional integrity and the reflective mirrors of relationship did their job, and in the dawn, my professional career was birthed.

The mirrors of illusion forced me to look at the link from my primary love template to the victim/perpetrator paradigm so the young men could feel safe enough to let me serve as a guide. Facing our internal shadows deepens resolve and strengthens our courage to walk through any jungle. Plotinus echoed this thought when he said:

> What is the Good for such a man? He is himself his own good.
> The life that he possesses is perfect. He possesses the good, insofar as he is not in search of another.

To remove whatever is other in respect to his own being, is to purify oneself. In simple relationship with you without hindrance in your pure unity, without the thing that it is mixed interiorly with this purity, being you only in pure light . . . you became a vision. Although being here, you are ascended. You no longer need guidance. Fix your gaze. You'll see.[10]

FEAR AND COURAGE

Failure is an extremely important tool and, if handled properly, improves our emotional, mental, and spiritual hygiene. Everyone needs to wash up, take a shower, and pick up around the house periodically. Removing the dirt and debris of life freshens things up and makes us more wholesome. Taking the time to release unproductive habits, poor attitudes, and immature beliefs that fail to support our highest interest rejuvenates us.

Fear of failure can motivate us to change in a positive way, so it is also a necessary ally. The willingness to admit or recognize a problem, take responsibility, and make corrections requires courage. The Cowardly Lion in *The Wizard of Oz* provided a wonderful example for how confusing and chaotic emotions can be. Considered the king of beasts by others, the lion assumed his fears made him inadequate. Unaware that courage is the willingness to act in the face of fear, he bullied others in a misguided attempt to mask his fears. Confusion continues for many men and women just like it did for the Cowardly Lion who didn't know how fear activates its opposite—courage.

Cowards fail to develop the courage it takes to express healthy anger and overcome fear. Conquering an adversary or a bad habit takes dedication, focus, and drive. Determination and willpower are positive forms of aggression that are necessary for survival in a competitive world with limited resources. Success, breaking barriers, or challenging the status quo requires courage and healthy forms of aggression. Self-control, fearlessness, and personal power are necessary to achieve an athletic or artistic accomplishment . . . or any dream for that matter. Anger in its empowered form is a comrade that will fight for your life and help you overcome any adversary or adversity.

Suffering points to our imbalances, while anger can be used as an excellent indicator or a warning signal to point out failed behaviors and unmet needs. A newborn shows an endearing form of anger by turning red in the face and screaming until the infant stops breathing. All this is due to a failure of a caretaker to address a primary need— whether food or being burped, comforted, or changed. That courageous temper tantrum gets his or her needs met. The newborn takes control of his or her environment and other people through anger as a form of communication. Birthed from fear and failure, courage and aggressive strategies are effective for success and survival. For adults, though, unmonitored infantile anger can corrupt a worthwhile goal. Due to its quick, mercurial, and lethal nature, expressing unmitigated anger fails miserably as a long-term means to get our needs met.

PASSIVE VERSUS ACTIVE ANGER

Aristotle described anger's challenges, which confronted me early in my career, this way: "Anybody can become angry—that is easy, but to be angry with the right person and to the right degree and at the right time and for the right purpose, and in the right way—that is not within everybody's power and is not easy."[11] The residents at the treatment centers and psychiatric hospitals I had the opportunity to work with taught me that anger has many guises, like the illusions within their primary love templates and various victim/perpetrator paradigms. I learned that chronic hopelessness, unexamined pessimism, and violent fantasies are passive forms of anger and need to see the light of day like any shackled prisoner in Plato's cave. Some concealed passing fancies or secret angers from the outside world could easily be swept away by a good night's sleep or in their dreams. Others have repetitive angry fantasies, addictive impulses, or repressed rage, which become problematic storage containers for their subconscious mind and/or physical body if too much anger accumulates.

Passive anger, if chronic, leads to physical illness. A medical researcher once said to me that, under a microscope, a cancer cell looks like a condensed ball with an attached pointer. She described how a cancer cell injects what she called its DNA message of hate into a healthy cell, which then forgets its origins and transforms itself into a hate ball. I have noticed a similar pattern with my clients recovering from cancer. The client would know what would make them feel happy, healthy, and whole but consistently failed to meet their own needs. Chronic neglect, negativity, and the absence of love can cause us to forget our origins, create physical symptoms, and eventually develop corrupted forms of anger.

Passive anger can be just as potent as violence yet avoids open conflict through procrastination, helplessness, and powerlessness. Polite society often considers victims as noble innocents suffering through no fault of their own from the slings and arrows of some outrageous fortune or exploitative dark force. Promoting one's suffering or claiming victim status often elicits compassion. Victims tend to be convinced that any behavior based upon retaliation, self-sabotage, and general violence toward the aggressor is justifiable. Thus, internal rage can lie underneath a passive presentation. Confronting a victim about a possible area of personal responsibility is a dicey proposition because righteous indignation jumps up and admonishes the whistleblower for being unsympathetic like their abuser.

Many countries, for example, claim victim status and glorify a struggle against tyrannical forces or terrorist organizations threatening the safety and security of their citizens. Some shamelessly expose the human rights violations of adversaries while conveniently failing to look at their own behaviors perpetuating the conflict. In situations like these, the detractors are vigorously attacked for failing to honor their claim of *victim status* and immediately dismissed for being disloyal, unsympathetic, unpatriotic, and on the wrong side of right.

Anger is traditionally identified as active by nature with perpetrators exploiting others, but the passive forms of anger fueling the victim side of the victim/perpetrator paradigm are just as problematic. Passive anger relies on the human instinct to provide compassion to those who suffer. Spouses, minorities, politicians, and even countries corrupt compassion by claiming victim status as a passive method to attack an adversary as payback. Calling an adversary a *victimizer* and providing consequences for transgressions has become a popular pastime for passive combatants. Individuals and now countries jockey to promote branding campaigns depicting suffering citizens to garner support and discredit adversaries as a deliberate strategy for future retaliation. Victim status has become a badge of martyrdom, and the competition for these badges is fierce. Spin campaigns to change world opinion and right wrongs often feel like strength, but often effectively shield the martyr from self-driven dark retaliatory impulses.

Righteous indignation arises from suffering, which blinds people so they can't see their reflection in the mirrors of illusion. The insidious nature of internal rage infects both the perpetrator and victim because the cycle is set in perpetual motion by everyone pointing fingers and flip-flopping roles back and forth endlessly. Victimhood is a form of passive anger, which elicits aggressive urges within a perpetrator to fulfill self-fulfilling prophecies of doom and gloom. Pleading innocence and demanding unconditional support, a card-carrying victim twists every negative event as more victimization evidence.

People who walk away from conflict or make intellectual commitments without checking to see if their heart *is into it* fear emotion and fail to express healthy forms of anger. Many men are emotionally dissociated, afraid to explore their sensitive nature privately, much less reveal it to anyone else. Unfortunately, because we treat our beloved the same way we treat ourselves, the lie we tell to ourselves is shared with our partner. Fears need to be faced and feelings expressed to create safe boundaries and emotional honesty.

Many women accuse men of being *passive-aggressive* when their lover repeatedly breaks promises, forgets commitments, and remains emotionally unavailable. Men often report that they don't feel angry, never intentionally ignore requests, and suspect memory failure, while women are convinced aggression is involved due to resentment of some sort. I've treated many men who struggle with intimacy-related issues and look passive-aggressive due to a lack of self-awareness. Many men neglect to check if they are holding back passion for projects and forgetting promises for this reason rather than passive aggression. By ignoring their heart's lack of interest and saying no to their partner's initial request, some men who walk away from conflict fail to take responsibility for their emotions. I prefer to call the pattern *passive abandonment*, since men generally abandon their internal emotions prior to abandoning a partner.

Anger pretends to be our protector and savior when we suffer from fear, loss, or abandonment. It pretends to rescue and deliver us to the promised land of love, safety, and security. It justifies its existence by reminding us that the world is dangerous: others carry weapons, and anger warns us that we should, too. Corrupt anger in its active form is a lethal knife with sharp edges on both sides, including the handle. The primal instinct to protect oneself by lashing out and inflicting pain is very seductive. Blinded by anger, the knife wielder fails to notice that their internal pain is self-inflicted.

Aggression in its corrupted form acts like a knife-wielding banshee that cuts the opponent, the wielder, and every bystander witnessing the event. Blood splatters on everyone in proximity, traumatizing all as victims. A natural tendency of humans is to try to dissociate from the emotions generating from an angry perpetrator. Unfortunately, seeds of viral anger are planted in every drop of blood with the potential to produce a virulent virus. Anger's painful lessons can infect everyone involved like a malignant cancer. Witnessing another person wince in pain and cringe in fear of future attacks creates multiple sad results. The person being "stabbed" suffers as well as the bystanders witnessing the violence. The knife wielder often experiences a release of internalized rage. This motivates the perpetrator to seek as much pain from the victim as deemed necessary in a vain attempt to satisfy an unconscious rage. All abuse, torture, and victimization of others originate from dissociated cycles of violence based upon the delusional aspects of the victim/perpetrator paradigm.

Many of us use anger as a motivational tool to accomplish goals. But recycled anger and churning rage produce hatred. Bitterness is focused hatred that became brittle with age. Like the hunter roasting a dead animal over a raging fire, the longer anger cooks on the rotisserie, the blacker and bitterer the carcass becomes. Life doesn't grow in these raging fires; only death, division, and destruction. Bitterness is not our friend, has no loyalty, and fails miserably as a successful strategy toward a worthwhile goal. Focused rage and hatred will teach us many lessons that engender pain, but there are gentler ways to grow and eventually become incorruptible.

People can mistakenly believe that redemption, peace, and prosperity are achieved through anger and retaliation. Immature leaders attempt to gain power by using hatred to galvanize their nation to unite against an adversary. Some groups think this honors ancestors and rights the wrongdoings of the past. This recycled rage in actuality cements the bond to the past but unfortunately continues to promote generational suffering.

Socrates said, "For that kind of release is not at all possible or noble; rather, the kind that is both noblest and easiest is not to restrain others, but to equip oneself to be the best possible."[12] Anger is like salt because we need it to survive. Toxic anger is like an overseasoned meal that unsettles our stomach. As with salt, anger requires an equalizer of prudence.

THE CODEPENDENT RELATIONSHIP OF DOGMA AND ANGER

Clans and countries have always feuded. When fear and anger from being marginalized or victimized are daily events, we tend to gravitate toward tighter circles and closer clans to the exclusion of more and more people. Even science-fiction writers have expanded on this idea when imagining the conflict of human versus alien encounters. These stories become best sellers because this timeless formula has global human appeal. As Plato aptly expressed it, "When the tyrant has disposed of foreign enemies by conquest or treaty, and there is nothing to fear from them, then he is always stirring up some war or other, in order that the people may require a leader."[13]

Many religions preach about being loyal and faithful. There is little tolerance for soul-directed behavior or perspectives differing even slightly from accepted dogma—that is called blasphemy. The concept that the divine is not complete or sufficient without a subservient human, who is required to do what he or she is told and judged as being good or bad, sets up an unfortunate chain of events. How can people have tolerance for spouses, neighbors, or another country when the God of our religion has no tolerance for divergent opinions? Is the divine really this controlling, or is our anthropomorphic attitude so embedded that humanity is unable to imagine a leader being any other way? In 1848 Alphonse Marie Louis de Prat de Lamartine offered the following perspective about power in his essay: "It is not only the slave or serf who is ameliorated in becoming free. . . . The master himself did not gain less in every point of view . . . for absolute power corrupts the best natures."[14] In a letter to Bishop Mandell Creighton written thirty-nine years later in 1887, Lord Acton added his perspective: "Power tends to corrupt, and absolute power corrupts absolutely. Great men are almost always bad men."[15]

Permission to dictate and dominate another through dogma has bred intolerance and stifled intellectual diversity since ancient times. When the God of our religion can override personal experience or what our soul senses, then it is just a short logical step for those in power to do the same with the huddled masses. We have all seen charismatic political and religious leaders use dogma to purge that society of any adversary or minority group by promoting their vision of perfection. When heads of families, political leaders, and religious hierarchies are corrupted with delusions of grandeur, we naturally expect to engage in similar victim/perpetrator paradigms with spouses, children, or the people governed. History is full of religious inquisitions, political purges, and sanctioned executions of people with divergent attitudes. The intention to unite is good, but corruption is the side effect of absolute control and its supporting dogma.

Unfortunately, throughout history people have suffered greatly from dogma, doctrine, and draconian tactics used to maintain order through threats and terror. "The end justifies the means" or "This is God's will/ promise for our people" are clichés that tyrants use to *protect* their country or agenda from adversaries. Fearsome *bad guys (terrorists)* are presented to the public and their dastardly deeds exposed. "Us versus them" is a powerful idea that creates a justifiable reason to organize armies. Bad guys offer a tyrant an opportunity to vanquish the bad guy and look like a hero.

Rallying the troops for defense, reinforcing religious dogma, and righteous indignation are reliable strategies employed by most despots to justify their autocratic existence. The fear-based concepts of danger, loyalty, and control have dominated the way people have related to one another for a very long time. Do we have the courage to evolve beyond what our ancestors taught us? Is there a voice inside that is tired of the old, fear-based thinking of a corrupted slave-owner who seeks power through control? Wise leaders like Plato and Plotinus have passed on philosophies, democratic principles, and immortal wisdom that advanced the human condition and prompted civilization to accept oneness and diversity within humanity.

Discerning reality from illusion and productive versus unproductive forms of anger is extremely difficult for us all. Safety and security are universal imperatives that motivate us to seek power to control our circumstances, but we have to look beyond the terror of the perpetrator to ascertain why the social system went corrupt within the individual. That key is found at the source of the original wound that our pain and suffering are guiding us to see. Sometimes the source of pain can be retrieved through dialectic discovery, and other times it surfaces when we examine what motivates our behavior or emotional responses.

REFLECTIONS OF LOVE AND MISERY

I believe that we come to experiment, explore mysteries, enlighten ourselves, and add our heroic story to our ancestor's storyline. Occasionally our experiments pull us into the depths of illusion and slingshot us higher into the light. Other times we become mired in division quicksand until we tire of it and try something different. Other people become mirrors so we can experience our reflection. Divinity reflects all of our stories back to us so we can experience the fullness of our actions. Since the divine has little interest in humanity becoming programmed robots, we do not have to be perfect or adhere to a particular dogma for this to occur. How we react to the mirroring of our beliefs back to us becomes the emotional material we must sort out. Our primary love templates provide the initial keys needed to open the treasure box of self-discovery. Understanding how life works is as simple as this because the divine does not punish. We actually draw to us antagonizing and spectacular events to wake us up, transform illusion, and transcend our delusions.

Plato said, "There must always remain something that is antagonistic to good."[16] The level of illusion or the depth of separation between the divine and a human is as unique as an individual snowflake. Our soul is connected to the omnipresent wisdom of divinity and has intentions, which are frequently unknown to us. Spiritual exploration guides our experience, and once we go on a spiritual quest, we often wonder what in the world is going on. On the soul level, we are all like the child experimenting in a magic shop who knows he will go home safely with his parents after he is done playing. Illusion allows us to individuate from our birthplace, which is the entirety of the divine, and experience the process of becoming spiritually and fully aware while trapped in the illusion of being a separate being in a physical body. Illusion reveals distorted reflections to motivate our personality to seek solutions. Suffering pushes and prods us to explore alternate venues to unify our body with our soul and all of divinity.

In short, when we hurt, we must remember our *sunlike* qualities or continue suffering, as Plotinus reminded us long ago:

> If we could behold him who gives all beings their perfection, if we could rest in the contemplation of him and become like him, what other beauty could we need? Being the supreme beauty, he makes those who love him beautiful and lovable. This is the great end, the supreme aim, of Souls; it is the want of this vision that makes men un-happy. He who desires to see the vision must shut his eyes to terrestrial things, not allowing himself to run after corporeal beauties, lest he share the fate of Narcissus, and immerse his soul in deep and muddy pools, abhorred of Spirit. And yet we may train ourselves by contemplating noble things here on earth, especially noble deeds, always pressing on to higher things, and remembering above all that as the eye could not behold the sun unless it were sunlike itself, so the Soul can only see beauty by becoming beautiful itself.[17]

Life on earth is an experiment with love and mirrors. We are born into a family and create a primary love template that mirrors love to us with all its splendor and delusions. Transforming the illusions inherited from our family, which stick like Velcro, into self-determined, autonomous loving solutions requires developing a basic understanding about the nature of dualism and the following reciprocal relationship between illusion and light:

- **LOVE:** As children, we accept both the good and bad experiences within our family as a form of love.
- **MIRROR:** Like a seductive siren, illusions reflect mirages posing as love to help us experience the shadows we mistake as goodness.
- **LOVE:** With maturity we learn to recognize the shadows we Velcro to our primary love template and develop incorruptible responses.

Remembering our divinity despite the confusing models from our family mirrors of both love and illusion is an important paradox to master. While on earth, we are constantly being supported by our soul and directed through all the mirrors and pain to return to the wholeness of the experience "we are all one."

If we cut our finger with a knife or burn our thumb on a stove, everyone knows the nerve receptors in our hand say "ouch" and provide valuable information necessary for survival. When a dentist injects the painkiller Novocain into our gum before drilling a tooth, problems associated with too much numbing can arise. Who hasn't inadvertently bitten their cheek because they couldn't feel it? Problems occur when people are numbed to psychological pain in similar ways, and this perpetuates the dissociative tendencies associated with victim/perpetrator paradigm. Emotional reactions are the nerve endings of our being and let us know what feels good and what doesn't. Addictions similarly fill our psychological voids with substances and behaviors, but they merely mask the symptoms of a greater problem. All we need to do is listen carefully to the pleasure and pain sensors of our feeling nature. If something hurts, choose a wiser path that works better, just like pulling your finger away from a sharp knife or taking your thumb off a hot stove.

Choosing wisdom over pain is easy to say but hard to do. The following meditation occurred to me while examining the source of my emotional wounds. Suddenly, I realized many of my injuries occurred from my own hand. My internal mental voices included a victimized child and an antagonistic adolescent mired in illusion birthed from my primary love template and victim/perpetrator tendencies. Furious with my inability to discern wisdom from the illusions running around in my brain, I created the Wise and Loving Inner Voice Meditation (appendix B). Sorting out wisdom from illusion is an invaluable practice that leads to incorruptibility and its awesome power. We will discuss how humans become incorruptible in more detail later in this book. Pain and punishment are often considered to be the tools of justice. This is actually untrue because the real tools of justice come from an expansive heart that has the ability to empathize with and have compassion for the pain of another person without being corrupted by the experience. Power is what the victim and the perpetrator both desire. Once we experience and sustain our power in an incorruptible form, the seduction to recycle suffering endlessly can end gracefully and effortlessly. We are not there yet, and so people continue to impose judgments and punishments upon themselves and their neighbors, unaware of the historical inspiration demanding retaliation and retribution. We just need to be informed so that we may decide, deep down inside on a soul-level, to make choices that lead to substantive change, without using suffering as the primary motivator for others to change.

LIBERATING DYSFUNCTIONAL PATTERNS

My mother's dysfunctional pattern included criticizing friends, foes, and family members without mercy. Disdaining and rejecting her judgmental behavior, I decided to never treat other people this way. Instead, my primary love template became a passive form of disowned anger that my mother modeled, and I ultimately became self-critical of my stuttering, judged others privately, and internalized my anger. Complaining to my friends, mentally dressing down others, and funneling my anger into sports provided little relief. Sustainable change occurred in my life when I broke free of my template by empathically connecting to the pain that my inner child received from my negativity and inspired the Wise Lover, Wounded Beloved Reconciliation (chapter 3). Healing my wounds and taking responsibility increased my incorruptibility, which helped me to overcome my dysfunctional victim/perpetrator paradigm.

Here are some perspectives and a few examples of the typical steps to transcending a template or paradigm:

1. The reptilian or primitive nature of the brain operates like a computer that evaluates, interprets, and decides *why* things happen based upon past data we have collected and uses those data to predict future outcomes.
2. Emotional trauma activates the adrenal fight/flight/freeze program, which produces adrenaline that anchors the template for that event into our biology.
3. Recycled pain solidifies emotional memories that become crystallized emotion embedded within mental pictures or snapshot decisions about life. Snapshots become scripts used to define, describe, and/or reenact past events in future situations and may generate hyper-vigilance. Soul-level focused behavioral, emotional, and mental connection can override an encrypted template;

however, the empathy and passion to heal need to be stronger than the initial incident.

4. When the perception of the precipitating event/events that created the original template transforms, wounds heal and new outcomes become possible.

Our most precious illusions are relived again and again when we replicate what was essentially done unto us, ad infinitum. We tend to treat others similarly to the way we treat ourselves. This is true for family members and especially lovers. Cultural, ethnic, and familial cycles of pain, fear, and anger are passed on from generation to generation through these primary love templates that can evolve into the insidious victim/perpetrator paradigm. But we can move beyond our caregivers' models by clearing the corrupted paradigms inside our own bodies, hearts, and minds.

Liberation from our family models occurs when we learn how to stop recycling ancestral pain. Self-responsibility teaches us to trust our own instincts. When we learn to communicate with the physical, emotional, and mental aspects of our being, including our soul, wholeness occurs and henosis returns.

Quick and direct access to the wisdom within our soul is greatly facilitated when we love ourselves and approach life similarly. However, the nature of duality attracts the perfect contrast designed to prod our personality to surrender and transcend illusion to the ultimate destiny, love. Confucius accurately described this: "By three methods we may learn wisdom: first, by reflection, which is noblest; second, by imitation, which is easiest; and third by experience, which is the bitterest."[18]

Pain or pleasure, evil or wisdom; the choice seems obvious . . . or does it? We get so enchanted at times that it is difficult to sort out if wisdom or pain is our primary teacher. Taking responsibility for our actions is necessary, but our susceptibility to the illusions of our primary love templates adds a degree of difficulty. Children accumulate wisdom through love and pain and often get confused about the role the first love template plays in order to recycle that drama. Maturity develops through the wisdom gained through the paradoxes spawned by the continuum of our successes and failures.

THE PARADOX OF THE HUMAN SOUL

People usually want pleasure but respond to pain immediately. I think that is why Plato saw pleasure and pain as two sides of the same coin and suggested that scratching an itch was pleasurable due to prior irritation caused by the itch. Plato's perspective on the purpose of pain as quoted by Plotinus is as follows: "Since evil is here, 'haunting this world by necessary law,' [Plato's *Theaetetus* 176a] and it is the soul's design to escape from evil, we must escape hence. But what is this escape? 'In attaining likeness to God,' we read [Plato's *Phaedo* 82b]. And this is explained as 'becoming just and holy, living by wisdom,' the entire nature grounded in virtue." [19]

Love is a real sustaining energy pulsating through creation, and perhaps this love is what animates the soul like breath and blood animates the body. Plotinus believed in the concept of *logical interpenetration*, which states that everything is simultaneously *something* primarily and *everything else* secondarily. *Ova-la* is a Greek word for an item's *essence, nature, or that which belongs to itself*. In Latin, the equivalent word is *substantia*. Both convey the concept that the *essence* of our blood, for example, is its vital force. Plotinus believed that ova-la interpenetrates all matter similarly to the Upanishadic principle that suggests that every self is present in every other self; every other self is present in oneself and all selves are identical or one at their core.

Immeasurable by current scientific standards, this energetic presence of love vibrates within every atom in the universe like a divine fingerprint. The unifying message of love's *ova-la* throughout divinity is a homing frequency to humanity—every cell of our being is also infused and will respond to the heartfelt embrace of love like ants are attracted to sweets at a picnic. Scientists have noticed separate heart cells in a Petri dish without physical contact immediately beat together in rhythmic unison. [20]

Plotinus offered an analogy about the life of a soul on earth in *The Enneads* when he described what happens to us at birth: "The soul in its nature loves God and longs to be at one with Him in the noble love of a daughter for a noble father; but coming to human birth and lured by the courtships of this sphere, she takes up with another love, a mortal, leaves her father and falls." [21] Picture a space shuttle leaving the divine space station, flying to another planet as an autonomous vehicle, and attempting to survive in a foreign environment without support from its mother ship. Our body is the vessel, and our soul is sealed inside that space shuttle. Illusion and division are designed to awaken a physical desire to seek our soul and eventually return to the mother ship (henosis). When our personality becomes one with our soul while trapped inside a body, we can unify with all of divinity. Plotinus described this evolutionary process in the following way: "The soul loves the Good (the One) because, from the beginning, she has been incited by the Good to love him. And the soul which has this love at hand does not wait to be reminded by the beauties of this lower world, but since she has this love—even if she does not realize it—she is constantly searching."[22]

Humans are programmed to accomplish many goals, and on the soul level, the primary goal is to realize our own divinity. Cinderella myths where a humble individual discovers that he or she is really a king or queen in disguise, worthy of all the riches and honoring that rightful position, speak directly to our soul. Fairy tales of slaves and servants having hidden royal birthrights are so appealing because the plot resonates with the story of our soul. Spiritual and philosophical masters rediscover this truth when establishing communication with the "mother ship" and experience a profound form of love expanding in the heart. Illusion vanishes like darkness at dawn and all that remains is unity, wholeness, and henosis.

The soul knows little about our biological experience but wants to express its loving nature and explore love in all of its forms. Our soul knows that nothing we do, not the suffering we endure nor the pain we inflict on others on earth, will positively or negatively influence the truth that we can do nothing that will exile us from the divine. We make our personal journey into illusion to remember our origins and return home.

It's extremely difficult for our personality to consider any perspective other than its own. We need support to sort out love from illusion and imagine the possibility that our soul wants us to add our epic story to a grand library of love shared by all. Everyone loves a heroic story about the courage it took to master all the mysteries and tame mythical dragons during a heroic journey home.

The divine and our soul are composed of the same loving ova-la, but a lower octave is necessary to individuate and have our human experience. Consider the possibility that we are all aspects of divinity, which shares our experiences through us. We are travelers on a personal journey into darkness to explore a principle, an ideal, and love in all its forms to share our experiences with divinity and the divine back home. Of course, the pain of living in a world of illusion can make cowards of us all—but not on a soul level.

THE RELATIONSHIP OF THE SOUL TO OUR PERSONALITIES

A human being is programmed for earth—survival, fear death, love, live in community—so gaining the panoramic perception that our soul enjoys is not simple. Bodies die, but our soul is immortal. Suffering does not deter the soul, since it is focused on a big picture with goals that our human nature is usually oblivious to. Plotinus described the goal of the soul as henosis, which included the emotional maturity to seek oneness and unity.

Since part of us is immortal and the other is human, the marriage vow "until death do us part" can take on new meaning. In essence our soul marries our body and departs at death. Our soul accepts and completely loves our humanity, but it also loves all of divinity and its family of souls. Plotinus did not believe that pain is processed on the soul level the same way we process pain at the biological/psychological level. He thought that there is a natural split between the temporal agony the personality experiences when seen through the timeless perspective of the soul. The pain on the physical plane is very real, very true, and very important. Plotinus's take on this subject is as follows: "We may treat the Soul as in the body—whether it be set above it or actually within it—since the association of the two constitutes the one thing called the living organism, the Animate. Now from this relation, from the Soul using the body as an instrument, it does not follow that the Soul must share the body's experiences: a man does not himself feel all the experiences of the tools with which he is working."[23]

But the soul uses pain, suffering, disease—as well as pleasure, power, and success—to persuade our personality to break its destructive patterns and addictive delusions. Mid-life crises, for example, often awaken memories that spur us on to pursue a previously dormant longing. Challenging events, like a near-death experience, the birth of a child, or an outstanding accomplishment, stimulate growth and satisfy our spiritual longings.

And while the personality struggles with these obstacles, the soul is molding our mental, emotional, and physical body into an enlightened being. Pain and pleasure are a big deal to the body, but the soul never loses sight of its master plan.

Plotinus describes our spiritual agenda in the following way:

> What could be more fitting than that we, living in this world, should become like to its ruler, to the Being in whom, above all, such excellence seems to inhere, that is, to the Soul of the cosmos and to the Principle ruling within it, the Principle endowed with a wisdom most wonderful?
>
> It is from the Supreme that we derive order, distribution and harmony, those virtues which are a principle of symmetry and beauty in us as long as we remain here; they ennoble us by setting bound and measure to our desires and sensibility, and dispelling false opinion, and this by sheer efficacy of the better, by the fact that the measured is lifted outside of the sphere of the unmeasured and lawless.[24]

THE ABANDONMENT IMPRINT

Birth is a spiritual journey into physical form after leaving a home where we were bathed in love and oneness. Leaving henosis and residing in a physical body immediately creates a lasting abandonment imprint, which includes separation anxiety and existential agony. The painful remnants of this primal process are directly related to what Saint John of the Cross famously termed "the dark night of the soul."[25] That term stuck and many poets and authors adopted the phrase to describe challenges during significant Job-like hardships, when nothing we do seems to be working.

The dark night of the soul is the recognized description of what is occurring, but it's actually a misnomer since our soul never suffers or actually leaves henosis. The confusion occurs when the human psyche registers the event as an especially "dark night." The promise of mortality and lost love severs awareness of our divine nature. But in this instance, shocks occur when we physically experience our primary abandonment template. Separation anxiety erupts from trace memories from this template that formed as we left henosis to become human. A similar jolt occurs when we separate from our mother at birth. The anxiety generated from these separations initiates the driving force behind our instinct to bond with friends, family, and lovers.

Healing occurs through loving connections and sympathetic resonance. Abandoned fragments of the self seek wholeness. Embracing our pain with supportive behavior, a loving heart, and eternal wisdom can transform illusion when we embody henosis. Incorporating these principles and learning how to be whole, when our soul or the divine supposedly isn't around, requires significant trust. The challenge is to remember our soul is always present and the divine never abandons us. Aristotle had brilliant insight on this topic: "We must no more ask whether the soul and body are one than ask whether the wax and the figure impressed on it are one."[26]

This awareness is necessary to navigate through the darkest illusions this world offers. The mirrors of illusion and life's experiences can be brutal. We come to earth to forget our origins, remember our spiritual home, and come to the realization that we were never, ever, for one microsecond, abandoned. We are also here to love and use our hearts, mind, and body to find the source of the deepest truths about our true nature. I would describe what we are doing as playing a game of hide-and-seek with divinity and our soul. Everyone goes through this process so that we can adequately heal the existential agony ourselves. When we truly accept our destiny by healing the abandonment imprint, we experience our own divinity. Immune to illusion, we fulfill the purpose of the dark night of the soul.

One of the reasons the story of *The Wizard of Oz* endures so powerfully in our culture is that it aptly describes our soul's journey on earth. Just like Dorothy, we land in Oz and can return home whenever we want by clicking our ruby slippers. Everyone has a trusty toolbox of reliable habits, rituals, and solutions near and dear to our hearts. When trouble erupts, some of our strategies are useful, but many are not. The dark night of the soul reveals the cracks in our foundation and shakes lose every habit, paradigm, and mental construct built on illusion.

Darkness blows up our emotional security blankets like the locusts, floods, and plagues that afflicted Egypt in biblical times. Pain and suffering humbles everyone—including powerful pharaohs. A problem of epic proportions always narrows our attention and pries open closed minds. The desire for relief motivates us to reexamine every delusion weighting us down.

When life kicks away our crutches, many collapse and believe that the divine has abandoned us. Rise up and reexamine every template, paradigm, and principle to sort out if it retains value. Surrendering every sacred cow, like power and control, will help you determine what creates more love or recycles pain. It's a grand occasion worthy of celebration when we can withstand all of the enchantments of earth and remember *there's no place like home*. Dorothy enjoyed this celebration when she woke up on the farm with her family and said, "Kansas is a lot like heaven, isn't it?"

It takes massive amounts of courage to master the multitude of illusions this world has to offer. Succumbing to the hatred, strife, hopelessness, and agony of feeling abandoned is very seductive. Alone in the darkness, some begin to question whether or not "Kansas" exists. The dark night comes in the form of illusion, so that the sunlight of our soul and the divine can shine through our mirages. It's the crowning achievement to fight off all the yuck illusion could muster so that we can develop the love in our heart, the brains, and the courage necessary to return to our divine home, just like Dorothy.

The dark night of the soul can be the last hurrah or test of illusion to overcome before the dawn of our new life. When storm clouds bring chaos, nothing is working, and you do not know what to do, remember to access your wisdom within like the Scarecrow, the love within your heart like the Tin Man, and face your problems with the determination of a courageous Lion. When the world crashes down around you from a wrecking ball, it's a signal to your mind to give up every delusion of control and surrender to new possibilities and unforeseen solutions, just like Dorothy did throughout her adventure. Storms create a field where rainbows can shine. Illusions are storms, and henosis resides in the peace, love, and harmony *under* and *over* the rainbow.

RECONCILING WITH THE FORM OF ILLUSION

Dorothy Gale reminds me of a shopper who enters a store to buy one item and never gets swayed by all the sales gimmicks and promotional come-ons designed to tempt her. Shoppers can be seduced by the illusion that they can save money by buying more merchandise than they need. Fear of losing a good deal can corrupt the common sense of a consumer in a department store just as assuredly as it did the Wizard when he was offered a cushy position as Supreme Ruler of Oz. I have noticed in my practice that unaddressed emotional needs often activate primitive reptilian appetites if a person chronically avoids those emotions. Addictions are like sales clerks offering snake oil to mask our pain while failing to solve our core problem. Illusions of grandeur are as enchanting as spells from the Wicked Witch, as the Wizard of Oz would no doubt attest. Shopping at the illusion store for temporary remedies will only make our problems worse. Avoiding emotions, especially repressed rage, is like ignoring the gravel rattling under our car as we drive off the road. Addiction and avoidance is like the sales clerk selling you a set of earplugs rather than offering directions to help you return to the yellow brick road to get home.

The form of love is like a warm embrace, while the form of illusion resembles a smack in the face. Since recognizing illusions is so complex, use the form meditation to ferret out delusion. Throughout the book you will see seven more form meditations, like the following one about illusion, which focus on the key principles explored in most chapters. For now, just read the meditation and let the ideas open up your awareness. Try reading this form aloud with the intention to own the message and find the illusion in any situation. Take a break and consider your illusions after reading this meditation.

Experiential practices using breath, movement, and intention can transform illusion. The Camel Wave Meditation (appendix A) is a powerful healing modality that employs these reliable methods to help you find your deepest illusion. The Wise and Loving Inner Voice Meditation (appendix B) is an additional practice designed to help you discern which internal voice within your brain provides loving wisdom or more illusion. I also suggest taking a break after reading this and any other form meditation. Let your memories and thoughts flow. Then move on to the next section.

When you feel the need, you can return to this form meditation about illusion and reread it over and over. When Plotinus said, "Our concern, though, is not to be out of sin, but to be god,"[27] I believe he was encouraging us to not merely avoid illusion but to let our principles and values become a beacon in the darkness.

FORM MEDITATION: ILLUSION

Opposition and contrast create masterful training programs. Pain is designed to oppose love so we humans can know love. Illusion is an enigma because the creative force that challenges humanity balances the equation of love through the creation of its opposition—misery. Shadow and light come from the same source. It would be impossible to choose love, or at least entertain the possibility of a choice, without opposites or contrast. Can love exist without indifference? How can I find goodness in my life without something else to choose?

Illusion provides the experiences I need to master on the path toward love and wholeness. How could I understand what a privilege it is to choose love if I have never suffered from a lack of love? Exploring the purpose of pain through the mirrors of relationship has been the path of all of humanity, since the very beginning of time. Pain allows good to be experienced as good and gives me the contrast to know that what I am experiencing is more spectacular than terrible.

The form of illusion warns me about trouble ahead similarly to when gravel rattles the undercarriage of my car if I am in danger of driving off the road and into a ditch. Wake-up calls may look like failure or self-sabotage to someone on the outside looking in but are merely reminders that I missed my mark. Life provides mirrors that reflect my perspective back to me. I need to accept what is mirrored back to me as a warning sign, like the gravel that tells me to avoid the ditch. Pain signals that I am in danger of recycling my suffering. Painful reflections offer course corrections and alter my perception of the world—for if my illusions remain a mystery, that pain continues until I solve my mistery.

Failure enflames my delusions and blows back pain to reveal my own reflection.

If I hate, I may be hated.

If I betray, I may be betrayed.

Until I heal what closed my heart to love, I may experience the mirror of being unloved.

The mirrors of illusion let me see my reflections and encourage me to return to my divine nature. In this way, the form of illusion is one of the best allies I have on earth because it reveals where my shadows lie. If I'm blind to darkness and ignorant of my voids, I can fill with negativity and ignore the mirrors of illusion warning me of impending trouble ahead. If I am suffering, I may be susceptible to exploring quick fixes, sexual delights, overindulgence, drugs, alcohol, and exciting games that exhaust my body and stimulate my mind but create more suffering. Mistaking inebriation as passion is easy sometimes. I am learning that my addictive impulses indicate I am avoiding what is generating my unpleasant emotions. I choose to resolve my personal love templates, personal paradigms, and unsolved mysteries.

In the equation of love, pain provides equilibrium and is an aspect of the divine; therefore pain and love are part of divinity. It's not about punishment or retribution for my wrongdoings; the form of illusion teaches me about reciprocity. In this capacity, pain humbles the rich or the holy; no one is spared, and it guides us on our path to fully experience love while in human form.

The mirrors of illusion greet everyone with a puppy's playful inquisitiveness and enthusiasm in reverse. When the form of illusion enters a room, it starts sniffing out everyone's shadows—just like a puppy checking out an interesting scent. Illusion immediately gets to work to make sure I and everyone else have the opportunity to experience our failures at full measure to help us transcend our delusions and move toward our destiny. No one is spared from this process of discovery.

Pain is a personal wake-up call requesting that I refocus my attention. Pain provides a service indicating where I missed the mark to transcend my delusions, like an annoying smoke alarm warns about an impending fire. The form of illusion is the fire and the bringer of fires to guide me out of the cave of illusions and into the light. This is always done in love, since the heat has a positive intention to burn away the dross of delusion, stimulate new growth, and return me to the path of reunification.

Earth is a living experiment for my soul to explore love and light through darkness and despair. Despair is the Petri dish or embryonic fluid that births some of the most beautiful creations on earth. Some people collapse from pain and believe there is no divine presence when tragedy visits them. It is important to remember that the negative reflection banging at my door is love in disguise and a delusion to master. With henosis, the goals are unity, wholeness, and reunification. The crucibles of pain and failure exist for the purpose of revealing the illusions blocking my path to become aware that I am one with my immortal soul.

3

MERGING HUMANNESS WITH LOVE

THE FORM(S) OF LOVE

Maintaining our principles and divine connection while accepting whatever happens with love in our heart is a challenge for all of us. When we can remain loving in the midst of fear, death, and all the pain earth has to offer, our illusions will melt into nothingness like a wicked witch doused with water. Pain is a teacher, illusion provides the curriculum, and a degree in incorruptible love is what we receive upon graduation.

In his *Symposium*, Plato expanded our perspective about the nature and purpose of love in the following way, "'Love' is the name for our pursuit of wholeness, for our desire to be complete."[1] In order to experience wholeness, we need to explore why we create barriers to love. Hidden behind each barrier erected and each crisis we knowingly or unconsciously create is an opportunity to remember our wholeness. Suffering recycles our illusions and dysfunction until this pursuit is completed. Once the purpose of pain and the mirrors of illusion are understood, the next challenge is to explore love's many forms.

Matters of the heart, willpower, and human passion lose vitality when empirically quantified into bits of data and intellectually dissected with dispassion. Everyone knows that love exists, but science struggles to provide evidence-based proof. Many romance novelists and mystical poets, such as Rumi, have described what love is, how it works, and how to become better lovers. There are countless ways to express love:

agape love, unconditional love, pure love, innocent love, divine love, tough love, and codependency. The list goes on and on. The precise, indisputable definition is not as relevant as considering how our experiences create love or fail to do so.

Since survival is a primary human imperative, our brain is exquisitely programmed to look for patterns and make associations for prediction and security. Similarly to how a computer analyzes data, the brain uses current and historical information to compare and then synthesize information into belief systems to comprehend our current conditions and predict future outcomes. Previously I used the term *primary love templates* to describe the original instinct to accept parental love models. Additionally, our brain, especially after any particularly dramatic event, will make decisions based upon what occurred for safety and security considerations. Those decisions interpret a positive peak moment or a traumatic crisis, which is subsequently programmed into mental conclusions or belief systems I call *personal paradigms*. Negative personal paradigms can reinforce a victim or perpetrator mindset, for example, and are limited to the wisdom and emotional maturity of the individual at the particular moment in time when the paradigm is created.

The gentleness typically associated with early childhood and self-realization can become distorted due to negative belief systems. Chronic suffering and early traumas become primary love templates and personal paradigms. When pain is partnered with love for the long term, the sweetness and goodness of love feels foreign. Chronic pain can trigger a programmed belief: *after sweetness prepare for suffering*. When this association cements into place, we instinctively create shields to prevent love from entering our heart in order to avoid the anticipated pain. Until we liberate ourselves from these dysfunctional templates and associated paradigms, we may conclude we are unworthy of love and continue to seek suffering because we sincerely believe the initial sweetness will be taken away if we fall in love. Some shun love due to fear that the pain would be too great when it's ripped away. Complications occur with religious programming, which implies that suffering leads to holiness or is preferred by God. Promises of heavenly rewards in the afterlife can be comforting initially but ultimately confound because on some level we may intuitively sense the following:

- The divine is love and nothing else and derives no pleasure from suffering.
- Love is what we are in life and what we are after our death.
- From a spiritual perspective, suffering is just gravel next to the road warning us if we get off track to return to the pavement.

When Plato introduced his Theory of Forms, he believed in our soul's inherent goodness. Whether or not we feel worthy of a life full of goodness is often based upon our familial, societal, and/or religious training. The quality of our personal relationship with the divine and what we believe to be our own philosophy about our lovability exemplifies autonomy and sovereignty. The word "sovereignty" has multiple meanings, but the type of sovereignty I am referring to implies personal authority, self-responsibility, and self-determination.

Prosperity, happiness, and joy are our birthright. The task is feeling lovable while facing invalidating parents, family members, organizations, strangers, friends, and supposed allies. Incorruptible self-worth and wholeness have the power to change a primary template or paradigm in the blink of an eye. In that blink, we can transcend those proverbial cave shadows, release our shackles, and experience henosis. Even though many of us were taught to judge, shame, and punish ourselves for flaws, acknowledging our faults with love is like waking up in a divine embrace.

Love begets love, and overwhelming force begets a variety of reactions including passivity, resistance, and counterforce. Snapshot conclusions and personal paradigms predict how the world works and are encoded in our youth during a life-changing event. Power and force are symptoms of anti-wholeness, so resisting the urge to control the "ocean swells" is the task. We can't control the tide of human desire; the challenge is catching a good wave and surfing the sea to where we want to go. Forcing anything on another person, even with earnest intentions, is a flawed strategy. When humanity is ready and accepts love or goodness as its primary teacher, the need for pain as motivational incentive will cease and our world will change accordingly.

Pain and pleasure have a reciprocal relationship on opposing ends of the same continuum, but Plotinus pointed out: "Pleasure and Pain belong neither to the Body nor to the Soul, but to the compound, that is to say, to the Soul present to the Body, or the Body present to the Soul.

The higher or reasonable Soul, in which our personality resides, does not [experience] these sensations, though is aware of them. The higher part of the Soul wears the Body, with its pleasures and pains, like a garment."[2] In other words, when we die, we will take only love with us; therefore love, like the soul, is immortal, whereas pleasure and pain are only relevant during our life on earth.

UNLOVABLE AS A PRIMARY LOVE TEMPLATE

As a therapist, the most prevalent afflictions I have noticed people struggle with are self-criticism and self-worth. Shame, judgment, punishment, and self-sabotage promote pain and the need for redemption, which will keep healers, therapists, and the medical communities in business until something changes. Shame, for example, deeply affects our self-esteem because its toxic message basically implies every emotional reaction or action taken is wrong. On the other hand, love in its purest form says we are okay just the way we are. Previously, I mentioned the importance of accessing an original traumatic event to retrieve the initial belief system buried within a primary love template. When an original illusion is revealed, problems and dysfunctional belief systems due to shame and unworthiness can be addressed. The following case study illustrates how a primary love template healed during a mutual process of dialectic discovery.

Mary was a thirty-two-year-old divorced mother of two who sought psychotherapy due to a plague of debilitating panic attacks after a romantic breakup. Mary had suffered similar attacks previously, after her husband had divorced her a few years earlier. We had had good rapport prior to the session when a massive breakthrough occurred. Paralyzed in anxiety, Mary was in crisis and wanted to heal the original trauma underlying her panic. Mary narrowed her attention before we intentionally went back to the first time she had ever felt similar panic in her life. This was accomplished through the process of dialectic discovery combined with a guided visualization where she split her awareness into two aspects of her personality to seek healing. Summarized, here are the main points:

Her adult observer (the lover). *Mary initially accessed the wisest aspect of her personality that possessed the will and maturity to* *actively nurture and heal her trauma. This gave us access to an observing aspect of her personality that was able to witness and briefly revisit her original panic associated with abandonment. We used this connection as an emotional bridge to return to the first time she had experienced debilitating panic.*

Her inner child (the beloved). *Aspects of our personality struggling with illusionary beliefs are sometimes represented as an inner child holding primary memories that react powerfully to similar events and the danger experienced at ground zero of their original trauma. I guided Mary to go to the first time she had ever experienced a similar emotion, which turned out to be her primary love template.*

Our goal. *We initially sought emotional release, which often uncovers the original belief system within a primary love template. Mary revisited her original trauma and the abandonment she had experienced in subsequent relationships throughout her life. Once her dysfunctional belief system surfaced, she could release the template and make a new decision.*

A solemn stillness filled the room as Mary and I revisited ground zero of her original trauma. Her adult observer reported she saw herself as a newborn in the hospital while her birth mother was deciding to put her up for adoption. Mary suddenly experienced herself as a beloved newborn making the following decision, "If I was a more lovable baby, then Mom would keep me." As soon as Mary was aware of her "decision," her inner child burst into gut-wrenching wails for forty minutes as she processed her agony associated with being abandoned at birth but also, more importantly, her conclusion that she was unlovable.

Later, her observer aspect reported to me she was awash in grief initially but then was flooded with images of her submissive behavior in subsequent relationships. Mary recalled spending her life doing anything anyone wanted her to do, hoping to receive love and thus recycle her unlovable/abandonment issues from birth. Ignoring her needs in every romantic relationship, Mary had always felt invisible and was troubled by repeatedly experiencing the men she loved taking her for granted—her *primary unlovable template* was that powerful.

Mary experienced the full potency of her lifelong template during her epiphany-style awakening. While safely exploring her dialectic discovery, she also released an internal decision that she was unlovable or worthy. Afterward, she began to meet her own needs in future relationships and expected others to do the same. Watching her turn her life around was wonderful to witness. I fully believe this occurred because she stopped recycling the life-script decision she made as a three-day-old.

Now, logic would say that a three-day-old infant would have no memory of such an event, but dialectic discovery is not about proving whether or not Mary's memory was 100 percent accurate. Instead, we focused on how Mary's *primary unlovable template* affected her intimate relationships and contaminated her ability to feel worthy. Dialectic discovery is a process of exploration and retrieval without theoretical expectations or scientific methods to satisfy. The proof is not in proving the event occurred; instead the proof is that her suffering subsided. Allowing Mary to process her emotions without skepticism helped her feel lovable and worthy. Together we marveled at her remarkable recovery. Mary witnessed and then processed the agony associated with her initial perception, which reprogrammed the illusion, released her template, and changed her life completely.

Mary's recent rejection re-created primal suffering, and her panic attacks were a formula—which I believe was divinely designed to obliterate her original "unlovable" delusion and buried crystallized emotion (discussed in more detail in chapter 4). Through her passionate resolve and focused attention, Mary rewrote her debilitating infantile conclusion and the traumatic picture was gracefully removed from her memory. The salient fact was that she consistently met her needs afterward, consistently spoke up, and set appropriate boundaries with others in the months to come. Her courage to explore the emotions within her core opened the door, and verifiable evidence of her ongoing success was the only proof she or I needed.

We are a divine being living in a physical body, and when we remember love, transformation can occur and internal shackles release. I imagine this process Mary experienced as an infinity symbol or figure eight that links her adult observer (lover occupies the first loop) to the illusion that created her inner child's suffering (beloved occupies the second loop.) Her loving heart created a healing multiplier effect that resembles a divine vortex (energy circling at an expansive rate) at the center of the figure eight.

WISE LOVER, WOUNDED BELOVED RECONCILIATION

Love is the most powerful force in the universe. Awareness is the ability to witness with compassion and completely accept stunted aspects of our personalities without expectation. When we use our ability to split our consciousness into a wise observer, separate from our suffering, we can witness our wounded self, and this action gives us a method to heal early trauma. The terms I use for these two parts are "lover" and "beloved," which mean "the ability to give and to receive love to ourselves and others." Mary's Wise Lover was her mature adult that accessed and witnessed her "unlovable" belief with heartfelt compassion. Abandoned at birth, her Wounded Beloved then re-experienced multiple rejections and panic attacks associated with her "unlovable" illusion. By processing and witnessing her (beloved) inner child's emotions with love and compassion, the illusions associated with Mary's wounds released and a new day dawned.

Understanding the Wise Lover and Wounded Beloved relationship provides a reliable method to heal our/others' illusions with love and compassion. Intimacy includes the ability to fearlessly witness and experience another's love and suffering. A beloved's pain usually subsides in the presence of heartfelt love and sympathetic resonance. When we walk a mile in someone's shoes, our judgments reduce and empathy flourishes. A loving, mature adult can calm down others who are recycling infantile, childish, or adolescent stress responses. (See chapter 7 for stress responses and their remedies.) Intimacy skills are not only important with friends, family, and lovers, but also with our own primary love templates and immature aspects of our personality.

Use this graphic representation of what happens when a wise and loving heart embraces our wounded inner child or another in a field of love to explore your own experiences. The infinity symbol is used here to represent the power of love in its limitless form and the ability of love to transform illusion.

Any obsolete belief system, personal paradigm, or template based upon illusion can release and evolve with love, compassion, and understanding through the cherishing qualities associated with sympathetic resonance. Grace and healing may occur when our initial intentions are acknowledged, while we address every delusion and belief system recycling our suffering. When the wise adult observer (the lover) summons

Figure 3.1.

its nurturing ability and willpower to bear witness and then embrace our wounded inner child or fragmented part (the beloved) in the midst of its suffering, any illusion can be healed and new decisions made. When love and awareness heal personal delusions, our heart actually melts the crystallized emotions and frozen traumatic memories recycling our suffering.

I've seen other templates such as Mary's panic response successfully rewritten and watched the people heal and overcome emotional trauma using this dialectic discovery technique. Modern psychology is around 150 years old and is constantly discovering new theories and dismissing others about the causes of chronic mental illnesses. A professor told me in graduate school that kind words from a warm heart produced results very similar to those produced by a professionally trained psychotherapist. Healing is a process, which includes many factors science has yet to quantify. Heartfelt presence and inspired wisdom can heal internal suffering when we are ready to accept the gift. After participating in hundreds of similar sessions, I am firmly convinced that perception becomes our reality and we each perceive the world differently in our own unique ways. Clients access personal subjective memories, so proving what actually occurred is a pointless exercise. The benefit of dialectic discovery has been proven to me time and time again. When we embrace our pain with a loving heart, illusion transforms and wounds heal.

THE HEART REVISES OUR TEMPLATES FOR LOVE

The human heart is an amazing organ that mechanically circulates vitality but metaphorically generates love, which provides the humaneness in our humanity. Hearts can beat as one and mirror the same loving frequency found throughout divinity—this similarity is not accidental. We are all spiritual beings exploring love in countless forms, and our heart makes life and wholeness possible. The union of heaven and earth is an analogy that mirrors our decision to create henosis with our body and soul.

When we love someone or something dearly, we usually say we do so with our heart *and* soul. If our heart is missing, our passion, dedication, and follow-through quickly die. When Mary decided she was unlovable after her mother rejected her, she had to heal her heart from that delusion in order to thrive again. The interplay between Mary's beloved inner child, who thought she was unlovable, and her soul that knew otherwise became her focus. Mary's strategy to be invisible in relationships resulted in her abandoning herself before anyone else did. The negative experiences from the men in her life recycled her *primary unlovable template*, which provided valuable mirrors and incentives to transcend her original abandonment wound and its illusions. When Mary released her *unlovable* decision after her mother's abandonment at birth, she started to love herself without abandoning her needs . . . perhaps for the first time.

When I restrained the boy in the institution in Ohio, a similar dynamic occurred. I stayed with him and provided behavioral limits with love in my heart, which helped melt his frozen emotion, which had crystallized around his heart. In this situation, restraint and love's nurturing powers created safety. His wounded inner child then released its emotional burdens, which were too heavy for him to carry endlessly. No matter how hard he fought, I did not lessen my grip until he talked about his rage, which caused him to hit others and smash property until someone took the time to embrace his heart. When his pain erupted into uncontrollable sobs, mucus, and tears, I held him like a cherished child. Frozen tears and heartfelt agony, which had never seen the light of day or known safety, were released. This gave his heart the space to feel worthy of love.

Both Mary and the young man's experiences were similar. With Mary, dialectic discovery took place through an imaginary dialogue, and with the young man, the dialogue occurred after physical exertion and heartfelt connection. Both experiences offered the space to transcend a lifetime of suffering and self-sabotage and eventually transform their primary love templates.

Our heart is a difference maker for any endeavor. We say things like "I knew in my heart I had to . . ." or "My heart was not in it" or "I didn't have the heart to do it" for good reasons. However, heartfelt passion can be expressed positively or negatively with corresponding results. Intention ignites the engine of ambition, but desire or suffering will also do the trick. Perception informs our experiences. Focused intention, heartfelt passion, and dedicated action toward a desire can create our dream. Our life experiences are a continuum designed to lead us to transcend situations and/or scars, which repeat until the original wound heals. Once a wound transforms, we no longer need to repeat our templates or paradigms. Liberation from our trauma and drama can lead to a desire to have a personal relationship with the divine. As an intimate relationship develops, an internal stability anchors within our core. This knowing begins when we believe, beyond a shadow of a doubt, that we are worthy of love. Another person or merely reading a book does not make this happen. It's perceived viscerally in the cells of our body through a deeper sense of knowing.

Pain and suffering reveal the illusions within our love equation. We are each born into families that provide models for our primary love templates. Voids occur when we are told lies about love while illusions separating us from our heart and soul are promoted. Lies about our divine origins are presented as "truth" until we distinguish our reflection from other's delusions. Illusion plays a starring role by helping us to discover what we *are* by exploring what we are *not*. This continues until we find our true love and possess the courage to rewrite our personal storyline. Everyone makes forays into the darkness and the collective din, while illusion provides mirrors so we can see our reflections. Illusion offers challenges and then invites us to experience incorruptible forms of love.

Romantic relationships start with a honeymoon phase in which everything initially looks wonderful; this phase can last from a few weeks to over a year or two. Once we feel comfortable and committed, the dross of illusion burns off. Committed lovers are simply integral players in the same story, mirroring fears, insecurities, hopefulness, and soul-level dreams to one another for the purpose of transcendence. Immature individuals tend to push sensitive emotions into the shadows. When we face our fears and confront illusion, we can find the truth that is able to transform and transcend problems. Buried feelings and disowned emotions have a purpose and are problematic if we lose sight of what motivates our behavior. Concealing our unresolved emotional issues from strangers is a relatively simple endeavor, but it's nearly impossible to accomplish with our intimate partner. A few decades ago, I made a remarkable discovery while teaching a relationship course for couples experiencing chronic conflict. Now, I am convinced we pick partners that not only make our heart sing, but also ones who will push buttons and point out our dysfunction. Since humans are compelled to express our deepest desires, intimate relationships provide excellent mirrors so we can transform, transcend, and sift through our unconscious illusions.

Standing in truth and addressing our delusions is an extremely difficult task that is put before all of us. After treating hundreds of couples embroiled in chronic conflict and examining relationship dysfunction, a consistent pattern emerged. Eventually in session, I help clients identify their core emotional need, primary love template, or personal paradigm that exists underneath a couple's presenting problem. When each person's core issue is rendered down to its essence, a similar shared skeleton issue between the couple always emerges. Gender presentations and intensities can vary widely, but it seems to me our soul chooses someone perfectly suited to mirror our deepest illusion to us.

The form of love provides an intimate partner that will push our buttons to help us root out illusion. This process is particularly active in intimate relationships and with family members, who unconsciously mirror core unresolved issues to one another until they heal them. The popular knee-jerk reaction to judge, blame, and/or feel victimized by our antagonist will, in return, provide the perfect opportunity for both participants to see their unconscious material reflected in another person. When we judge someone vociferously, we would be wise to assume that person is a mirror—reflecting some aspect of a personal core issue.

Mild frustrations often ignite buried emotion and/or previous traumas from primary templates and victim/perpetrator paradigms. Unresolved, unconscious emotional material is guaranteed to be involved when a relatively small event instigates significant conflict. Thus the response to the minor disagreement is magnified out of proportion to the current conflict or situation. The hallmarks of this type of regression are infant, child, and adolescent stress responses (discussed in chapter 7), which innately prioritize protective and security considerations over equanimity. Unseasoned combatants mistakenly believe that their job is done once they identify their adversary's distortions and related delusions. What many lovers fail to realize is that their anger, conflict, and heightened emotions are opportunities for each person to grow. Examining our illusions helps us distinguish fact from fiction to create an incorruptible form of love.

Try this quick comparison to check if your gut reaction to a "crime" someone committed is truly objective or contaminated by unresolved emotional material:

1. Rate your emotional state to the "crime" on a scale from zero to ten.
2. What number would polite society provide for the same "crime"?

Any numerical difference between you and polite society reflects the presence of your unresolved issue.

Illusion will always provide mirrors so we can see our reflection to help us find and address our unmet needs and unresolved emotional material. For example, let's say your emotional reaction to someone's "crime" is *nine* while most people would rate the same offense at *five*. Pounding at someone with a level nine intensity, when your adversary believes they deserve at best a level five reply, will stimulate defensiveness and a possible victim/perpetrator (pitch and catch) type of retaliatory response. More desirable outcomes occur when you address the historical material or emotional allergies creating your four-point multiplier and reach a state of equanimity before you address your adversary from a level five or lower.

When I worked with the angry young men in Ohio, my unconscious anger, hidden vulnerability, and victimization trauma from my stuttering history mirrored and then triggered a similar rage and a perpetrator paradigm within the residents of the treatment center. The mirrors of illusion are very efficient; we expressed our fear/anger to each other through the victim/perpetrator paradigm and eventually found a proper home for our emotions. Again, the mirrors of illusion provided opportunities for us to see our reflection, which gave the angry young men and myself an opportunity to become whole. When I finally faced my fears, my inflated reaction to the "crimes" the adolescents committed got in line with the rest of society. Once I became immune to those terrorizing tactics, I reached my full potential and transformed my role from victim to mentor. For more than forty years now, I have taught thousands of other clients how to transform fear and heal vulnerabilities. Initially, I needed to take the responsibility to heal my core issues, past wounds, and illusions before I could help others reach their full potential. When two or more people accomplish this feat together, as happened in Ohio or with couples, a powerful surge of love, compassion, and incorruptibility strengthens the personalities of everyone involved.

Love provides powerful mirrors that ferret out illusion to create more love. I remember participating in a ten-minute laughing meditation with a large group of people and being surprised when some people were crying and in pain at the end of the laughing meditation. Suffering surfaces when love fills a heart that needs cherishing, which is why crying occurred during and even after the meditation. Pain activates our illusions, which respond like rats crawling out of hiding when a vortex of love appears. Love cleanses every heart, especially those overloaded with suffering. When illusions leave and divisions heal, hearts reopen again but are stronger and fortified.

Uniting our spiritual and physical nature is a solitary journey made easier with a quiet mind able to listen to our soul. However, this emptiness is difficult to sustain. Many of us think self-love, self-esteem, and self-responsibility are difficult tasks, which require a great amount of work and diligence, but we *don't* need to deserve, pray, or beg for an outstanding life, and henosis is ours for the taking. *Illusion* blocks wholeness and suffering reveals its hiding place. Empower yourself by removing every illusion blocking your ability to give and receive love freely.

In the fairy tale *The Wonderful Wizard of Oz*, Dorothy loved and courageously helped her friends achieve their goals to become whole before she returned to Kansas. We can follow her example when a Kansas twister picks us up and throws us into our own Oz. All we need to do is get back on our feet, dust ourselves off, and follow the yellow brick road to henosis. A crisis is an opportunity to solve the mystery unfolding before us. When a problem occurs, just stop, look, and listen to find the jewels hidden amid your rubble. We can assume love is knocking on the door in the disguise of an illusion, reminding us that we veered off the yellow brick road. Accept what happens gracefully, meditate for wisdom, and let the knowledge gained redirect you.

We fail to grow when we pretend that our symptoms don't exist, so embrace each opportunity to mature, which our problems provide. In *The Essential Rumi*, which contains remarkable poetry and quintessential prose about the mystical union with the Beloved, Rumi said, "God turns you from one feeling to another and teaches by means of opposites so that you will have two wings to fly, not one."[3]

WHOLE HUMANS

Love is fundamental to our explorations into how humans become whole and eventually incorruptible. Love is like water because it is forceful beyond measure and yet its basic nature is to yield and seek the low places. Its fluid nature melts into other structures and gives life to everything it touches. Whatever happens is perfect when we love because, like water, love never loses its constitutional integrity and will continue to exist in its next location. Water moves through the membranes of the body freely, without obstruction for the most part, allowing life to enter the dark places shrouded in illusion. People die without water, and our heart and soul would suffer from a dearth of spirit without love.

Love is the most powerful force in existence; even animals rush to our side when we suffer. Who hasn't felt better when a pet or a friend offered us love? Like a monk lost in prayer, we too can whisper the endearing phrase *there's no place like home* and try to remember love exists everywhere. Once we know we are worthy, we can let love nestle in like a loyal pet. Like an eternal river, love fills the low spots within our heart to remind us we never left our wholeness or our loving home in henosis. Love soothes the paradox of simultaneously being both human and divine. Plotinus said, "It [soul] is said to be buried in a cave, but, when it turns to intelligence, to be freed from its fetters and to ascend, when it is started on the contemplation of reality by recollection . . . souls then become, one might say, amphibious, compelled to live by turns the life there and the life here."[4]

Frogs can live both on land and in water and are called amphibians. The concept of *living a double life* stems from the Greek word *amphibios*. The philosophy of both Plato and Plotinus addressed the dichotomy of our human and divine nature. They said the body has appetites, which are variable, volatile, and temporal, while our soul is incorruptible and knows henosis intimately. The phrase *voluptas in stabilitate* was used in antiquity to describe the relationship a soul has to the divine forms of pleasure, love, and happiness. Plato and Plotinus thought the soul stabilized our humanness and that love was the elixir drawing our body, mind, and soul toward henosis. Loving ourselves without conditions gives us access to our soul and eventually wholeness. Subsequently, loving others and our beloved will feel natural and uncomplicated. Unity reminds us of our pre-birth experiences awash in oneness. Breaking free from templates and paradigms based upon illusion helps us reach our reunification goal.

Plato and Plotinus believed that by living a virtuous life, standing in our truth, and embracing what best serves the whole, humanity would experience *voluptas in stabilitate*. Here is my summary of what I believe they were saying:

- Hold on to your principles and allow love to transform and transcend illusion.
- Remain connected to goodness, oneness, and all of divinity.
- Embrace everything with love and then surrender to what transpires.

When Plato and Plotinus truly became incorruptible, illusion had no power over them and they were compelled to share and illuminate others with their wisdom.

Tragedy is derived from the Greek word *tragos*, which literally means *he-goat*. Dorothy was tragically orphaned, and her heart *could* have shut down in a reptilian stress response and remained closed. When she was re-orphaned in Oz, a primary love template could have prevented her from realizing she was worthy of good fortune or seeing Kansas again. Perpetrators seek scapegoats and victims to discharge rage upon. The importance of remembering this eternal wisdom cannot be underestimated, and I honor those authors, healers, and philosophers who have kept the healing elixir of love alive. I have seen many clients sabotage a good relationship because their lover activated every unexamined delusion about their vulnerability and unworthiness. Trauma victims often push love away due to an emotional black hole in their heart that is loaded with suffering. We create protective mental fences around our hearts until we heal the primary wound and learn to love our flaws, claws, and self without conditions.

Hearts close and love is kept away due to fear that the devastation would be too great if love is again withdrawn. Dorothy provided a fairy tale model of how to overcome this illusion, but my client Mary, who was put up for adoption, had panic reactions after being reabandoned until she released her unlovable decision. Mary surmised she was unlovable when her mother rejected her.

Through dialectic discovery, she revisited her primary love template and found her associated illusions flowing from the belief she was unlovable. When she learned how to truly love herself, Mary felt worthy and eventually sovereign. Over time love will trigger every enchantment we have about love, just like Mary experienced.

AN EXPANDED FORM OF LOVE

The form of love enables us to conquer illusion and rise above division and prepares us for a good fight for our survival. Often conflict looks like a challenge to love one another more, but it is usually a reminder to develop more self-love. Humanity is an aspect of divinity disguised as friends and strangers. We can emulate henosis by becoming whole ourselves. What occurs in our internal world appears in our outer world. Whatever deepens our ability to experience joy, happiness, and love needs to remain in our life. Patience, forgiveness, and the absence of shame are qualities that dramatically improve the quality of our life. When the decision about which road to take becomes confusing, take the time to focus inward and choose activities that reinforce the fact that we are worthy and lovable. When we, as individuals, believe in our worthiness and lovability, any primary template or personal paradigm about love can transform.

The form of illusion reveals our delusions so we can experience expanded forms of love. Use the following form meditation to enhance your ability to love. For now, just read the meditation and let the ideas open your awareness. Try reading this form aloud to own the message. I also suggest taking a break after reading this and any other form meditation. You can also use the form of love with the Camel Wave Meditation (appendix A) to deepen your ability to love. The Wise and Loving Inner Voice Meditation (appendix B) will help you discern which internal voice within your brain provides useful directions about how to become more loving. These tools can be useful when seeking a loving solution to a sticky problem. Explore the freedom of examining the ideas, the feelings, and the thoughts that the forms trigger. Then move onto the next section.

When you feel the need, you can return to love and explore its forms over and over.

FORM MEDITATION: LOVE

A vital goal of being human is to master earthly forms of love. Honoring, nurturing, and truly respecting myself gives me the muscles to love my neighbor and eventually all of creation. The ability to love is a precious gift in life and is the only treasure I can take with me when I cross over after death.

My goal is to embody love completely in my mind, heart, and soul. Maturity is directly related to my ability to maintain incorruptible principles in the face of life's slings and arrows. Discerning my shortsighted delusions and illusions from long-term solutions enables me to overcome my trials with love and awareness.

Most of us were taught as children to love one another and open our hearts to family, friends, and lovers. Embracing someone else is a formidable challenge all by itself, but the most difficult challenge to master is to love myself.

Love is the quickest route to evolve into a blissful state of being. Transforming illusion into love is one of the primary mysteries blocking my realization of henosis. Treating a negative personality trait as a friend or figuring out which belief system recycles my problem is a good starting point. When I can embrace my flaws with compassion and acceptance, love occurs with ease. When I treat every positive or negative aspect within in a loving way, I accept myself as I am. This delicate process creates the template and the requisite learning curve to develop the skill set and balanced wisdom necessary to learn how to apply this skill with another. The secret of turning my life around from a world of hurt, betrayal, and abandonment into a loving one lies within this understanding.

Family, friendships, and intimate relationships are sacred mirrors reflecting my successes and failure to love. When I embrace the annoying habit of another person as a mirror of my own frailties, problems transform easier as I become more capable of bringing compassion and deeper forms of incorruptible love to my relationships. The illusions hidden within my personality are challenging to reveal, but they also provide solutions to the problems I have recycled with others. Judgment, righteousness, and my victim/perpetrator paradigms generate separation. When I love and accept my failures, my heart opens; my compassion for others deepens, and more desirable outcomes occur.

Successful relationships with friends and lovers provide templates on how to direct these concepts toward humanity and the world at large. When enough people consistently apply this approach as a daily practice, suffering is transcended and the whole world will become more loving.

Love challenges me to embrace my enemy with a softened heart. The act of loving is a shortcut to my divine roots where I can exude the purest expression of my divine essence.

The following affirmation reminds me to surrender and love mindfully in troubling times:

My divinity within knows that there is wisdom afoot, which is intangible to my personality. I align myself with the divine and my soul to discover this presence in my life with wisdom and love. I accept what is happening to me with grace, acceptance, and a knowing that the divine is love and the answers to my questions will come eventually.

I am love, divinity is love, and that is all there is. My divine soul longs for henosis while in human form. Love is the answer, the question, and all there is in the universe. I seek the wisdom while on earth to know, understand, and live this truth.

I ask the divine to help me align to oneness and love. I appreciate your assistance to hold love, be love, and accept that I am nothing but love. And so it is.

4

THE CHERISHED HUMAN

THE FORM OF CHERISH

Plato called the divine "Goodness" and the "Form of the Good" to describe what Plotinus later called The One. In ancient Greece, "agape" was the word Greeks used to describe the exquisite and remarkable form of love humans experienced from and toward the divine. Agape love describes what psychology textbooks refer to as unconditional love. "Cherishing" is a more recognizable term, so going forward I will use "cherish" to describe this similar irresistible loving force. Plato likened the loving energy from the divine to the sun shining on everyone and gave the Form of the Good preeminence over the other forms:

> What gives truth to the objects of knowledge, and to the knowing mind the power to know, is the Form of the Good. As it is the cause of knowledge and truth, think of it also as being the object of knowledge. Both knowledge and truth are beautiful, but you will be right to think of the Good as other and more beautiful than they. As in the visible world light and sight are rightly considered sunlike, but it is wrong to think of them as the sun, so here it is right to think of knowledge and truth as Good-like, but wrong to think of either as the Good, for the Good must be honored even more than they. . . . As for the objects of knowledge, not only is their being known due to the Good, but also their real being, though the Good is not being but superior to and beyond being in dignity and power.[1]

In studying the works of Plato and Plotinus and observing the progress of my clients, I recognize that moving straight to goodness is a quantum leap for people in the midst of suffering. Positively reinforcing and cherishing the gradual steps toward success constructs a gentle bridge from suffering when people confuse love with pain and struggle to remember how "good" actually feels.

Love is a tiny word but a daunting emotion to master because it is the most complicated, convoluted, irresistible force in the universe. Just as we have a biological instinct to breathe, so we also have a divine instinct to love. Getting to that wonderful state of love, though, when blinded by illusion is challenging. Sometimes we just need a practical stepping-stone such as feeling cherished, which can restore our balance when challenges and crises take our breath away.

RECEIVING THE FORM OF CHERISH

Cherish is an expression of love and includes blessing what we give or receive with an open heart and equanimity. Breathing in love, circulating it within, and extending it to another allow hearts and souls to flourish. Unfortunately, conditions and expectations from friends, family, and society burden love with paradoxes and contradictory messages. Divergence threatens the social status quo, so what happens most often is that relationships either adapt or are suffocated by expectation and control.

I stutter. When I hammered at words in my youth, for example, soft listening eyes showed me that they were indeed windows into a soul. I could tell within seconds of meeting someone if they were cruel, compassionate, or could be trusted. Some kids and adults would become impatient, frustrated, or unconsciously smile while I hammered my words. People with closed hearts often have cruel or empty eyes that reveal an inner savagery or emotional vacancy. Stuttering frequently triggers knee-jerk reactions from observers. Some people enjoyed my plight or dismissed me, so I frequently felt invisible.

Some people would remain present, soften their eyes, and compassionately wait for me to finish my words without a hint of internal discomfort. A few would try to help me finish my sentences. That was okay, but I always finished my sentences myself because I felt incompetent if I accepted their assistance. I cherished the enlightened ones who patiently waited for me to finish my thoughts. Those with open hearts accepted my stuttering and waited to hear what I had to say, embraced that discovery, and possessed an intellectual curiosity about me. When I experienced acceptance, I cherished that person for tolerating my flaws without judging or fidgeting impatiently.

I know my dad cherished me because when I stuttered, his eyes always had a loving sparkle in them. He waited patiently. A thoughtful and sensitive man, he comforted himself with alcohol like many men of his day. Unfortunately he didn't know how to consistently cherish my mother's heart or his own.

Mom's heart just didn't seem to have any room for compassion. Her father died during the Depression after a long bout with tuberculosis. Her dreams of escaping a harsh life died along with him. At the age of nineteen in 1936, she gave up her college scholarship to support her mother and three younger siblings. Underemployed, bright, and angry, she was uncompromising, just like the world she experienced in her youth. Unhappy, unaware, and a devoted Catholic, she prepared us for life by role-modeling selflessness, tenacity, and persistence.

Convinced that the word *yes* never graced her lips, I tested my theory repeatedly. She foiled every ingenious attempt I could think of to get her to say the word and provide the love I craved. Her typical response to a discussion of this nature would've been, "Cherish . . . forget about it; there's too much work to do to waste any of my time on your childish games."

People always seemed too wounded or self-absorbed to totally entrust my heart into anyone's care. Then I met Toby, our neighbor's dog; he "adopted me" and became my beloved friend. One day when I was walking to my friend's house, two stray dogs approached and started growling at me in a menacing way. Alone and terrified, my heart cried out silently for help. Toby appeared out of nowhere, fought off the dogs, and rescued me. He taught me a lesson about fearless loyalty and the intangible, quantum connection between all living things. Perhaps we are all connected through our ability to care about what others feel, I thought. Toby sensed my terror, and his noble act won my heart. I've cherished my furry companions ever since and have learned many additional lessons about love and the ability to cherish from the animal kingdom.

The ability to love and cherish in the midst of everything, including suffering, is what I believe Plato, Plotinus, and every other sage want us to achieve. When we accept ourselves the way we are, then it's easier to accept others similarly. Toby was a living example of how love begets love, just like those wonderful people who let me finish my sentences.

CAN I CHERISH MYSELF FLAWS, CLAWS, AND ALL?

Stuttering was such a struggle for me in grammar school that the Sisters of Notre Dame recommended that I repeat third grade. Speech therapy in the early 1960s was primarily a warm heart and soft eyes in a kind soul. Two other students with significant lisps and myself were driven to a local public school twice a month for group therapy with a speech therapist. Our hearts were cared for, but the strategies employed in those days never worked very well.

My classmates and I had public problems others could witness, but psychological trauma or poor coping strategies are invisible to polite society and are either addressed or ignored privately. Speech therapy required me to discuss my impediment openly, but the therapist never explored what occurred within me internally that had started my stuttering engine. Privately I criticized myself unmercifully; I hated myself for my failures and continually clawed for control.

Graduate school placed me with a field placement supervisor who mentioned how lucky I was to stammer because it provided a built-in anxiety barometer. Part of me wanted to punch him in the mouth, but I knew better. He said problems fester when hidden and misery multiplies if left stranded in the shadows. Public embarrassment and humiliation were powerful teachers, and stuttering eventually became a gift when I learned how to cherish my suffering.

Unfortunately, humans have a knack for self-sabotage and are often left fantasizing about ideal love scenarios or reenacting unproductive primary love templates. Our parents offer blueprints for the form of love whether we are aware of this occurring or not. When we fall in love, our beloved pries open our heart during the honeymoon phase and activates every unrealistic illusion or fairy tale we have about finding our true love. Many people mistakenly believe that our partner is the answer to our prayers because, during that initial phase of love, a void seems to be filled or the cracks within our heart temporarily masked. Who hasn't been disillusioned when inexplicably our lover horribly disappoints once we gave them our heart? That lover jumps, falls, or smashes the pedestal we had created for them, taking away our fantasies about finding true love.

Everyone has delusions about love and what romance will do for our hearts. Disillusionment inevitably occurs, and couples seriously question the relationship when conflict arises and the honeymoon phase ends. When those major triggers occur, the good news is that a more mature phase in the relationship, the cherishing phase, can begin. Cherishing our own flaws mirrored to us by our partner is difficult to do. It is important to remember that conflict leads to what our relationships require us to heal within ourselves.

Love, presence, and innocence are treasures to behold, but trauma and human drama can cause hearts to close. "Once bitten, twice shy" is an idiom that describes the natural human instinct to protect oneself. This is why compliments for occasional verbal fluency or well-intended encouragement from a kind soul never penetrated my stuttering defenses. Gracious publicly, I never lowered the protective shield closest to my heart. As Rumi said: "The cure for pain is in the pain."[2] Romance provides opportunities for our heart to become incorruptible in our ability to love. Partners mirror their unresolved issues to one another. Lovers reflect what needs to be cherished and healed within the other. After forty years of treating couples, I believe that souls are matchmakers. Our soul leads us to a romantic partner who will activate our deepest illusions about love so we can learn to cherish what we find most heinous within our own heart. Throughout my career, I have noticed from my own dialectic discoveries that couples have chronic conflict around the *same* core illusion. Partners in the relationship provide a valuable service to each other by mirroring different versions of the same core illusion to one another that each is challenged to transcend. Our eyesight is often 20/20 about another person's issues, but most of us need glasses to find, examine, and transcend a similar core illusion hidden within ourselves.

Deep in contemplation one day, while using the Wise Lover, Wounded Beloved Reconciliation (chapter 3), I began my own self-induced dialectic discovery to uncover what stuttering provided me besides lessons about humility, frustration, and shame. Speech therapy taught me the benefits of emotional release, heart connection, and the courage it took to speak publicly. When my disassociated emotional download came, I remembered how much I hated myself for my inability to control my circumstances. Recalling my unmerciful self-criticism that clawed for control, I realized that I had never truly accepted myself . . . flaws and all.

It eventually dawned on me that *I* was by far the worst bully of them all. Every negative thought about myself was like a gut-punch to my inner child, who was powerless to stop the stuttering much less my malicious self-evaluation. For the first time in my life, I felt the consequences of my misguided attempts to claw at myself with criticism. Learning how to accept my flaws led to loving myself and relinquishing my propensity to judge others, which had burdened my relationships since youth. Worthy again, I felt the agony that I had unwittingly perpetrated against myself, cherished my flaws, and decided to stop my attempts to control through perfectionism. My reawakened passion signaled my heart to love in a way that had not been possible before. My protective shield was no longer necessary when I learned to love myself . . . flaws, claws, and all. My heart opened, and through my own internal dialectic discovery, I could not only give love but also receive love when I learned to cherish my imperfections for the first time.

CRYSTALLIZED EMOTION

Herein lies the mystery of why we reject love and react paradoxically when tender loving care is what our heart desperately needs. Once bitten, a human heart is very tender and quite shy. The heart will close after significant trauma, and trust issues arise that can evolve into a pattern of protection, which includes sabotaging that most precious human experience of love. This pattern of protection repeats until a way is found to transcend suffering and cherish our original wounds.

We are each challenged by self-inflicted injuries that developed from misguided interpretations, conclusions, and delusions about love that are rooted in emotional material from past experience, which crystallizes over time. Recycling the suffering from a previous love injury can activate shields to protect our heart and prevent further harm. Shielding mechanisms like a victim/perpetrator paradigm or primary love template can wound a lover, when our defenses rise up unexpectedly.

When intense emotions are burned into our memories, our mind makes snapshot conclusions that can become framed photographs and mental programs. Trauma and suffering can evolve into encrypted, crystallized emotion that recycles defensive reactions to present situations. Memory lapses and dissociation are shields protecting us from crystallized pain until we reaccess that original event. But shields do *not* protect forever and actually *postpone* suffering until we release the emotions, revisit our mental conclusions, and take those pictures off the walls. Beloved partners, family and friends, or some stranger or event will often trigger our unresolved trauma and reopen these wounds. Addressing them with love and acceptance is how to cherish them. When our wise lover reconciles the wounded beloved (chapter 3), defensiveness and the need for protective shields can be reduced.

Here is how crystallized emotions melt:

- By accessing a nurturing, emotionally mature aspect of our personality that has more internal strength and heartfelt passion than manifested during the original event, we can melt the resulting emotion that was internally crystallized into a primary love template or victim/perpetrator paradigm in the aftermath of the precipitating event.
- By cherishing with heartfelt sympathetic resonance the entire residue from our traumas, including the associated mental conclusions, the frozen, crystallized emotions melt away and disassociated decisions can be rewritten as our wounds heal. Removing embedded emotional material and its associated memories opens the gates for omnipotent wisdom to spontaneously erupt and unravel illusion.
- By improving our ability to self-cherish, we can increase our adaptability and emotional maturity.
- When our wounds, or those mental snapshots we once used, are replaced with loving solutions, we regain the ability to react to similar experiences more productively.

Intellectual understanding is a tool of our brain's left hemisphere and does not typically have enough potency to melt crystallized emotion, which resides in our right hemisphere. However, the simple action of cherishing and processing our emotional material experientially will access our right hemisphere and can be very productive. (Brain hemispheres will be discussed in more detail in chapter 7.) The Camel Wave Meditation in appendix A is a practical healing modality I designed for an individual to use with the eight form synopses mentioned in this book. Sometimes though, when our wounds are deep and the patterning is destructive, we do need additional objective help and heartfelt compassion from others. I do recommend that you seek a trustworthy friend or professional counselor for assistance in cherishing an encrypted negative event and its associated crystallized emotional material. By loving our flaws and claws similarly, we gain strength, courage, and the ability to rewrite a primary love template or a related victim/perpetrator paradigm.

No matter how well intentioned a lover or in my case a speech therapist might be, a heart will remain closed until our private conclusions based upon crystallized emotion are rescinded. Releasing the emotional residue and addressing our illusions by cherishing them accomplish this. When I played the private blame, shame, and dissociation game around my stuttering, my heart never really opened, and I deflected love or any form of encouragement. By accepting my flaws, claws, and all, I cherished my heart and let love in.

The cliché is true: give and you shall receive. Cherish is too precious to have it work any other way. Cherish forms a bridge into henosis and wholeness.

THERE'S NO PLACE LIKE HOME

Since the dawn of time, safety, survival, and perpetuating the species have been the primary imperatives of humanity. Material possessions, personal satisfaction, and security considerations continue to dominate the popular "survival of the fittest" philosophies. Throughout history, most societies around the world treated citizens like ants: the survival of the colony, clan, or country superseded any consideration about cherishing each and every individual. Plotinus reminds us about unity within plurality, when he said, "There is one identical Soul, every separate manifestation being that Soul complete. The differentiated souls issue from Unity and strike out here and there, but are united at the Source much as light is a divided thing on earth, shining in this house and that, and yet remains one. One Soul [is] the source of all souls; It is at once divided and undivided."[3]

In the *Matrix* films, Neo struggled initially when he was informed he was "the One," but eventually he lived up to his birthright, cherished unity, and led humanity out of illusion. Plato described how illusion imprisoned mankind two thousand years ago and would have loved the following statements spoken by Morpheus and Agent Smith inspired by his Allegory of the Cave.

> **Morpheus:** This is your last chance. After this, there is no turning back. You take the blue pill—the story ends, you wake up in your bed and believe whatever you want to believe. You take the red pill—you stay in Wonderland and I show you how deep the rabbit hole goes.

> **Agent Smith:** Did you know that the first Matrix was designed to be a perfect human world? Where none suffered, where everyone would be happy. It was a disaster. No one would accept the program. Entire crops were lost. Some believed we lacked the programming language to describe your perfect world. But I believe that, as a species, human beings define their reality through suffering and misery. The perfect world was a dream that your primitive cerebrum kept trying to wake up from. Which is why the Matrix was redesigned to this: the peak of your civilization.[4]

Do you reject the notion that humanity refuses to be cherished and chooses suffering over happiness? Powerful people force others to do their bidding and have throughout history, like the Agent Smith tyrants did in the *Matrix* films. Dictators may start with great intentions, but something usually snaps, corruption ensues, and tired paradigms of enslavement, exploitation, or manipulation of weaker members of society inevitably recycle. Engineered societies promote philosophies about "the needs of the many outweighing the needs of the few," often believing that rules and regulations are the only glue keeping marriages, religions, and even their country together.

Laozi hit the mark when he said, "The more that laws and regulations are given prominence, the more thieves and robbers there will be."[5]

Ironically, as a whole we are being treated as a solitary entity, but unfortunately something vital is missing. When most of us struggle to get by, fear and anger come to the rescue to handle the terror felt inside. To regain control, many ethnic groups and countries require strict obedience and compliance, which limit the ability of an individual or a civilization to innovate and evolve. When unquestioned compliance to ancient traditions is the expected and rewarded social norm, innovation suffers and societies decline.

Everyone needs community, and rules can be successful tools for humans to coexist with one another. Many times a society has a legitimate, positive goal behind its controlling tactics, but an underlying flawed belief system lies within restrictive societies and misses a critical and immensely important point. The desire for peace, love, and order exists deep within the spiritual core of every human being. We come from oneness. Henosis is our birthright and the home we long for while we learn to cherish others and solve the riddles within our experiences. At the core, humanity *instinctively* wants to share resources, experience love, and cherish others. We are all creators, and we naturally want to cooperate and support one another without coercion, fear of punishment, or isolation as our primary motivators to do so—that is, until we are trained by others or suffer from narcissistic wounding and act otherwise.

Failure is a vital activity because accepting mistakes helps us develop self-esteem, which leads to success. This is how we develop the necessary skills to create unique solutions to unforeseen problems. Though it may require internal rewiring, once we cherish our illusions, our soul knows the way back to henosis. Neo demonstrated this phenomenon brilliantly when the bullets Agent Smith fired to kill him in our current paradigm fell harmlessly to the ground when he mastered his fears and accepted his fate. Exposed to love and the light of day, illusion quickly returns to its origins: smoke and mirrors.

USING THE FORM OF CHERISH

As previously mentioned, Plato considered Goodness the most powerful force in the world and likened divine benevolence to the sun. Plotinus once said, "Our world is not separated from the spiritual world. . . .

We deny that God is in one place but not in another."[6] Plato and Plotinus gave us a useful analogy when they likened the sun to how the divine emanates love. Beyond the sun, similar to the moon orbiting earth, our ability to cherish waxes and wanes like lunar phases. This is because our moment-to-moment and day-to-day ability to cherish will vary based on the circumstances we experience. Criticizing our "failures" or championing perfectionism misses the mark.

The following fairy tale about apples offers cherishing information. Sometimes solutions to problems and ultimate success are impossible without friends, adversaries, and antagonism.

Imagine, for a moment, somewhere over the rainbow that apples are humans living in an orchard cherished completely. Every person is a beloved apple in a beautiful orchard so vast that some say it never ends. A thriving environment of lush soil, bountiful rain, and copious sunshine nurtures each apple with loving, exquisite care. Cherished, these apples flourish until they reach maturity. Ripe and perfect in every way, the apples eventually fall from the tree, land on earth, and thus lose perfection.

Lying on the ground, bruised and battered from the fall, the heart of each apple remains strong initially because it was cherished in the orchard. "Apples are good through and through" happened to be everyone's primary love template. But, with time, many fallen apples forget the orchard and their enlightened motto when the earthworms and illusion antagonize them. The bumps and bruises were bad enough, and now creepy, crawly things that never existed in the orchard get under their skin. The mind does funny things when earthworms and creepy illusions challenge an apple's sovereignty and orchard unity. When delusions inundate a grounded apple for too long, some apples blame, feel victimized, and question their orchard origins to explain the fall.

Rare apples remember that all the fruit from the orchard is perfect and even bad apples are part of a bigger whole—the orchard. Many apples fail to realize that worms motivate us to remember wholeness so we can return to the orchard sovereign and incorruptible. Focusing on ugly worms under our skin gives an apple the illusion it is flawed and corrupted. And when a worm pokes its head out for everyone to see, many people fail to remember it is just a primary love template and refuse to cherish themselves or anyone else infested with worms.

In conclusion, some apples cherish every apple on earth and thus remember their divine origins. Placing our attention on the perfectly good part of our companions' apple core and accepting worms as illusions until that apple remembers being cherished in the orchard pays love forward. When apples cherish, the antagonistic worms and the personal illusions eventually disappear for their beloved companions. *Eudaimonia* is a Greek word similar to cherish, often translated as "happiness" or "welfare," but some say *human flourishing* more accurately captures the meaning. Cherished apples intuitively understand this principle and accept their worms, flaws, claws, and all. It is important to see the proverbial good part of each apple even when the worms are at their worst. Then everyone flourishes.

We can learn to cherish more by embracing our earthworms with a warm heart and soft eyes. However, the apple and orchard fairy tale is a shortcut to the form of cherish distilled into just a few paragraphs. Forms in ancient Greece were realized wisdom, and by cherishing, we'll explore its form meditation.

The Camel Wave Meditation (appendix A) uses movement, a form meditation, and conscious breathing to release crystallized primary love templates and personal paradigms such as a victim or perpetrator mindset. Read the following form meditation and let the ideas penetrate into your being so that the next time you are in a tricky situation you can use the form of cherish to help soften your suffering. You may also choose to read it aloud to amplify the message. I also suggest that after reading a form meditation for the first time, you take a break and reflect. You can work with the Camel Wave Meditation or try the Wise and Loving Inner Voice Meditation (appendix B) to help you develop a practice to discern which internal voice within your brain provides loving wisdom. Let flow the ideas and feelings that the form of cherish triggers. Then move on into the next section. When you feel the need, return to the cherish meditation and reread it.

FORM MEDITATION: CHERISH

Every atom of all of creation—including me—is appreciated, valued, and honored. Every experience of love and angst brings the paradox of both wisdom and delusions to unravel. I know that no matter what occurs, the divine is with me. I know the divine cherishes me, and I, the human, cherish the divine. Our cooperative relationship creates the foundation for a spectacular partnership.

In the English language, "cherish" is a word I can use to capture the quintessential quality of the divine's love for humanity and all of creation. Even if I am in the midst of a challenge to shift, I can cherish my emotional reaction like I would a giggling child or recall how I felt cherished by a pet that adored me. Being cherished is uplifting, but now I also want to learn how to cherish the people I touch in my everyday life. My challenge is to develop the strength to reach a state of wholeness where I cherish and expect nothing in return. Can I willingly surrender to the wishes of another while, at the same time, honoring me and accepting that what happens is okay, even though others are indifferent to me? I choose to be objective and observe my judgments, indifferences, and rigid reactions blocking my ability to love or cherish.

Even when other people react or judge me, I achieve tranquility and fulfillment by cherishing my own divine/earthly nature. I also appreciate when the divine, or anyone else for that matter, accepts or cherishes me during my darkest moments. Being "real" by maintaining my principles and values creates more integrity within me. But sometimes I do wonder why it's so easy for a human to compromise their principles and personal integrity to receive a momentary illusion disguised as love. Cherishing everything and everyone around me in a competitive world that enables people to hurt one another is sometimes extremely difficult to do. Sometimes, scars exist inside me that make it difficult to love or trust another and that's okay. I will be gentle with myself especially if I am finding it challenging to cherish someone who has harmed me. My goal is to cherish everyone to the best of my ability in each moment.

I recognize that some days I have difficulty receiving love. Early childhood experiences, trauma, or previous relationships have left me with emotional scars that have led me to develop behavior patterns that rationalize, defend against, and/or avoid intimacy. If my heart is too closed or self-protective, cherishing another is difficult, if not impossible, until I acknowledge and resolve the painful memories remaining in my heart.

My unhealed scars make giving or receiving love in some circumstances painfully difficult until I learn to cherish those scars by learning the lessons that increase my incorruptibility to every illusion residing within me.

But love just is. I don't need to do anything or be something to deserve or earn it. When I believe I'm worthy of being loved, I see others and myself through the eyes of divine partnership. To experience love (which I am coming to realize is the whole point of the soul becoming human) is to use cherish as the soul-infused quality that most closely resembles the way the divine loves me—flaws and all.

How often do I cherish my experiences without expectation and/or love myself without conditions? What is too much or too little or just right? How many people or things do I actually cherish in my world? Can I muster enough courage to discover what motivates an unsavory desire or cherish a failure hidden within the recesses of my heart? Some days I miss my mark and on others I am spectacular. Shame and blame create more of the same, so I plan to cherish others and myself courageously no matter what happens. If I am compassionate, celebrate my beautiful flaws with acceptance, and do my best to cherish them, love can burn away the illusion of separation. Then my positive lessons and growth-producing opportunities will flourish.

The dark aspects of human drama and the negative experiences of earth are created not to harm me but to guide me away from behaviors that recycle suffering. That guidance becomes exponentially more persistent and troublesome when I ignore, judge, and punish others or myself. I am willing to embrace my troubles, for they are partnered with the divine to remind me to love the aspects of myself that remain in illusion. When the world is mired in black-and-white thinking and division, acceptance creates openings for me to cherish others and create unique possibilities. Loving approaches create opportunities for light to emerge from darkness. Enlightened perspectives such as these allow me to discover what I previously thought unimaginable or improbable. When I love others and embrace my own positive and negative qualities, other people are drawn to take my lead.

Here, within cherish, lies the secret of love and success on earth. I want to accept this invitation to cherish. I will freely express my divine nature so that my world will flow with grace and ease and bloom like a flower.

Cherish is a gateway to love; love is a gateway to cherish. It is a continuum.

5

GRACE

THE FORM OF GRACE

Illusion often feels like a smack in the face, while love holds us close in a warm embrace. Cherish is a gentle form of appreciation—a conscious choice to love without expectation. Grace is spontaneous like a serendipitous kiss. Innocence, presence, and loving intentions are powerful grace magnets. Sometimes experienced as awe, we can prepare for grace by dreaming for our heart's desire. An elusive quarry, grace cannot be conjured or controlled. Grace and synchronicity inspire us to do or say the right thing at precisely the right time.

Ancestral templates and victim/perpetrator paradigms are always worth examining. Everyone needs a healthy home for every emotion, especially if feelings remain frozen. Crises create space for healing, and grace might show up anytime on the horizon. White flags, failures, and weakness are traditionally associated with surrender, but an underconsidered aspect is that opening our mind to new possibilities is a brilliant method to access grace and spectacular outcomes. Surrendering to a crisis to find a unique solution is the birthplace of innovation.

Socrates' famous paradox, "I know that I know nothing,"[1] is not sarcasm nor meant to imply that Socrates considered himself stupid; he simply articulated the most important insight from Plato's cave of shadows—by questioning all that is given as truth or absolute certainty, his mind remained open to every possibility. When Socrates famously said that he *knew* nothing, he reminded us to keep our mind open, like an

empty cup. Creativity, spontaneity, and originality are generally associated with grace and thrive with the psychological spaciousness of
open-mindedness. A closed mind comforts itself with certainty like a
cup of water filled to the brim; new information spills on the floor.
Clearing space releases tired ideas past their prime.

Willpower and human endeavor pale in strength compared to the
magnificent force created by a thunderstorm, tornado, or typhoon.
Amid tempests or during the calm that follows, peace can unfold, mysteries reconcile, and events synchronize without effort due to the form
of grace. Everyone fights for control, but surrendering to the storm of
love all around is exactly what is required. We have the ability to give
and receive love while we suffer and experience our divinity in the
midst of tragedy. Those failures, that crisis, the angst, a beautiful moment of bliss erased by a sudden devastation—all of what most people
would consider the absence of love may actually lead us to a spectacular
form of love called grace. In *our pursuit of wholeness*, a crisis can look
like a problem initially but gracefully transform into a blessing.

ONENESS IN DIVERSITY

Oneness in diversity is a paradox, which requires walking into a mystery. Paradox occurs the moment our soul experiences human form.
Wanting to experience henosis in a fragile body, the soul is subjected to
the distractions associated with physical survival and unconscious people. As infants, we naturally bond with our family and interpret *all* of
our positive and negative familial experiences as love. Discerning *which*
emotion or attitude is our own versus those originating from another
family member is a complex and often confusing consideration. As infants, we absorb the emotional milieu like sponges, and this milieu
serves as the source of not only grace but also primary love templates.

Conservative societies often expect children to act like lemmings and
follow traditions that may be counterintuitive to the innate sensibility of
the child. In such societies, trendsetters have little support or parental
approval and frequently walk alone. Paradoxically, infants are awash in
absolute oneness at birth, but individuation through self-actualization
must occur before they eventually return to the divine nature of complete oneness on their own. As an adult, to discern whether our current

experiences result from fate, grace, or our personal creations is a daunting challenge. Developing self-regulated common sense while trusting instincts to ignore parental programming is a complex task.

Adolescents frequently get into trouble with authority figures because of a propensity to say yes or no at precisely the wrong time. Puberty, peer relationships, and preparing for a career present difficult choices for every teenager. For example, in my sophomore year of college, I seriously considered dropping my psychology major because every one of the seventeen seemingly mutually exclusive psychological theories I was forced to memorize about the genesis of human personalities seemed completely accurate. Forced to drop my "one size fits all" illusion to continue my career, the enticing paradox *oneness within diversity* entered my life.

Human nature always captured my interest, and later in my own life, the paradoxes within Western and Eastern philosophy confused and intrigued me. Confucius and Laozi, in particular, were difficult to comprehend because they always seemed to talk out of both sides of their mouths. It took years before the wisdom those philosophers expressed became clear to me. Elders and sages, once they comprehend the subtle nuances between love and illusion, start talking about oneness within diversity and speak in paradox.

I had to experience life's complexities before I noticed how grace entered my life and helped me mature psychologically. When we solve our internal physical, emotional, and mental mysteries, our presence expands. Innocent longings and loving intentions invite grace and synchronicity. Merging our whole heart with the great vastness of the divine is one way to experience henosis. However, that does not complete our quest—the next challenge requires us to surrender the illusions preventing us from remaining there.

Grace is ubiquitous . . . like the air we breathe. It exists even if we fail to recognize it and just access grace unconsciously. Once we learn to recognize and accept the gifts paradox brings, our fears shatter and opportunity gains a foothold. In the words of the Scarecrow, "Everything in life is unusual until you get accustomed to it."[2] Once we get accustomed to one perspective, paradox comes along as an invitation to surrender to what is perfect in that moment, but the catch is that we are already powerful. During their ordeal, Dorothy and her companions learned that they already possessed what they sought—a brain, the heart, the nerve, and a way to get home.

PARADOXES OF POWER

Maturity usually is measured by decades of accumulated wisdom. The human brain categorizes information to gain knowledge to predict outcomes based upon previous experience. If our primary love template predicts love will not return, we may give too much or cling too tightly in a futile attempt to stay in a relationship. An inability to surrender inevitably leads back to primal fears and trust issues. Clutching, wanting, or giving too much in a relationship, for example, is an attempt to control love and mask unworthiness fears. Attempting to take or receive from another what we're unable to create for ourselves is the residue of an unresolved issue. Controlling others is an ageless strategy designed to overcome abandonment fears. Creating a unique perspective that differs from a scripted response requires an original solution from our intuitive ability, higher brain, and spiritual nature.

Paradoxically, surrendering control looks like the absence of power and yet is one of the most fundamental sources of personal power. Giving up our most treasured delusion strengthens us. When we don't know what's happening, it takes courage to seek wisdom by allowing the unknown to excite and inspire new growth. Empowerment occurs through self-actualization and discernment. When we empty our mind and renounce our addiction to control, our intuitive or spiritual nature is freed to explore the eternal wisdom that philosophers called a "Muse" for thousands of years. Ancient Greeks used the word *nous* to describe the purest archetypes, universals, or forms (Plato and Plotinus) located within the cosmos (divinity) as a whole. The Greek philosopher Anaxagoras defined *nous* as follows:

> All other things partake in a portion of everything, while nous is infinite and self-ruled, and is mixed with nothing, but is alone, itself by itself. . . . For it is the thinnest of all things and the purest, and it has all knowledge about everything and the greatest strength; and nous has power over all things, both greater and smaller, that have soul [psuchē].[3]

Over the centuries, phrases such as the *universal mind* or *nous*, the *collective unconscious* termed by Carl Jung, or *the way* in the *Tao Te Ching* by Laozi were used to describe the accumulated wisdom and unlimited potential within divinity. Intuition is an abstract form of guidance that unifies our physical, emotional, mental, and spiritual aspects, which initially work together at birth but unravel with life experience. With radiant wisdom and love, our soul has the ability to access grace with much more refinement, especially when our body aligns its power with divinity.

Our soul is supple and accommodating and intrinsically knows how to surrender to henosis. Our soul knows that whatever happens, it is for the best, while our personality struggles with the concept of grace and trust. When we surrender to the often-illogical, transcendent guidance of our soul, intuition blossoms. Love is best expressed as a reflection of our soul rather than just being a job that one must do. Following our instincts and protecting ourselves is important, but grace suddenly appears in ways unknown to our rational mind. Love, paradoxically, especially expressed as grace, is a force without force that we can either accept or reject.

To the soul, the idea of surrender to the divine is as silly as needing to orally tell your foot to move—the soul and divine are inseparable. But our human personality wants to get accurate answers about how to access grace, which creates conflicts of interest. Inherent wisdom flows without effort and intellectual control. Who hasn't experienced this during a difficult conversation with someone important? Once we stopped overanalyzing every possibility and accessed our natural instinct, positive intention, and intuition, the right words appeared without difficulty. Laozi described this process in the following way, "With an open mind, you will be openhearted. Being openhearted, you will act royally."[4]

Since "we are all one," we have access to the same "computer database"—or the collective experience, wisdom, and grace of our forefathers, foremothers, and the divine—whenever we want, without having to experience or think through every possibility. Ants and bees are brilliant models of how the collective of humanity functions. Like an instinctual ant, we have the ability to tap into and access the information to know what we need to do without all the effort and struggle it took others to achieve it individually—this is our legacy, not a paranormal phenomenon. Eternal wisdom is an entity *and* exists within, as the Scarecrow, Tin Man, and Cowardly Lion characters demonstrated in Oz. That trio of misfits released the illusion that only a wizard could solve their problems. But solving life's challenges through personality, power, and intellect alone can lead to a lifetime of struggles. Abandoning the notion of rugged individualism allows us to connect to the wisdom of the ages through henosis, which empowers through grace.

The loving energy of the divine exists in every cell of our being. The earth challenge is to love, be loved, and let love inspire more love in the process. Allowing love from another into our heart necessitates vulnerability and trust. It enlivens us when we clear the debris blocking the path to receive love, which allows grace to flow more freely. Children, for example, surrender instinctively to nurturing teachers and loving parents. Children thrive from the experience by trusting that all of their needs will be met. The path to henosis invites us to empty our mind, renounce our defenses, and surrender the attachments that block divine love from penetrating our hearts at the deepest levels. The paradox of surrender provides the container for wisdom to connect or penetrate without attaching.

Plotinus describes how grace tips the scales toward love in the following quote:

> The Good is gentle and friendly and tender, and we have it present when we but will. Beauty [realized love] is all violence and stupefaction; its pleasure is spoiled with pain, and it even draws the thoughtless away from The Good as some attraction will lure the child from the father's side: these things tell of youth. The Good is the older—not in time but by degree of reality—and it has the higher and earlier power, all power in fact, for the sequent holds only a power subordinate and delegated of which the prior remains sovereign.[5]

The following examples demonstrate grace in action.

THE DOLPHIN DIAGNOSIS

During a dolphin encounter camp I attended in the Florida Keys some time ago, the program leader shared an account of a crisis that transformed into a blessing. In a previous camp, a woman had slipped into the water with captive dolphins and had immediately complained that a dolphin had rammed its rostrum into her chest. After recovering her equilibrium, and with assurances from the leader of her safety, the woman had gone back in the water. The same dolphin immediately hit her again, in exactly the same spot. Her pain intensified so significantly that the leader thought her rib was broken. Later X-rays revealed no damage, but the doctors discovered she had a suspicious spot on her chest where the dolphin had hit her; it later tested positive for cancer. Previous mammograms had failed to detect a problem that the dolphin seemed to have found. Following the diagnosis, the woman had her cancer treated successfully, all thanks to a dolphin that detected it at an early stage. The woman and the program director were both grateful. What had initially appeared to be an unusual dolphin assault was actually a diagnosis, or I would say a form of grace. Situations like this reveal mystical agendas related to our suffering that may not be obvious immediately, if ever. Depression and a sense of abandonment may set in after we endure a significant amount of pain with no obvious resolution. Objectively looking for hidden jewels and remaining positive during a crisis is quite challenging and takes an enormous amount of intestinal fortitude. Like clueless adventurers with special needs, we are all blindfolded travelers called to trust what our eyes cannot see.

To have faith in something foreign or trust that our misery could have a perfect purpose requires courage. This is the nature of the proverbial opportunity within every crisis. Tragedy and turmoil challenge what we believe to be certain and may inspire the creative momentum to break even the rustiest heart open. Crisis pries open our mind to possibilities *beyond what the eyes can see* and/or what can be quantified by scientific method. Plotinus provided clues about transcendence when he said, "You must close the eyes and call instead upon another vision that is to be waked within you, a vision, the birth-right of all, which few turn to use."[6] If our purpose for existence is reunification (henosis), wholeness develops when we know we are worthy of experiencing love, happiness, and grace. Determining which of our thoughts and what behaviors nurture or support self-worth is critical for our well-being.

Have you ever watched someone in the depths of a personal crisis (like the death of a parent, spouse, or child) show exemplary wisdom and equanimity? This is the person who, with an admirable elegance, expresses grief while simultaneously being mentally aware of all that is occurring. Can you imagine anyone thanking the divine for the opportunity to love and cherish a beloved, so much so that the pain of their leaving is worth the experience? It would take a herculean effort, the love of a saint, and the wisdom of Plotinus to achieve that level of grace in that dire circumstance. Consequently, pain can make us ugly or we can become one with the pain, which opens us to the way to transform our suffering into noble, graceful, precious experience. Grieving the loss of a loved one provides an opportunity for us not only to experience how much we have loved, but how much we *can* love.

Grace, like love, is an enigma—many people have attempted to describe and compare precisely what these two qualities are; however, few of us have spent the time to grasp how the undertones work. Though we may say that people "exude grace and elegance" in their mannerisms, movements, and actions, we rarely explore the mechanisms at play that have created this dynamic. Because we name our daughters Grace, usually we see grace as a feminine thing, but the feminine connotations associated with the word do not always apply when grace visits us. *Divine* is an androgynous term unless we preface the words with the masculine and feminine adjectives. Therefore, "divine grace" is androgynous because both men and women experience it equally.

THE WRECK

In 1970, on the way to play a game against Utah State University, the Wichita State University football team's airplane crashed into a mountaintop forest. Trees ripped off the wings, and the tail section of the fuselage cracked open upon impact.

A nineteen-year-old linebacker named Glenn, who sat in the rear of the plane, was one of nine survivors. He and his buddy instinctively crawled, hoisted, then pushed each other through a gash in the fuselage of the wrecked plane just after the impact and were surprised to find that the plane was suspended in the air by a tangled cluster of broken trees. The two men climbed on top of the plane, jumped to the ground, and began to help teammates to escape. As they encouraged a stewardess struggling to free herself near the front hatch, Glenn and his buddy noticed a fire engulfing the tail of the plane. Terrified and dazed, they witnessed the ruptured fuel tanks explode into flames. Things had got-ten tragically worse. Glenn and his friend helplessly watched their worst nightmare occur. Many teammates were still trapped on the plane. Thirty-one people died in the crash. Glen, through grace or a miracle, was treated for a broken foot and a gash on his head but was not seriously injured.

The Aftermath

A man's man, even at the age of nineteen, Glenn was fearless and clueless about emotional trauma. Considering himself lucky to have survived, he tried to bury the image of the plane going up in flames and all those painful memories. To move on with his life, he quit the football team, which for him was a logical decision because most of his friends were dead. Glenn didn't buy into any of the "survivor's guilt" theories and quickly married his girlfriend. When he struggled to cope or if the memories were triggered, he called himself a wimp and bucked up/ froze up like men are expected to do. Glenn became a hardworking, tireless professional who numbed off his flashbacks and emotions with alcohol. He described himself as "selfish" during those initial years after the accident, which attributed to the dissolution of his first marriage. Blaming himself for his symptoms compounded his problems.

Historically, men have been trained to be self-reliant, self-responsible, and in control. We need to realize it takes strength to admit to a problem and solving it frees us from bondage. Otherwise those unresolved issues infect our relationships with family members, friends, and lovers when we become unconscious, self-destructive, and self-centered.

The Vietnam War was in full swing when the plane crashed in 1970, and veterans were coming home with the same trauma-induced symp-toms that Glenn had experienced after the crash. During the early days of outpatient psychotherapy, mental health professionals had little understanding of what was going on with trauma survivors. We are learning, but veterans still struggle with flashbacks, addiction problems, and high suicide rates. PTSD has always existed. Trauma survivors and vets need assistance to create healthy ways of responding in relation-ships.

The Reconciliation

I met Glenn twenty-plus years after the accident. His second marriage was failing, and the source of his problems led back to the plane crash. In our sessions, we accessed the original point of impact and released the emotional debris alcohol tried to bury. With the courage of a linebacker, he faced the buried trauma that had profoundly affected his ability to have intimate relationships with self or others. Glenn turned his life around when he released a decision he had unknowingly made during the crash.

Through our mutual dialectic discovery and using the Wise Lover, Wounded Beloved Reconciliation (chapter 3), Glenn realized that he was still carrying his teammates in his heart. His loyalty to his teammates had fueled his decision to hold onto them as the loving act of a true friend. When he let his teammates go, he could finally grieve. Cherishing his noble intentions and unexpressed pain made him whole again. Subsequently, Glenn gave himself permission to love again. When he truly became aware of his selfless dedication to his teammates for all those years, his vitality also returned. His illusion of selfishness was replaced with the realization of his selflessness. Now he had the opportunity to create space in his heart for himself, his wife, and his children. Glenn was always a successful businessman and selfless team player who led by example throughout his career. When trapped in the illusion about his selfishness, he struggled with the addictive issues he had used to deal with his overburdened heart. The courage he accessed to heal his trauma helped him to start sharing his emotions with his spouse, family, and friends. He always took care of others and finally learned how to take care of himself.

Many years later, when a commemorative video about the airplane crash was televised, his son, a decorated Special Forces veteran of the Iraq and Afghanistan wars, asked Glenn about the crash, when he noticed tears welling up in his father's eyes. In this case, an innocent question was the grace that helped both father and son explore the private places where warriors and survivors bury their pain. They talked together about tragic events, about friendships and innocence both had lost. Grace came to them that day as a turning point. When hearts touch, love heals the burdens that are too heavy for us to individually bear.

Glenn had a "Fisher King" wound that never healed, and grace helped him find his "Holy Grail" when he remembered how much love was woven into the fiber of his being. As he recalled his loving nature and applied what he learned to his personal life, Glenn started to thrive and experience inner peace again.

With time, Glenn's positive and persistent nature helped him remember who he was and completely accept his sensitive nature again. Grace and love work together to make humans whole. Plotinus spoke eloquently about unity and its tenacity to find the eternal good:

> As long as unity exists it produces: but it exists forever; so, therefore, do its products. And so great is it in power and beauty that it remains the allurer, all things of the universe depending from it and rejoicing to hold their trace of it and through that to seek their good. To us, existence is before the good; all this world desires life and wisdom in order to Being; every soul and every intellect seeks to be its Being, but Being is sufficient to itself.[7]

In other words, Glenn couldn't forget who he was forever.

THE SAFE

When I was nine years old, a thirty-five-pound fireproof safe flew through the wall of my parent's bedroom into an adjoining bathroom in the middle of the night. Startled, frightened, and completely awake, my sisters and I heard my parents fighting again, this time about closet space. At some point my father screamed, "I'm leaving . . . and I won't be back!" I heard the ominous sound of his determined footsteps walking toward the garage door, so I called out to him. I was terrified that my dad would leave. My heart raced when the steps stopped, and I felt my father pause and heard his footsteps come closer. A large shadow darkened my door and stoically sat down on my brother's empty bed. I didn't like Mom's yelling or Dad's drinking, but my love for both of them was unshakable. Since I couldn't imagine living without my father, I innocently mustered the courage to say, "I got space in my closet for Mom's stuff." Time stood still until I heard my father quietly sobbing. As an adult, I understand now that his heart had released the pain fueling his rage. His sorrow and our love for one another filled the room, washing away my fear. That moment will remain with me forever. Dad's pain was expressed as rage, and when our hearts touched, emotions flowed and reconciliation entered. I'll never forget that peaceful moment with my father. A loving force replaced our mutual terror, and I believe that force was a form of grace. After what seemed like an eternity, Dad slowly got up and quietly went back to his bed without saying a word.

Looking back at that night, I see that presence, innocence, and pure love went toe to toe with a Goliath called fear. The deep connection between my father and me lasted until his death. I'll never forget my father crying for his friends and seeking consolation from me, a mere teenager, after he had to let three accountants go in his role as vice president of operations. A sensitive, loving man and loyal friend, he always shared his emotions with me. He felt responsible for his employees who worked by his side for decades; in the early 1960s, he had created a new computer system with IBM for the wholesale drug industry that had made his friends' jobs obsolete. He did not like that the world was starting to replace good men with machines. Dad and I loved each other without hesitation, talked about our troubles, and always supported each other's dreams.

Sometimes there are no words for our emotional pain, and we say or do the stupidest things because our heart can't imagine doing anything else. The hole in the wall was fixed in the days after the safe fell through, but hearts take more than a patch to heal. A long time ago, I learned that being present and innocent and expressing pure love are indeed more powerful than a thousand safes flying through walls. The grace was that, in my innocence, I knew what to say to help my dad and myself. Everyone was richer from the experience.

THE STATE OF GRACE

Some creatures are instinctively classified with the qualities of grace, but I don't think anyone would say an albatross landing is always graceful. We do associate butterflies and dolphins with grace because these creatures mirror childlike innocence. As I stated earlier, powerful emotion expressed with presence, love, awe, and appreciation is a grace magnet.

At a museum butterfly exhibit many years ago, I noticed that some of the kids were covered with butterflies and others were not. As a school chaperone for my daughter and her classmates, I spent some time observing what was occurring and enjoyed wondering why butterflies land on some children and not others. What I discovered was that the children who were covered in butterflies were the awestruck ones who stayed present and appreciated every butterfly that "graced" their bodies. The kids who were desperately trying to make the butterflies land on them by sticking their arms out at them were unsuccessful. What I saw is that innocence and awe attract while control repels.

I have experienced the same phenomena in the ocean with wild dolphins and whales. Swimming with awe, love, and appreciation in a state of grace attracts an encounter with these majestic cetaceans. Attempting to grab or chase a dolphin or whale produces the opposite result: they will leave you. So, in summary, successful experiences of grace are attracted by three attributes: innocence, love, and presence.

Trying to control, coerce, or direct the behavior of another being comes from a place of neediness and ignores the fact that the object of our love *chooses* to be with us. Cherishing from a state of awe and accepting whatever is happening with wonder opens the space for divine grace. Presence is the ability to be completely aware from moment to moment with wonder, awe, or whatever emotion bubbles up—including fear. Intending everyone to experience his or her divine potential that is in alignment with his or her soul is an expression of love. Appreciation is a form of humility that accepts whatever happens without expectation.

The beauty and elegance of this process can feel foreign, so most people attribute grace to divine origins. Wholeness embraces the entirety of our experience; therefore, we are the messenger of grace, the message of grace, and the recipient of grace. The day Glenn's life was spared, he received divine grace not only in the midst of terror but when he reopened his heart. That led the way for more grace in the form of a poignant bonding moment around shared grief with his son to bring that event full circle. My father's tears shed in the midst of his rage and my fear provided an opportunity for grace to enter both our lives. If my dad had left that night, something far worse than a hole in the wall might have occurred. That is the miracle of grace: it appears to only last for a fraction of moment, but in that moment, whether painful or beautiful, something extraordinary occurs that often sends our life off into the most perfect places. Presence, love, and appreciation offer an invitation for grace to enter our lives, which opens a gateway to henosis.

CAN WE CREATE THE FORM OF GRACE?

The form of cherish is something we can choose to do; however, the form of grace is different. Grace is like a child who kisses a grandparent spontaneously or a butterfly that lands on your nose unexpectedly. Forcing a child to kiss a grandparent makes everyone feel uneasy, and thrusting an arm at insects wildly to entice grace or synchronicity is another fruitless strategy. We can ask for grace, say grace, or prepare for grace to come by entering a state of presence, love, awe, and appreciation catalyzed by the following form meditation; but the butterfly that is grace can land on our nose or kiss us at any moment unexpectedly.

The potential failure of Glenn's second marriage offered an element of grace, eventually leading him to release the teammates he still carried in his heart. Then he could finally reopen his heart and grieve. When my father threatened to leave our family after throwing a safe through a wall, grace inspired me to find the words to say to him amid our mutual terror and guide us back to safety. Glenn and I accessed the form of grace and tasted henosis briefly. Love and innocence helped us stand strong in the midst of our mutual storms. Plato said, "Virtue does not spring from riches, but riches and all other human blessings, both private and public, from virtue."[8] Our experiences on earth are our riches—the love is invaluable. Life consists of a series of dress rehearsals, and grace checks if our presence, our innocence, and the love in our heart are incorruptible.

For now, just read the following form meditation and let the ideas settle into your heart and mind. Try reading it aloud to own the message. I also suggest taking a break after reading this or any other form meditation. You can also use the Camel Wave Meditation (appendix A) to deepen your experience by combining the form with an ancient breathing method. Reviewing the Wise and Loving Inner Voice Meditation (appendix B) will also help you develop a practice to discern which internal voice within your brain provides loving wisdom. Explore the freedom of letting the ideas, the feelings, and the thoughts that the forms trigger simmer. Then move onto the next section.

When you feel the need, you can return to the form meditation for grace and reread it.

FORM MEDITATION: GRACE

Even if something horrible crashes upon me, the form of grace offers inspiration. I used to believe that synchronicity originated from outside sources, like a muse whispering in my ear telling me exactly what to do. Interestingly enough, the Greek translation of the words "to inspire" describes the process of "breathing in the divine," which in fact is exactly what is going on when I am inspired and how grace feels sometimes. When I experience grace, I am one with divine universal wisdom. Scribes have written about muses being the source of their inspiration throughout the ages, but grace was possibly what they experienced.

Cherishing and presence magnify my capacity to attract grace, so I choose to be happily in a state of wonder while grace may choose to visit me. When I access a heightened state, which includes loving intentions and innocent inspirations for those around me, I occasionally have the potency to penetrate the defenses of the most hardened heart. Sometimes, in the midst of a ferocious storm, grace visits me when I have heartfelt intentions and can remain present, loving, and appreciative of whatever happens without expecting a specific outcome. Standing strong in the midst of dire circumstance that I do not understand requires trust and mighty confidence. Here, in the presence of grace, I enter a place of peace so powerful that walls crumble; righteous indignation and the struggle to hang on or control become passé. Grace helps me recognize my fears, anger, and angst and encourages me to allow those feelings to wax and wane so I can discern love from pain. Focusing upon my suffering or lost opportunities activates the mirrors of illusion reflecting my façade of control.

Negative outcomes are sometimes part of the path, where grace leads me toward a heightened state of resistance to illusion. I choose to explore my ability to overcome obstacles and eventually incorporate maturity and wisdom rather than recycle my illusions. For now, I also choose to dream with a passionate heart and with love on my mind to prepare myself for a state of grace uncorrupted by expectation. I forgive myself for my failures and now wish for something more. Awe, presence, love, and appreciation create wonder, and like a child enraptured by a flock of butterflies, that innocence and wonder are the seeds that grow grace. All my powerful loving intentions have the same potential to access grace.

Grace has a sublime quality that guides me to do what I need to do at precisely the perfect moment. I expect to be inspired by synchronicities and to explore the unplanned sequences of perfectly timed events. Those inspirations provide me evidence that grace comes in many forms to enrich my life. Songbirds in a meadow and animals in nature instinctively know how to cherish a cool breeze or appreciate the sun during a rainstorm. I too can position my focus to allow the grace of the breeze to hit just the right spot and let the sun shine in the midst of a rain shower without questioning or wondering why it occurred or if I deserve such a gift.

6

MINDFULNESS, SOULFULNESS, AND EQUANIMITY

Mindfulness is a very popular word today with many definitions. I add the concept of *soulfulness* to the term of mindfulness. Soulfulness is a lifelong process of deepening our awareness of our soul and embodying its immortal wisdom. "Mindfulness" and "soulfulness" are two words that describe our attempt to merge our human and divine nature. *Equanimity* unifies all our diverse parts by balancing mindfulness *with* soulfulness until we become mentally, emotionally, and physically incorruptible—eventually indistinguishable from our soul. Soulful objectivity helps humans transform suffering into opportunity, transcend illusion, and eventually experience love everywhere. This is the challenge within equanimity.

Generally associated with the philosophy of Buddhism, the term "mindfulness" is a popular method to still the mind and live in the moment. In the late 1970s, mindfulness entered the mainstream with a definition that went beyond a religious practice to access eternal wisdom. Mindfulness became a pragmatic, contemporary way to develop presence and equanimity. Harmony and internal balance enhance our ability to discern love from illusion. Pain has a destiny and will without fail point to our imbalances, which can be reconciled with mindfulness, soulfulness, and equanimity.

In this book, "mindfulness" does not refer specifically to a meditation practice or the Buddhist tradition, but the aspiration to soulful objectivity and equanimity about what occurs in our life. Profound passion and sincere emotion are often described as soulful expression. Since our soul remembers what enduring love is and its illusions, soulfulness includes a deep desire to embody the enlightened qualities of our soul in each moment. Mindfulness can also imply spiritual purpose, and I believe soulfulness is a more accurate word to describe the herculean effort to let our divine nature guide our human activities. The reciprocal relationships between love, illusion, and henosis are potent. Going forward, mindfulness, soulfulness, and equanimity will be used interchangeably.

THE FORM(S) OF EQUANIMITY

When every thought, word, or deed expresses our purest attempt to love, to be loved, and to allow love to grow, henosis is realized. Mindfulness and soulfulness are the essential qualities of equanimity, which includes the realization of our physical and spiritual nature coexisting together in perfect harmony. Every one of us must interpret what love is and what it's not from the convoluted messages from mass media, religious dogma, and the sometimes-dysfunctional models from our family. Most of us look for love in the wrong place at one time or another during our lifetime. Addictions, material possessions, and personal relationships offer shallow promises and often provide only temporary relief. Many people mistakenly believe that love originates from the outside world, from another person or a pleasurable activity. Unfortunately, it often feels that way in our daily lives, but it's important to remember that our exterior reality mirrors our internal psychology and personal philosophies until we evolve and mature spiritually. When we love ourselves, act responsibly, and apply the wisdom gleaned into a daily practice, we can access love in exquisite forms. Owning our creations is important because saying one thing and living a lie requires dissociation and delusion to account for our disharmony. When we completely own our experiences, the pursuit of enduring happiness can be taken on as a loving pleasure, just as the many other routine tasks of life. Animating every aspect of our being with love as our only motivation is a spectacular way to live a life as a conscious soul. Imagine for a moment how our most mature version of ourselves would communicate with our soul to answer the following questions:

- What does equanimity and wholeness mean to me?
- Do I give and receive love as easily as I breathe?
- When I am in love, how mindful am I of my needs?
- Can I nurture my own dreams as well as others'?
- How often is an intention to love my only motivation?

Like the cliché of kids in a candy store, eyes can get bigger than stomachs. The real test comes when and if we are willing to take responsibility and develop inner mastery. The heroes and heroines of legend unmask illusion, embrace self-discovery, and embody mindful/soulful practices. We can emulate those storylines by creating balance within our physical, emotional, mental, and spiritual natures. Loving oneself mindfully is contagious and leads to a generative love that nurtures others. Spiritual masters loved themselves, walked the walk, and practiced equanimity prior to experiencing henosis.

Spiritual teachings like "turn the other cheek" offer guidelines and great promise but are not easily accomplished. Ridiculed for stuttering in grammar school on a regular basis, I hated my predicament and hammered at words uncontrollably in front of friends and foes daily. The following story describes how the form of equanimity paid a visit and helped me overcome my problems with bullies.

EQUANIMITY VERSUS BULLIES

My own personal journey of discovery about vulnerability and reluctantly dealing with bloodsucking bullies led me to discover the qualities of equanimity at an early age. What I learned during my childhood helped me immensely throughout my life. Due to the severity of a significant stuttering problem, I attended weekly speech therapy during school hours from 1958 to 1960. Terrible anxiety, fear, and anger would well up inside me whenever I had to speak. I hated myself for my failure to speak normally and despised the bullies who preyed upon my weaknesses.

Of course, I became the butt of many Porky Pig (a stuttering cartoon character) jokes. Afraid to speak in class due to the students' ridicule, my teachers concluded I was a slow learner and recommended that I repeat third grade. Fortunately, my mother took me to a reading tutor that summer, which allowed me to advance in school and build some academic self-esteem.

During my Catholic grammar school education, I learned that Jesus "turned the other cheek" and prayed for his tormentors because "they did not know what they were doing." But after years of prayer for my stuttering to stop and my adversaries to become more enlightened, I finally gave up after a particularly devastating attack.

My "turning the other cheek" strategy had worn thin after three years of bending over backward in front of my adversaries and hating myself every day during the process. I felt unappreciated, afraid, and alone with only my private prayers offering solace. And since offering my pain to the divine and imagining a higher place in heaven as a reward for my efforts produced no discernible decrease in verbal abuse from others, I went to my dad for help. My father had been the commander of a U.S. Coast Guard PT boat during World War II, made good money playing semipro football during the Depression years, and was a man's man by everyone's account. His brother entered the U.S. Navy in 1918; at eighteen, as lead motor mechanic, he helped set a world record for continuous flight for an amphibious aircraft. Uncle Art would walk on the wings while *in flight* to repair engines, before he died testing a new seaplane in 1919. The men in my family were leaders and I knew it. The primary family template taught me that men faced their problems head on. My father was my hero, and he was more than willing to teach me how men solved these problems. Taking me outside, he showed me how to punch when I was eight years old. He gave me careful instructions on how to use my legs as a power base and use my whole body to deliver the overhand punch that any good boxer worth his salt would deliver.

Once I knew how to demolish my adversaries, I figured they would never mess with me again, as my dad promised. We practiced together until I was ready to shut up any jerk that gave me lip.

Sure enough, when the first bully started up with the abuse, I punched him in the face without blinking an eye. He shut up right quick, and I started looking around for anyone else cruising for a bruising. While I was riding high on my initial rush of satisfaction for standing up for myself like a man should, another kid came by and made the mistake of ridiculing me. He got the medicine he deserved.

But then my world came crashing down around me like a ton of bricks. The new bully had pointy shoes and kicked me in my private parts like a kangaroo. Collapsing to the ground in a heap of agony, all I could do was tear up and try to catch my breath. I felt stupid curled up like an armadillo on the ground at the feet of my perpetrator, before a nun mercifully took me into her classroom to recover. Rocking in pain and holding back tears, I had a long time before recess ended and thought hard about what I was going to do next before the bell rang.

Since my "turning the other cheek" plan hadn't worked out and my father's strategy to stop bullies had a major pitfall, I needed help big time. My fervent prayer to the divine was for another idea to stop the bullies because I knew I wasn't going to fight again. Embarrassed to my very core and believing that I had failed my father, I never told him what had happened or complained about bullies again.

A month later, four boys started to make fun of me as I approached the school entrance. I spontaneously decided that I wasn't going to give them the pleasure of seeing me scared, mad, or fearful of them. I calmly walked up to them, looked them in the eye, and shrugged my shoulders before I said, "You're right; I have a stuttering problem." The original perpetrator tried to get a rise out of me again and one of his friends stopped him by telling him to lay off.

That was the last day I had trouble with the vampires sucking the blood out of me for my stuttering. Happy and unaware of my dialectic discovery, I later realized that I had stumbled upon a universal truth about bullies: they feed off the emotional reactions of their victims like vampires sucking blood. It was clear to me that bullies got an emotional release from their dissociated fear and rage and experienced relief when witnessing someone else's pain. My pain had a destiny.

This explains why the victim/perpetrator paradigm has been such a prolific and insidious problem throughout the history of humanity. Every cycle of abuse and victimhood has this pattern of perpetrators needing victims, and vice versa, to experience and express the emotions they dissociate. The soul is interested in helping both parties heal the issues, which is why we are attracted to one another. When a victim remains calm during an attack, a perpetrator gets bored quickly and moves on by discharging their dissociated pain, anger, and rage onto someone else.

As a child, I could never pronounce a fifty-cent word like equanimity or comprehend what it meant. But it turns out grace let me stumble upon the following timeless principles held within the form of equanimity, which enabled me to stop the bloodsuckers when I took the following four steps:

- reconciled my internal fear, rage, and judgment, which attracted the bullies;
- ended my self-imposed perfectionism and began to practice self-acceptance;
- admitted my flaws to the blood-sucking bullies with a carefree calmness and equanimity; and
- held true to these principles in the unholy presence of the perpetrating heathens.

I have taught these four principles that lie within the form of equanimity to everyone I work with who struggles with bullies and emotional vampires. When the targeted individual can remain emotionally neutral and look the vampire in the eye in complete acceptance and ownership of the problem, the perpetrators consistently stop, get bored, and move onto a more satisfying victim.

It is hard to imagine loving someone without conditions or a bully overlooking our imperfections and cherishing us just the way we are. We pile criticism onto ourselves mercilessly in our misguided attempts to become "worthy" of love while all the while claiming to know better. But our soul will hear nothing of it while our ears sting. Love takes many guises, and the form of equanimity is an eloquent form of love within the totality of henosis. I would have never guessed that the ideas just mentioned would stop a bully when I was curled up on the ground at the feet of my perpetrator at the tender age of eight. Little did I know that the form of grace and what some call the *zone* had found me.

PSYCHOLOGICAL HENOSIS (AKA THE ZONE)

Who are "we"? . . . As pure souls, we were Spirit. . . . We were a part of the spiritual world, neither circumscribed nor cut off from it. Even now, we are still not cut off from it. Now, however, another person, who wanted to exist and who found us . . . has added himself on to

> the original person. . . . Then we become both: now we are no longer only the one we were, and at times, when the spiritual person is idle and in a certain sense stops being present, we are only the person we have added on to ourselves.—Plotinus[1]

Since every one of us is a divine being in a physical body, our existence is a royal marriage between heavenliness and earthliness, or we could say soulfulness and humanness. Life challenges us to return, like a prodigal son or daughter, back to our original nature. Approaching problems with mindfulness, soulfulness, and equanimity is a formula that can transcend our patterning and allow us access to the power of henosis to achieve remarkable results. Seasoned dance teams are accessing this unified field when dance partners express refined motor instincts through movements propelled by grace. Athletes frequently experience the beneficial effects from physical and psychological henosis (commonly referred to as being in the "zone") when accomplishing amazing feats with ease and minimal effort. Zen masters describe this same phenomenon as "no mind," when body, mind, and soul merge as one to access powerful intuitive skills. The "field" scene in the movie *The Legend of Bagger Vance* (2000) aptly illustrates this magic:

Bagger Vance: I think it's time.

Rannulph Junuh: Time for what?

Bagger Vance: Time for you to see the field.

Rannulph Junuh: The field? I see it, yards long, it's got a little red flag at the end . . .

Bagger Vance: That ain't it. If you had, you wouldn't be hacking at that ball like you was chopping weeds.

Rannulph Junuh: Just give me the club.

Bagger Vance: Sorry I bring it up. Take that, hack away.

Rannulph Junuh: All right, what's the "field"?

Bagger Vance: Fix your eyes on Bobby Jones. Look at his practice swing. Almost like he's searching for something. Then he finds it. Watch how he settle this up, right into the middle. Feel that focus. He's got a lot of shots to choose from . . . duffs and tops and skulls. There's only one shot that's in perfect harmony with the field. One shot that's his authentic shot. That shot is gonna choose him. There's a perfect shot trying to find every one of us. All we got to do is get ourselves out of its way and let it choose us. Look at him, he in the field.

You can't see that flag as some dragon you got to slay. You've got to look with soft eyes. See the place where the tides, and the seasons . . . the turning of the earth . . . all come together. Where everything that is becomes one. You've got to seek that place with your soul, Junuh. Seek it with your hands; don't think about it, feel it. Your hands are wiser than your head's ever gonna be. I can't take you there . . . just hopes I can help you find a way. It's just you . . . that ball . . . that flag . . . and all you are. Seek it with your hands; don't think . . . about it, feel it. There's only one shot that's in harmony with the field. The home of your authentic swing. That flag . . . and all that you are. Even a blind squirrel finds an acorn now and then.[2]

What Bagger Vance wanted Junuh to experience was that no-mind state of being paradoxically referred to as mindfulness and equanimity, a perfected balance where all that is becomes one within our soul. The beneficial aftereffects of this union allow us to experience a soul-infused life, or put another way: the "henosis zone." We experience these moments when we merge our heart and soul as Plato accurately described long ago. To explore the infinite where every possibility exists, our soul needs to be involved. When our behavior, emotion, and intellect truly unify, these become the base or stabilizing legs of a three-legged stool. Once harmonized, the three legs attract our soul, which has access to Bagger Vance's zone.

A STABILIZED STOOL: DEFINITIONS FOR EACH LEG AND OUR SOUL'S ROLE

Behavior

Real estate professionals have a cliché for success: location, location, and location. The three rules for a successful life in my opinion are behavior, behavior, and behavior. *We are what we do* is an equally important guide toward unification. Consistent, conscious, and compassionate behaviors are necessary for a successful life and ultimately henosis.

A by-product of henosis is a state of being in the "zone" that makes us ready to receive the grace of that "one perfect shot" trying to find us. Grace spontaneously assists our efforts to unify our behaviors, emotions, and intellects into soulfulness. The activities we consistently *do* trigger internal emotional and intellectual aspects of our personality that either support or recycle traumas resistant to this amazing zone. Consistent behaviors will flush out our hidden emotional and intellectual illusions from concealment. Exposed, our illusions respond like rats running for their lives on a sinking ship. The pattern of illusion is to attempt to block any healthy behavior because the instincts of illusion are like rats focused on survival similar to the will of the human to live. When cornered, a rat will come out of its hiding place and fight for its life. Our illusions live in our brain so they are smart and outthinking them is virtually impossible. But illusions are also our friends—when we see what illusions reveal about physical, mental, and emotional maladies, we are ready to heal to return to union with our soul. Healthy behaviors, mindfulness, and equanimity are important keys to wholeness. In regard to behavior, consider what Steven Covey said, "To know something but not do is really not to know."[3]

Emotion

Emotions are powerful reservoirs of our expressive feeling nature, serving as signposts that lead us to address our unmet needs, wants, or underlying desires. Positive and negative feelings are like traffic signals that turn red or green or flash caution to motorists waiting for instructions at an intersection. Positive feelings tend to reinforce (green lights), while unpleasant or painful emotions provide motivation for us to stop, learn, and listen. Anne Frank said, "But feelings can't be ignored, no matter how unjust or ungrateful they seem."[4] It is wise to determine what our emotions are saying and what needs to be done to go forward again.

Accepting the waves of emotions without stifling our suffering is the essence of equanimity. A feeling is like a baby that needs to be cherished for us to grow into emotionally mature adults. Love feels wonderful, but every emotion needs to be acceptable. Negative emotions help us identify the sources of suffering and stop our recycling. Flushing out illusion and every resistant behavioral or intellectual "rat" blocking our relationship with our soul is a worthy goal.

Intellect

Decisions are made based upon sensory and emotional input. Our intellect evaluates every event before, during, and after it occurs like a computer and stores the data. After accumulating this information, our intellect decides what actions to take and develops theories about how the world works to create a primary love template or personal paradigm to make future outcomes more predictable. These theories become our ensuing beliefs that function like software programs embedded in the left hemisphere of our brain repeating past perceptions, unable to adjust to new and unique circumstances unless they are consciously reviewed by our right hemisphere, which has access to our emotions. These templates reflect the wisdom that was based upon our life experiences at the time the "beliefs" were encoded into memory. A saying attributed to Confucius brilliantly explains this: "To be wronged is nothing unless you continue to remember it."

When we rewrite an encrypted primary love template or personal paradigm mired in illusion, we claim sovereignty. Mary accomplished this feat when she stopped trying to become more *lovable to her mother* by becoming a doormat in her intimate relationships. When she released her trauma associated with feeling unloved, she became visible to others by cherishing herself despite the pain she endured around her adoption. Junuh found the field when he stopped thinking about golf and let golf play him. When I rewrote my victim/perpetrator paradigm, the bullies left me alone.

On the topic of unifying our mind, Plotinus said, "And the needs of the body and the passions make us have continually different opinions."[5] However, positive thoughts and actions will trigger or activate any behavioral, emotional, or mental template or paradigm based upon illusion that we possess. Like a rat running for higher ground on a sinking ship, illusion will crawl out of the woodwork to devour anything threatening its existence. Clearing out our inner saboteurs is necessary mental hygiene. Any instinct to resist love due to an early decision in life is best approached mindfully and with equanimity. When we have behavioral, emotional, and intellectual unity for a sufficient amount of time, our soul joins in and creates a multiplier effect, which I call soulfulness.

SOULFULNESS

In ancient times, the phrase "all roads lead to Rome" represented two realities simultaneously. Throughout the Roman Empire, all roads were designed to and literary did lead to Rome. And from a political and philosophical point of view, Rome was the epicenter of the ancient world at a crucial time in history.

Psychologically speaking, behavioral, emotive, and cognitive theories dominate the conversation about human growth potential and healing modalities. Of course, each camp is mired in the belief that its theory is superior to the others. My opinion is that all of them are equally valuable—they all lead to Rome. We are all travelers attempting to meet a basic need, yet each road requires mindfulness and equanimity to arrive at the desired destination that I call soulfulness. When our metaphorical three-legged stool and soul agree on a plan and remain in complete harmony, dreams anchor on terra firma.

One could assert that the soul does not exhibit behaviors, feel emotions, or have an intellect; yet it does reside within a physical body that is constantly distracted by these aspects. Once we have the discernment to identify and then deal with all the distractions from our human experiences, then we invite our soul to join along. It holds the keys to unlock henosis, a soul-level destiny humanity has desired since the time of Plotinus. He said: "All things and events are foreshown and brought into being by causes; but the causation is of two Kinds; there are results originating from the Soul and results due to other causes, those of the environment."[6]

If or when the divine matches our efforts and joins the chorus, we can reach the uncharted territory where miracles happen; our mindfulness, soulfulness, and equanimity work together, uniting heaven and earth to make us whole.

"MATCH PLAY" IN THE FIELD

When our behavior, passion, and intellect align with the soul, our intentions are broadcast to the universe and act like a tuning fork attracting matching frequencies. Our individual harmonic and state of wholeness will excite and invite nearby forks, which spring to life in response to our desire similarly to the marching brooms that responded to Mickey Mouse's enchantment as a sorcerer's apprentice in the 1940 film *Fantasia*. Avoiding yet another painful episode or the same old drama requires a noble plan that benefits all. For example, many people mistakenly believe happiness is linked to their social status or material possessions. Plotinus suggested we aspire to the Higher, when he said: "Of men, some enter into life as fragments of the All, bound to that which is external to themselves: they are victims of a sort of fascination, and are hardly, or not at all, themselves: but others mastering all this—straining, so to speak, by the head towards the Higher, to what is outside even the Soul preserve still the nobility and the ancient privilege of the Soul's essential being."[7]

When I overcame my propensity for self-criticism and accepted my stuttering imperfection, the victim/perpetrator paradigm lost its hold over me. Mary stopped attracting "lesson relationships" when she revisited her primary unlovable template, reconciled her misguided perception, and followed through with corrective behaviors. Panic motivated Mary to review her suffering, transform an unlovable illusion, and eventually fully experience love. Like tuning forks entraining to similar frequencies, the vibration we broadcast will attract suffering until primary love templates and victim/perpetrator paradigms are replaced. Mary and I practiced what I call the three rules of success that also apply to relationships: behavior, behavior, and behavior. After addressing our suffering, we experienced the inner peace, mindfulness, and love within henosis.

Any practice that becomes dogmatic or boring to our personality creates diminishing matching spiritual energy, which produces poor results. New Year's resolutions frequently fail for this reason. Our bodies, hearts, and minds need to completely align and anchor a unified frequency over time to engage the necessary matching spiritual energy to get us over the hump. Mindfulness, soulfulness, and equanimity balance every equation with an expression of our true essence. Spectacular outcomes flow when we keep our ears to the ground, listen with child-like playfulness, and express what our soul wants to have happen. When trouble occurs, remove what's not working and surrender to new possibilities.

Sorting through the rubble of your failed dreams and listening to your heart for your initial need, want, and desire is an excellent method to maintain your positive intention. Then create a new plan with more potential. Bagger Vance was correct: "There's a perfect shot trying to find every one of us. All we got to do is get ourselves out of its way and let it choose us."[8] Renounce any illusion that your personality dearly holds onto and invite your soul to join as you unite heaven and earth. Expressing your divine nature through balanced action, emotion, and thought is the essence of mindfulness and soulfulness—the hallmark of equanimity.

Experiencing pain without yearning or longing for something different is a very difficult task. Accepting full responsibility for our problems without blaming or self-criticizing is also difficult. Our human nature wants to eradicate suffering around the world—especially the suffering we personally experience. When in extreme pain, we may seek justice or retribution, but those methods rarely provide enduring solutions, as humanity has experienced throughout its violent history.

Resolution usually contains seeds of acceptance, responsibility, and compromise. When equanimity is practiced, both pleasure and pain are recognized as necessary aspects of growth.

Renouncing societal urges to seek retributive and retaliatory solutions to human suffering is very beneficial. However, incorporating love and mindfulness into a daily practice is not a simple mental exercise. Cultural biases and popular "eye-for-an-eye" philosophies are strongly rooted even in the fairy tales we were exposed to as children. *Noble heroes accomplish feats and get rewards, and bad guys are annihilated or stopped and wow . . . everyone lives happily ever after, the end.* Primary love templates, victim/perpetrator paradigms, and even bedtime stories address human cruelty and provide equanimity models. Now, let's look at a very familiar fairy tale, starting with the basic storyline.

HANSEL AND GRETEL: MODELS OF EQUANIMITY

"Hansel and Gretel" takes place during a famine, and the story is about the poverty-stricken children of a poor woodcutter and a heartless stepmother. The stepmother convinces the father to abandon the children deep in the woods, so that the starving couple can survive on their remaining meager food resources. A witch lurks in the woods and has built a trap to lure in hungry abandoned children.

The Storyline

Overhearing their parents plotting to abandon them, Hansel and Gretel leave a trail of white pebbles as they are taken into the woods and find their way home. Foiled, the parents try again the next day, this time making sure the children don't have any pebbles. Instead, Hansel saves the slice of bread given to him for lunch, which he breaks into crumbs to make a trail. Birds quickly eat the breadcrumbs so the children cannot find their way home. When Gretel becomes disheartened and afraid during their night in the woods, Hansel comforts her and says, "God will not forsake us."

They eventually stumble upon a gingerbread cottage, constructed of sweets, in a clearing. Hungry and starving, they begin to eat the roof of the house. An old blind woman comes out and offers them more food and a warm bed. The children agree but soon learn her evil motivations; she is a wicked witch who intends to eat them. The witch locks Hansel in a cage to fatten him up and enslaves Gretel. Because the witch is blind, Hansel tricks her into thinking he is too skinny to eat by giving her a stick instead of his finger whenever she tests to see if he is plump enough. When the witch finally prepares a fire to cook him anyway, Gretel shoves the witch into the oven and frees Hansel. The children find precious jewels and more in her cottage and fill their pockets with the witch's treasure. Then a duck helps the children to find the way home. When they return home, they discover that the stepmother has died and their father has regretted his actions every day since he abandoned his children. He welcomes his children with open arms. And, of course, they all lived happily ever after.

SURVIVING ORDEALS AND ENDURING LOVE

Classic fairy tales like "Hansel and Gretel" engage our imagination because they contain eternal wisdom about children overcoming significant hardships despite their upbringing. Nestled within any immortal storyline, there are formable obstacles but also universal principles to enlighten us. "Hansel and Gretel" is a fable about innocence, grace, and survival that shuns the victim/perpetrator paradigm and models love and forgiveness. Let's explore this familiar fairy tale through the lens of children teaching lessons about the form of equanimity throughout the story.

When Hansel overheard his parents plot to abandon them, he used white pebbles and moonlight to return home with Gretel. When he was re-abandoned in the forest by his father the next day, Hansel left a trail of breadcrumbs and accepted his fate without whining, blaming, or yearning for another reality. Lost in the dark, Hansel comforted Gretel and said, "God will not forsake us." Even though Hansel and Gretel's personalities naturally freaked out after their parents abandoned them deep in the woods on two occasions and a cannibal witch planned to eat both of them, they did not judge, question the divine, or succumb to the popular victim/perpetrator paradigm. As the drama unfolded, equanimity would suggest there was good reason for their challenges, one that their souls found acceptable.

However, protecting one's life and self-defense is imperative for survival. Mentally accepting reality and preemptive actions designed to ensure survival are separate activities. Hansel and Gretel acted appropriately to protect themselves by using the pebbles and breadcrumbs, even though their plight eventually evolved into deceiving and killing a cannibal witch in self-defense. The children did not confuse intellectual acceptance with the necessary activities required for their survival, which allowed them to ultimately express the true nature of their souls in very challenging circumstances.

The mind is a tool of the physical world and therefore mortal, but our soul is immortal and has direct access to divinity. Knowing what nurtures our body and what diminishes soul connection provides crucial information. To return to henosis, we need to learn how to love, forgive, and release our illusions that seem so real and important to our mind. Hansel and Gretel did not hate their father for abandoning them. Judging him was a shadow on the wall, a temporal illusion within the victim/perpetrator paradigm they chose to ignore. Hansel and Gretel's beauty was the love beating in their hearts and their ability to forgive their father. Love in the form of equanimity allowed them to trust in divine benevolence and release judgment. Hansel and Gretel not only survived but also eventually thrived due to their soul's input throughout their ordeal.

The duck that helped Hansel and Gretel return home after "acing" the spiritual experience could represent soul-level grace or guidance. Returning home with jewels and earthly treasure was fortunate, but the enduring richness of reunifying a loving family and forgiving a regretful father was the most precious gift in this story. While experiencing life and death struggles within the human drama, Hansel and Gretel held on to their principles despite the illusions plaguing each adult in the story. Possessing soul-like wisdom beyond their years, Hansel and Gretel trusted in divine benevolence and modeled mindfulness, soulfulness, and equanimity for all of us to see.

When our soul has input into our everyday activities, we will not only survive but also thrive. The positive and negative aspects of life are breadcrumbs in the woods, temporary in nature and certain to wash away in time. We can learn from Hansel and Gretel by addressing our personal obstacles as a divine mystery and maintaining our equanimity. Allowing our soul to become more present in our life will teach us what really matters and help us to release our negative attachments. They accepted their fate, remained loving, forgave their father, and never lost connection to divinity. Returning home was a noble act of forgiveness, love, and equanimity, which some of us, similarly betrayed, would never have considered. Are Hansel and Gretel idealistic and more mindful than most of us? Perhaps. But fairy tales endure due to the immortal principles and wisdom held within them.

SOUL CONNECTION

> If we come to be at one with our self, and no longer split ourselves
> into two, we are simultaneously One and All, together with that God
> who is noiselessly present, and we stay with him as we are willing and
> able.—Plotinus[9]

Equanimity and mindfulness are innate qualities natural to our soul. Since our soul has a direct connection to the divine, we have immediate access to the transcendent and can incorporate its wisdom to overcome our illusions like Hansel and Gretel modeled. Listening to our soul's hummingbird voice whispering in our ear amid illusion's cawing crows and screeching monkeys in our head is the task. Think of soul communication as a friendly chat with a close buddy who recommends wholesome activities for your return to henosis. Remove the mystery, ritual, and hoopla if a meditative or religious practice feels burdensome. Ignore the critical voices and accept your loving hummingbird within whispering with integrity, honesty, and equanimity.

Illusions enchant humans and signal marching brooms and reflecting mirrors. A soulful intention has access to divine wisdom, which can enlighten and transform illusion. The singular focus of a predator stalking its prey is needed to listen to the hummingbird whispering within. Illusion is a formidable adversary, so attuning our body, mind, and emotional sensitivity to accurately assess loving wisdom from fiction is an important skill to master. Our soul will help us overcome illusion and love more completely to return to henosis in a physical body. When we actively work toward these same goals and help others, our soul and all of divinity automatically ping into aligning frequencies. When listening for your hummingbird's whisper, consider the following suggestions.

We are divine beings in a physical body, so imagine an energetic continuum that towers above your head with direct access to the divine at one end. Allow the other end to anchor into the physical center of the earth and visualize your body in the middle of a shimmering pillar of light pulsating between the two poles. Hang out with the divine like true friends discussing your passion. Then muster the self-discipline and start the necessary activities to create your dream on earth. Hold pure intention in your heart until you notice your emotional energy begin to travel and eventually anchor at both ends of the energetic continuum flowing parallel to your backbone. When dreams create love for yourself and others, heaven and earth align. Then listen intently for your hummingbird's advice once the energetic continuum is anchored deeply at both ends. Meditation and soul connection are invaluable methods to discern love from illusion.

DUALITY AND PURPOSE OF ILLUSION

In Sanskrit, the continuous flow of birth, life, and death in all its pleasurable or painful forms is called *samsara*. Our purpose not only includes re-creating henosis on earth but also overcoming suffering and the illusions perpetuating our primary love templates and personal victim/perpetrator paradigms. In other words, our soul plays hide-and-seek until we realize the purpose of pain is its transcendence. Samsara is a necessary aspect within duality because without pain and suffering, we would not know opposition in order to seek enduring love, bliss, and union. Otherwise, we could just remain in blissful henosis with the divine and skip the human drama many refer to as the choice between good and evil.

In the fourth century, a Christian monk named Evagrius Ponticus wrote about eight terrible temptations that plagued humanity. Pope Gregory the First revised his work, which became commonly known as the seven deadly sins. Over the years, countless authors, theologians, and philosophers have weighed in on the topic of dualism and the virtues required to overcome these "sins," which I call illusions because they are seductions giving humans a mirage of power and happiness. The Seven Deadly Illusions (Doesn't this sound better than sins?) are updated below with a counterbalancing concept based on the form of equanimity.

- **Lust** is an uncontrolled fixation with pleasures from outside sources such as money, power, addictive diversions, or material possessions that fill a void with short-term enjoyment. Our divine connection and/or true love of self can fill these voids in a more permanent and enduring way.
- **Gluttony** is the overindulgence of any substance to the point of waste or obsession to fill a void, which can be balanced by discov-

ering what we are hiding from that created the original pain or hunger we subconsciously feel an obsession to mask or feed.

- **Greed** is the compulsive pursuit of material possessions beyond what we can use or need; counterbalancing comes when we pursue and remove the source of our own disempowerments and/or inferiority beliefs.

- **Sloth** can be described as physical or spiritual laziness—characterized by a failure to use a talent, act on our passion, or do what needs to be done—that validates a subliminal lack of self-worth template or personal paradigm and is counterbalanced by successfully fulfilling our responsibilities until confidence and self-worth start to regenerate.

- **Wrath** is an inordinate feeling of hatred or anger that may include self-sabotage, active or passive violent acts or feuds, and obsessive fantasies with retribution or war that persist long after a grievous injury. Healing our emotional wounds and addressing the needs underneath our anger are necessary counterbalancing activities. By accepting that bad things happen and being mindful, we can forgo retaliatory justice impulses and the associated eye-for-an-eye philosophies.

- **Envy** is the desire for the traits, abilities, or possessions that another possesses while jealousy is the fear of losing something that we personally value. Both envy and jealousy usually stem from low self-esteem and discontent with our status or abilities but can be counteracted by cherishing what we have, accepting what is, and relinquishing a need to control others or the events around us.

- **Pride** is an imbalance of self-esteem, an illusion of superiority, and an obsession with the façade of appearances, which is eradicated when we cease to need validation of another person or group to experience confidence or feel empowered.

These Seven Deadly Illusions (sins) were on full display in the motion picture *Avatar*. Released in 2009, James Cameron's award-winning science-fiction film portrayed the classic struggle between love, illusion, and dualism on a planet called Pandora. Infected by the illusions listed above, the corporate humans were totally unconscious and spiritually bankrupt. The native population and a few human recruits provided some interesting examples of how henosis works in a fantasy context.

Connected to all of divinity, the indigenous population and the human recruits survived the chaos wrought by human greed, wrath, and pride and achieved a sustainable form of incorruptibility, which stabilized the unity or henosis within all life on Pandora.

To achieve a sustainable level of equanimity, practice thinking mindfully, acting consciously, and loving with your heart and soul—bridging the perceived gap between our human and divine natures is our purpose. The mighty task is to resolve our reliance on primary love templates or personal paradigms that re-create how we interact with people. In the case of Hansel and Gretel, this was a primary love template with a generous subplot of abandonment. In *Avatar*, it involved revising our definition of sentience to include an alien species that some considered inferior. What is recycled can seem so real, but those ugly witches and adversaries we battle are just antagonists in the form of mirrors and phantom memories; they are all opportunities to transform illusion and become more conscious.

Mindfulness, soulfulness, and equanimity help us become whole. When we feel overwhelmed or suffer from low self-esteem, incorruptibility, self-responsibility, and personal sovereignty enable us to regain equanimity. When our mind and soul align, illusions transform. Transcending the mundane is like rain on a sunny day—attitudes shift about the dreary rain in a spectacular way when the juxtaposition occurs. The combination of light and rain creates a positive mood because the paradoxical nature of that event is so uplifting. This sunlight metaphor symbolizes the act of revealing and illuminating our divine.

When we release illusion's hold and return to love, our soul awakens. When Hansel and Gretel faced suffering with love and equanimity, everything in the universe conspired to help them solve their problems. This is not just a fairy tale. The same thing happened to Mary and many others I have treated. In *A Course in Miracles*, it is written: "Your task is not to seek for love, but merely to seek and find all the barriers within yourself that you have built against it."[10]

ETERNAL BALANCE

As mentioned previously, the Greeks coined the word *amphibios* to describe a double life, and everybody, no doubt, has felt the dichotomy of expressing our divinity in a fragile human body. To this end, exploring the purpose of pain and examining how the curriculum of illusion leads a human to love is a paradox within equanimity. Mindfulness and soul awareness make us take notice of our tendencies toward self-blame, irresponsibility, or making others suffer. When passions heat up, the desire to engage in noble causes to eradicate worldwide suffering is tempting and can also create imbalances. Revisiting our core principles with soulful wisdom before engaging in an impulsive reaction demonstrates proactive wisdom. When we are deliberate and address problems proactively, equanimity can look easy.

A tipping point may occur when a substantial percentage of humanity reaches a state of equanimity. Perhaps then we will eventually stop throwing that cumbersome victim/perpetrator ball back and forth. Mindfulness and soulfulness, when practiced regularly, improve our equanimity. When self-responsibility, sovereignty, and incorruptibility (discussed in chapter 9) expand exponentially, henosis will be right around the corner.

Bagger Vance understood that some universal "perfect shot chooses us" when we access the "field." The combination of our behavior, emotion, intellect, and soulfulness is what attunes us to the field of both our angst from antagonists and the goodness of love. In *The Matrix*, Agent Smith sarcastically observed that humans *rejected* the utopia program. Are we so discombobulated we would reject peace for terrorism and the victim/perpetrator paradigm? However, people continue to seek equanimity and many want to return to the paradise of the Garden of Eden. I suspect Plotinus would say that the virtues explored within the form of equanimity and each of the other forms accelerates self-awareness and wholeness.

Wholeness is a complex journey with many twists and turns. Disappointment is an opportunity to practice equanimity. Humanity can decide to leave the victim/perpetrator paradigm ball lie on the ground. Focusing on the positive intention underneath our own or an antagonist's questionable behavior is helpful, but there is another method sitting on the table. Just forget about it, stop judging others, and move on to your next adventure based upon the knowledge that we are all perfect apples at our core. To cherish is our choice, grace chooses us, and illusion points out imbalances blocking our ability to love. Here, equanimity reminds us that in order to flourish, mindfulness and soulfulness need primary roles. Read the following form meditation and let the ideas open your awareness. Try reading this form aloud to deepen the message. I also suggest taking a break after reading this or any other form meditation. You can also practice using the form of equanimity with the Camel Wave Meditation (appendix A). The Wise and Loving Inner Voice Meditation (appendix B) will help you discern which internal voice within your brain provides useful directions or more illusion. Explore the ideas, the feelings, and wisdom within the form of equanimity. Let them simmer and then move onto the next section.

When you feel the need, you can return to equanimity and reread it over and over.

FORM MEDITATION: EQUANIMITY

Objectivity toward everyone and everything in my exterior world is a lofty, attainable goal. Mindfulness as an outward state of being creates equanimity within me and nurtures and sustains my interior tranquility. When my mind is calm and my heart emanates love, a state of equanimity engulfs me like a black hole in space where light cannot escape; but instead of light, I am engulfed by love. Here, equanimity becomes an ecstatic form of love occurring within me organically.

Equanimity is calmness as deep as the ocean; no matter how balanced I am with my words, deeds, or emotional maturity, there is much more to be accessed below the surface. This state of being is powerful yet virtually undetectable because everything remains the same on the surface, but the real stability is occurring in the depths within me beyond what the eyes can see. Mindfulness is an expression of my soul and life challenges me to exercise and master my ability to maintain this state of being regardless of my circumstances. Equanimity is an enigma I choose to explore to become incorruptible during life's challenges.

The riddle evolves and eventually is solved when my soul and humanness become whole. The importance of experiencing that moment of uniting is profound—I need to know what presence feels like so I can re-experience this black hole engulfing me with its immortal loving form. My heart naturally responds, and the fortitude it takes to maintain balance returns. Presence of mind restores balance and moderation, and as a daily practice, I feel courageous.

When navigating through suffering that sometimes I may not understand, I can resist rote programming messages, which lead to the victim/perpetrator paradigm. Humans tend to judge and hold grudges, but I know that life produces mirrors and reflections of my story that provide me opportunities to release and renounce my illusions. Intellectual acceptance and pre-emptive actions to protect and ensure my survival exist at one end of my equanimity continuum. Yearning for an alternate reality or dissociating from dangerous entities lies on the other end. I am love and accept the absolute truth about myself that is at the core of me. I am free to tranquilly address the problems I encounter; no matter how painful or difficult the situation, I choose to maintain my equanimity.

Enduring happiness and love exist within my soul and my personality. When I surrender my illusions and move from forgiving transgressions to a place where I accept that no one is to blame for my angst, I reach a state of equanimity more powerful than what has tormented me in the past. When my heart, mind, and soul unite, I am equanimity. My desire to dedicate my life to become loving and mindful calms the emotions within me, creates a deep presence within my heart, and invites my soul to shine.

When I attain the heightened state of being known as equanimity, I become one with all of divinity and every soul that ever experienced or transcended a similar challenge during their lifetime. My suffering is grace for it opens avenues for the love and compassion inside of other people's hearts to access mine. I have access to all the necessary resources and in unlimited amounts to assist my efforts to maintain balance, and I choose to be an example through my actions and reactions to others. We are all one, hurts and all. When I transcend, I open a way for others to transform and transcend at their perfect time. Thus, with equanimity, the secret of oneness, unity, and wholeness is realized within me.

Part II

We are divine beings living in physical bodies. Part I focused upon creativity within the invisible world (psychology, philosophy, and spiritual expression). Part II will now address how dreams actualize in the tangible world (manifestation, physical reality, embodying wholeness).

To maintain the principles and values associated with the forms of illusion, love, cherish, grace, and equanimity discussed in part I, emotional and psychological maturity is beneficial. The brain and its complementary functions are addressed in part II with practical advice to soothe stress responses.

Empathic people can absorb emotion from others, and the challenges associated with sovereignty within diversity are thoroughly explored with suggested solutions. Life sometimes strips away everything alien to the love within us. The chapter about the form of incorruptibility describes why this purification process exists with historical and current examples. The form of wholeness concludes the book and can spontaneously occur when we understand the purpose of illusion and eventually embody the principles associated with love and its multiple forms mentioned in this book.

7

THE BRAIN

Logic, Presence, and Emotional Intelligence

Many ancient cultures have attempted to explain complex subjects like why we exist, the nature of God, the nature of good and evil, and how our mind/soul transitions after death. Both the secular and religious explanations that survive today can be seen as arguable theories or debatable philosophies rather than verifiable truth. Throughout human history, spiritual sages and sincere prophets heard God's word and wrote about their impressions/instructions. Religious dogma ensued, which offered *cause and effect* consequences for certain actions. Secular and religious hierarchies took notice because when individuals were held accountable, governing bodies gained more control over their citizenry. Justification came from the order that evolved from chaos. The intention to create a civilized nation was served, but motivating the masses through fear and punishment spawned a host of problems. Head-scratching scripture and jumbled philosophy perplex humanity like jigsaw puzzles with missing pieces—throughout this chapter, we will explore how to develop the emotional maturity to mind the gaps.

But all those answers and opinions about God's plan are only theories. Attempts to "prove philosophies" usually fail, so many religions encourage followers to have faith, not proof. *The Promise of Wholeness* assumes that the divine and our soul exist and suggests that human bonding instincts reflect an innate drive for interconnectedness and ultimately henosis. Proving or disproving the various interpretations of the divine or oneness or the soul is not my intent. What inspired me to write this book is a heartfelt passion to reduce suffering, restore human dignity, and remind people of their divinity. My desire is to facilitate wholeness on an individual basis so humanity can eventually experience henosis collectively. Healthy spirituality is like the bird that sings before breakfast; we know love exists and the divine provides. Dogma is a story about rewards and consequences, which are manufactured ingredients for a bitter breakfast.

The ideal mind/body relationship in ancient times was "a sound mind *in* a sound body." Athletic ability and mental sharpness were prized Roman traits; today desirable traits include intuition, gut reactions, and heart intelligence. For thousands of years, intuitive practitioners taught humanity about the brain/belly connection, and current medical research studying stress-related maladies supports this ancient knowledge. Innovation and inspiration have a physical location, and our task in this chapter is to explore how our reptilian instincts, emotional intelligence, and higher brain work together. Intuition is a wonderful skill everyone possesses to one degree or another. When a settled mind aligns with an open heart and intuitively trusts its innate gut impulses, good things happen.

To fully understand perception, we must take into consideration how the brain processes sensory input, intuition, and our intangible guidance. Advances in MRI scanning techniques have helped neuroscientists advance our understanding about the brain and the effects of trauma. In this chapter, we will move beyond the more intangible aspects reviewed thus far and will explore how the brain processes physical experience and its emotional states. Suggestions and techniques for healthy stress responses, visualizations, and meditations for use by both laypeople and health-care professionals are provided toward the end of the chapter.

A STORYBOOK BRAIN DILEMMA

The Scarecrow in the original book *The Wonderful Wizard of Oz* was only two days old when he went off to see the Wizard with Dorothy to obtain a brain. After a successful stint scaring crows from eating the farmer's corn on the first day, the Scarecrow couldn't realize what to do when the lead crow figured out he was made of straw. As the old crow filled his craw with corn, he wisecracked to the Scarecrow about the importance of having a brain. As the story unfolded, it became clear to everyone but the Scarecrow himself that "he was the wisest man in Oz." Toward the end of the story, he was eventually recognized as such, but the Scarecrow deferred and always credited the Wizard instead. When it was the Scarecrow's turn to receive his brain, the Wizard gave him a melon-sized ball of pins and needles (called bran) in the original story and a diploma in the movie. He finally believed he had a brain when the Wizard recognized what was obvious to everyone all along.

Scarecrow: I haven't got a brain . . . only straw.

Dorothy: How can you talk if you haven't got a brain?

Scarecrow: I don't know . . . but some people without brains do an awful lot of talking . . . don't they?

Dorothy: Yes, I guess you're right.[1]

In the book, Baum illustrated the placebo effect, which occurs when we feel better because we *think* we are better, not necessarily because we received the proper medication or scientific evidence-based treatment. The placebo effect demonstrates the power of positive thinking, yet scientists and society often reject the results if the evidence isn't corroborated by experts and verified by numerous double-blind studies. Dialectic discovery and the placebo effect are akin in this regard. In *The Wonderful Wizard of Oz*, the Scarecrow demonstrates three possible placebo effects:

- The Scarecrow already had a brain and circumstantial evidence to prove it, but he let the crow bully him out of the perception that he had a brain. In this instance, the negative observation planted by the crow, which the Scarecrow accepted as fact, produced a reversed placebo effect. Since he was only two days old, that "illusion" possibly became a primary love template.
- The Scarecrow had a brain and had circumstantial evidence to prove it but refused to accept the possibility until someone whom he esteemed, the Wizard, persuaded him. As a result, the Scare-

crow created a personal paradigm, which included the belief he had a brain; this perception occurred through the positive placebo effect provided by the Wizard.

- The Scarecrow let the Wizard talk him into the delusion that he had a brain when he indeed did not have one. Thus, the placebo was the perception that he had a brain and so a transformation occurred due to his positive attitude without scientific evidence or physical proof of a brain. Thus the power of intention and the placebo effect created wisdom that Dorothy and everyone in Oz noticed.

The human brain gets equally confused when it is filled with divergent opinions and observations that turn out to be garbage. It is difficult to sort out if a modeled primary love template or personal paradigm is based upon a positive or negative placebo effect or an actual fact. Everyone has flying monkeys and wisecracking crows ripping apart our self-worth like the Scarecrow experienced. Some of us seek Wizards who replace our initial garbage with more garbage, so we need to access our own intuition and enlightened inner voice. Knowing how the human brain works helps us recognize wisdom from wasted effort. Understanding how the Scarecrow, who was later known as "the wisest man in Oz," could accept the notion that he didn't have a brain is an interesting question. How many times have we intuitively known what was true or what we should do but couldn't do it? Unproductive patterns, templates, and paradigms persist even though we know better. Both delusion and intention share our brain with us and possess the same intellectual capabilities, so we must objectively choose what to do with every faculty at our disposal.

LOGIC VERSUS EMOTIONAL INTELLIGENCE

"All the same," said the Scarecrow, "I shall ask for brains instead of a heart; for a fool would not know what to do with a heart if he had one."

"I shall take the heart," returned the Tin Woodman, "for brains do not make one happy, and happiness is the best thing in the world."[2]

An enjoyable debate about logic and emotional intelligence similar to the one modeled by the Scarecrow and Tin Woodman also occurs between the left and right hemispheres of our brain. Neuroscientists like I. McGilchrist tell us that language, logic, and the ability to sequence our experiences is located in the left hemisphere. The right hemisphere processes our feelings and records sensory experiences, but the left does the talking. The left hemisphere categorizes, organizes, and stores factual information and looks for logical patterns. It pays attention, remembers what we value, and applies solutions it already knows.[3] Without our left hemisphere's sequencing ability, we would not understand cause and effect, which is essential for learning. On the other hand, stress and trauma can distort our sensory perceptions and instill left-brain dominance.

The ability to seek novel solutions, explore divergent alternatives, and relish paradox originates within our right hemisphere. Pre-birth memories and all sensory experience including our intuitive/spiritual abilities are located in the right hemisphere. The human need for affection and empathy are located here.[4]

Nonverbal communication, facial expression, and the body language related to our emotions originate within the right hemisphere. It stores memories of our sensory experiences and attaches meaning to them. Distorted perceptions can lead to disproportionate emotional reactions without the sequencing ability of our left hemisphere. Our left and right hemispheres work together through the support of the corpus callosum. The corpus callosum inhibits each hemisphere from interrupting the task of the other.[5] This allows us to mentally surrender and spiritually meditate without simultaneous left-brain analysis. Let's look at the brain as a whole before we discuss any more details.

THREE MAJOR FUNCTIONS OF THE BRAIN

The instinct to survive and seek safety is biologically hard-wired into every creature on earth. Humanity has thrived in bonded groups that divvy up responsibilities and survival tasks. Because the need for emotional attachment is so fundamental, many of us will endure an abusive relationship to maintain bonds with friends, relatives, or lovers—pain is preferable to isolation or going it alone. Abandonment fears are very powerful, so taking responsibility or demanding accountability is more frightening to some people than silently suffering from the aftereffects of unpleasant emotions. Dissociation allows us to numb our pain as a survival strategy to remain in our group even while we suffer.

Neuroscientists have found that the human brain has three complementary branches with distinct roles. To make things simple, in the following discussion, common terms for these branches will be used rather than their clinical names.

- The **reptilian brain (dorsal ventral complex)** is our autonomic nervous system, which regulates our primary functions such as breathing, digestive system, and heartbeat. This is the part of our primitive brainstem that shuts down, dissociates, or immobilizes us under duress. Our brain can survive while underwater and unconscious in an icy lake due to the shutdown response.
- The **emotional brain (sympathetic or limbic nervous system)** is located in the middle of our brain and has the ability to mobilize us by releasing blood and glucose into our muscles when we are excited or need to compete. If our heart detects danger our fight/flight/freeze response releases cortisol and adrenaline to address the crisis.
- The **higher brain (smart ventral complex)** is geared to regulate our physiology for our social engagement system to create safety through facial, auditory, and heart connection. Internal self-regulation and the detection of social cues are located here and possess the ability to calm down the other two aspects of the brain.

By design, these three systems work in tandem by opposing and competing with one another to determine which branch should respond to a specific life experience. The system is perfect in design, but our brain can short-circuit or lock up when an overwhelming event occurs. Then we must rely upon only one or two of these branches. My clinical observations and discoveries will be offered as we explore these three aspects of brain function in the following sections.

FUNCTION ONE: REPTILIAN BRAIN

Our reptilian brain performs the vital functions associated with the passive reflexive regulation of our abdominal visceral organs such as our digestive tract and stomach. Ninety-five percent of the brain neuro-transmitter serotonin is located in the lining of our bowels. Our sense of safety and well-being is located here. Eastern medicine historically and now Western research has recognized the importance of our gut-brain axis. This is how we can simultaneously experience fear in our mind and butterflies in our stomach.

Similar in appearance to an actual reptile brain, it is responsible for autonomic respiration, heart rate, and blood pressure. This primitive aspect of our mind sees danger everywhere, processes new information very slowly, and believes the world remains the same as we personally experienced it in the past. The sedentary nature of our reptilian brain wants repetition and routine for pleasure and survival purposes. Prone to be rigid, it tends to be obsessive or compulsive as it tries to address or avoid the messy emotions located in our emotional brain. Our reptilian brain "checks out," shuts down, or dissociates during life-threatening or traumatic events. Corrupted reptilian fear can develop into a major depression, chronic hopelessness, and suicidal ideation. The best way to begin to feel safe again is by releasing our emotions by sourcing our emotional brain and accessing the healing wisdom of our higher brain.

A prisoner in Plato's cave with a dominant reptilian brain is prone to be sedentary, fear change, and abhor risky adventures, which may even lead to success, power, and productivity. Predictable comfort zones are a priority, even if they only produce pain. Like a frightened child, the reptilian brain thrives on routine and never questions authority or develops sovereignty. Immobilized and emotionally immature, the reptilian brain can shut down and/or remain shackled; it does what is expected and/or what others direct it to do. The reptilian brains of baby elephants are trained with shackles. As adults, elephants possess the brute strength to break free of those shackles, but because of that primary template early in life, they usually won't try. Childhood models and societal imprints on humans create immobilizing beliefs, perceptions, and even placebo effects that shackle us. Emerging out of deeply held irrational fears is almost impossible because safety and security are primary considerations to a heated-up reptilian brain. Perhaps the wisecracking crow planted the delusion that the Scarecrow didn't have a brain into his reptilian brain.

The reptilian brain and our higher brain oppose each other in a brilliantly designed check and balance system. When our higher brain comes up with a new endeavor or risky venture, our reptilian brain wonders what can go wrong and thinks of potential problems. This enables our higher brain to come up with well-thought-out strategies and effective countermeasures. When someone has an overfunctioning reptilian brain and underutilized higher brain, fear-based programming will rule over any risk-taking venture. Trauma can trigger increased left-brain dominance, which can result in the need for power and control and is associated with anger, hostility, aggression, and jealousy.[6]

Our emotional brain makes emotional value judgments on the objections, perceptions, and solutions presented by the reptilian and higher brains. Cartoonists have depicted this ageless debate as a devil tempting us to do the forbidden in one ear and an angel whispering the higher moral ground in the other ear. Who hasn't heard that little voice inside warning of potential trouble, which starts a debate with the adventurous risk-taker aspect within us that wants to try something new? Who hasn't regretted ignoring that little voice warning us of potential danger, which turned out to be right? Ambivalence is a symptom of our higher brain being immobilized by a flooded reptilian brain and unresolved emotional material overwhelming the emotional brain. The executive powers of our higher brain return once peace and calm return to the other two aspects. Good decisions are made by the cooperative collaboration of all three aspects of our brain.

FUNCTION TWO: THE EMOTIONAL BRAIN

The emotional brain mobilizes our body to respond to any physical or emotional demand quickly and efficiently. The human heart has a powerful physical connection and direct access to our emotional brain. An intrinsic nervous system allows our heart to sense and intuit information through its feeling nature prior to cognition. Has dread ever blanketed your heart or have you noticed it skip a beat *before* some bad news?

An intuitive heart has an intelligence of its own and stores its wisdom in our emotional brain's memory banks. Safety considerations are integrated with our feeling nature to improve future social exchanges. Emotions can be likened to weather patterns, which reflect and influence our perception of reality. Change occurs when we want something new and have the passion/dedication to make our dream happen.

The urge to leave our cave of illusions to experience the sunlight that Plato wrote about long ago originates from a mobilized emotional brain. Perception is the film studio where the pictures and places within our imagination have a playground to create, so we can adjust to or influence our universe. Everyone perceives the world differently, so the projection screens of possibility on our mental walls depend upon our current emotional state and/or historical material present that day.

We each possess an intuitive sensing mechanism that explores our environment through our feeling nature. Everyone has internal voices or instincts that suggest which hunch to follow or not, and our emotional brain is the staging ground where every possibility we imagine exists, waiting to be shaped into physical form. It is the sorting table or loading dock for all the various scenarios, potential outcomes, and expected or planned realities. If we are calm, cool, and collected, it is the home for our fertile imagination, where dreams are tried on for size so that we can later make informed decisions.

Traumatic memories can contaminate perception and trigger disproportionate emotional responses. When fear and/or frightening memories dominate our right hemisphere, obsessions about danger, panic, doomsday scenarios, and helplessness can overwhelm. If we fail to deal with our fear, a fight/flight/freeze response may ensue, which triggers our amygdala to release adrenaline, cortisol, and norepinephrine stress hormones into our body. Emotions and stress hormones accumulate if ignored and can erupt into a full-fledged panic attack. Chilling self-criticism, procrastination, and perfectionism immobilize and keep us frozen and isolated. Racing hearts and hypervigilance can trigger aggression, avoidance, and general defensive maneuvers.

The policeman who sold me my first Rottweiler had this to say about fear: "Guard dogs balance vigilance and survival fears every day." As we completed the sale, he asked me if I knew which puppies became the best guard dogs after he sold them to the local Air Force base. He said, "Scared puppies are the best. Fear motivates vigilance. When they mature, fear instills diligence, and their survival instinct, loyalty, and strength makes them great guard dogs." Similarly to a good guard dog, the calming influence of the higher brain is needed to create equilibrium and soothe fear.

Our emotional brain, which includes our hippocampus, the pituitary/pineal gland, and the hypothalamus, is our motivational passion center that makes "value judgments." When a peak or traumatic event slows time down or stops it altogether, our emotional brain is involved. Fear activates our adrenal glands or the black-and-white thinking of our amygdala. Fear activates stress hormones such as adrenaline and cortisol. Survival depends upon quick thinking and prioritization because our reptilian brain anticipates negative consequences and predicts fearful outcomes, which can activate the fight/flight/freeze response of our emotional brain without the required healing wisdom from our higher brain.

FUNCTION THREE: HIGHER BRAIN

The higher brain regulates our internal physiological states to match external cues from the environment and our social engagement skills. Speech, hearing, and our face/heart circuit are located here, which regulate our emotional expression and attention, and these emotional aspects transform thought into action. Our prefrontal lobes are excited by interesting challenges, anticipate future outcomes, and perform our highest executive tasks. Abstract thought, imagination, and limitless learning potential resides here. Creating a new perspective or regulating our breath and heart rate are a few of the tools our higher brain has at its disposal to calm down overstimulated emotional and reptilian brains. It can modulate, govern, or apply the "brakes" to a fight/flight/freeze or shutdown response if a social situation demands restraint. It is our higher brain that reminds us to take a deep breath to access our enlightened inner voice within that sees the bigger picture and knows just what to do.

Our higher brain uses social engagement, heart connection, and self-soothing to regulate an overstimulated aspect of the brain whose survival feels threatened. Right-brain, body-based synthesis needs to be processed through left-brain analysis to form knowledge that can be accessed through logic, sequence, and language.[7] The higher brain regulates our psychological state through our speech, communication, and facial expressions. Creativity needs calm and a delicate balance of passion, patience, and excitement. When we meditate, as Plotinus describes below, it is our higher brain that experiences transcendence, heightened consciousness, and henosis.

> When people are too weak for contemplation, they switch to action, which is a mere shadow of contemplation and of reason. Since, owing to the weakness of their souls, their faculty of contemplation is insufficient, they cannot grasp the object of their contemplation and be fulfilled by it.
>
> Yet they still want to see it; and so they switch to action, on order to see with their eyes what they could not see with their spirit. In any case, when they create something, it is because they themselves want to see it and to contemplate it; and when they propose to act, insofar as they are able, it is because they want their act to be perceived by others.[8]

If intoxicants, drugs, or alcohol numb the reptilian, emotional, and higher brain, ill-advised adventures can ensue. Without wisdom and reptilian inhibition present to create prudence, our impulsive desires, expansive emotions, or guilty pleasures within the emotional brain can party hearty. We have all seen an inebriated individual or heard stories about someone in such a state or actually drunk too much ourselves and said or done something we later regretted.

Outlandish behavior is attractive to a dissociated or inebriated mind because our intellect is compelled to express our deepest unresolved issues. Illusion plays with our head like a banjo player, and our intellect just masturbates to the music occasionally. Did the reptilian brain within the Scarecrow shut down his memory of having a brain? Could the bullying behavior of the crow have overwhelmed the emotional Scarecrow to the point that his brain froze? Was it the placebo effect or did the higher brain of the Scarecrow finally kick in when the Wizard recognized his intelligence?

Each of these three aspects of the brain seeks harmony and needs balance to overcome the larger challenges within the form of equanimity.

THE GUT-BRAIN AXIS

Often referred to as our second brain, our gut-brain axis has its own autonomous enteric nervous system and houses most of our immune system. The fact that serotonin and dopamine (the well-being neurotransmitters) are present in the bowels but affect brain function is fascinating. How do the brain and gut function together? Why do some people faint at the sight of blood or spontaneously upchuck when they witness someone vomit? Mirror neuron studies, somatic empathy, and quantum theory offer some insights.

Neuroscientists are mapping the brain with neuroimaging, MRIs, and a host of other technological marvels. Brain activities are recorded while a subject performs the task being measured to see which neurons activate and/or mirror another's neural circuitry. Physicists currently recognize that intention has a significant bearing on what becomes real. Similarly, through the *uncertainty principle* within quantum theory comes tangible evidence that the process of observing subatomic particles creates measurable effects. Another tenet within quantum theory, the *principle of superposition*, states that atoms exist in multiple potential states until observed.

Quantum *entanglement theory* states in effect that once two or more particles interact intimately with one another, a permanent connection and an ongoing correlation to each other's state/property occur. Additionally, the *principle of nonlocality* goes on to say that these particles maintain this intimate and immediate access to each other's state/property even while separated by vast distances. Einstein accepted quantum theory but initially dismissed the notion of nonlocality as "spooky actions from a distance." But scientists have repeatedly proven the efficacy of quantum theory and accept that particles are entangled intimately and interconnected through time and distance by the principle of nonlocality. I suspect that these principles have something to do with our primary love templates, mirrored empathy, and illusions that recycle until we superimpose new possibilities within each hemisphere of our brain.

I have noticed this phenomenon occur in psychotherapy, when a client emotionally regresses after accessing a traumatic memory. Poor decisions based upon unexamined life scripts occur during the resulting left and right hemispheric disharmony. Porges, in his groundbreaking *polyvagal theory* about the brain, coined the term "neuroception" for an initial life script or assumption.[9] Traumatic memories can superimpose illusions on our state of well-being and trigger primitive coping strategies. Imagine the possibility of a trauma-induced picture being created from a painful event and that this picture now hangs with other trauma memories in the right hemisphere of our brain. Searing emotion crystallizes and embeds *neuroceptions* with mental pictures. Emotional residue from previous trauma reactivates during a similar event in the future. These pictures not only contain the current troubling images and powerful emotions generated by the trauma but also every neuroception and life-script assumption buried within our left hemisphere. Conflicting thoughts paralyze and ambivalence immobilizes. So as I mentioned previously, stronger passion and dedicated willpower are needed to release any trauma-induced superimposed emotional, embedded illusion buried within our brain. When our misguided assumptions about the purpose of suffering are removed by compassion, our distorted self-portraits will come off the wall.

We often sense truth and integrity in our "heart, body, and soul," perhaps due to the principle of nonlocality. Initially, when clients come into treatment after things go south, I help them find their original positive intention, unmet need, and/or organizing principle within their left hemisphere that existed prior to their suffering. Then we access and resolve the related right-hemispheric emotional milieu. Personal love templates and/or personal paradigms based upon illusion release with heartfelt compassion by our higher brain. Next, we revisit the original positive intention and supersede the suffering by charting a new course of action. When suffering transforms and/or transcendence occurs, we feel better. That sick feeling in our gut subsides as we release and reconsider our trauma. When we emotionally mature, we view the world more objectively, and new possibilities superimpose on our illusions/delusions. The principle of uncertainty provides opportunity through observation, when the loving wisdom of our inner adult cherishes us and witnesses the mistakes we make with compassion.

These theories, principles, and technologies are a marvel; I am certain Plato and Plotinus would have much to say about brain mapping and quantum theory. Of course, Plato did not have modern technology and relied upon dialectic discovery as science, concluding that intuition plus reason originated human thought. He thought deductive reasoning provided the necessary logic to build upon the wisdom of previously accepted philosophy. "Anamnesis," for example, was the word Plato coined to describe the intuitive process of remembering preexisting knowledge hidden within the depths of our soul. Plato's inspiration evolved into the modern concept of "amnesia," which in English means *forgetfulness* or *without memory*. Both Plato and Plotinus agreed that any knowledge of our connection to others and the divine was perceived through our intuitive senses, aka the gut. Plotinus summarized Greek philosophy about the origins of inspirational thought when he said, "Knowledge has three degrees—opinion, science, illumination. The means or instrument of the first is sense; of the second, dialectic; of the third, intuition."[10]

Sensation and intuition are two of the four functions of our personality that the psychiatrist Carl Jung (1875–1961) used similarly in his psychological theory. When we *know* something without having a logical reason or knowing why, it's called a gut reaction, a hunch, or an educated guess. Knowledge that originates from the combination of our intuition, rational mind, and gut reaction is frequently referred to as common sense. Carl Jung noticed that aspects of our mind could access ancestral memory and universal experiences common to all mankind, which he named the collective unconscious. Intuition was considered trans-intellectual in these circumstances, while our instinctual nature involves precognition.

The more our spiritual and physical natures work together, the more perceptive or intuitive our emotional brain becomes. We can peer into windows of the unknown by using the extrasensory perceptive abilities we were born with, even if we, like the Scarecrow, do not recognize our own abilities. Extrasensory perception, the sixth sense, communicating with the Holy Spirit, and so on have been around for thousands of years. Here, I will merge those terms and simplify the concept by referring to it as intuition.

Regardless of our beliefs or arguments discounting intuition, we each have instincts or hunches commonly described as our intuition or sixth sense. Clairvoyance (seeing), clairsentience (sensing), clairaudience (hearing), and claircognizance (knowing) have become well-known terms to define some of the ways we receive information beyond the scope of our five traditionally recognized senses. Unfortunately, as of this writing, our sixth sense has not been accurately measured by science, which is why so many debate its existence. The ancient Greek philosophers felt direct knowledge (*nous*) could be obtained through inference rather than direct observation. They thought that a universal principle or form could only be grasped through a healthy balance of intuition, reasoning, and intellect. Since feelings were temporary in nature and originated from our senses, they were not considered very significant. Intuition and reason were more substantial to the Greeks because this is how one accessed the source of infinite knowledge.

Anyone in ancient Greece who experienced an explosion of creativity (*furor poeticus*) that accessed his full potential would thank the *Muses* for their inspiration. In Greek mythology, the Muses were goddesses who inspired literature, science, and the arts. Intuition is our "Muse" or union of our physical, emotional, and mental abilities that interacts with divinity to inspire us. Perception, intention, and our conscious or unconscious thought processes interact with pertinent information and assign meaning to our experience. Depending upon the individual, logic, intuition, or inspiration may or may not resolve our issue, so dialectic discovery is frequently involved.

The Wizard looked very real and frightening to Dorothy and her companions until the curtain was pulled back to reveal a small man. When Neo unhooked from the Matrix, he saw that the virtual-reality dream entertaining humans was an illusion and that humans actually existed in a state of suspended animation. The prisoners in Plato's cave thought the shadows on the wall were real until somebody was inspired, removed his shackles, and saw the truth. Enjoying the sunshine outside our rational mind, we too can experience something a cave prisoner never thought existed. Intuition, inspiration, and instinct are wonderful, but blending them with equanimity, balance, and moderation is extremely beneficial. I believe this equanimity blooms when we are able to become emotionally mature.

CHRONOLOGICAL VERSUS EMOTIONAL MATURITY

Our reptilian, emotional, and higher brains process information and make associations quickly like computers. Sensory management is paramount to the right hemisphere, so our left hemisphere assigns meaning to input we receive for predictive and survival purposes. Our psychological makeup and perception have a direct bearing on our emotions and the manner in which we experience life. There is a distinct difference between our *internal emotional reactions* versus *extrasensory input* from the environment. In his book *Metaphysics*, Aristotle described this difference in the following way: metaphysics involves intuitive knowledge of unprovable starting-points (concepts and truths) and demonstrative knowledge of what follows from them.[11]

Throughout my career, I have observed that our emotional maturity consistently waxes and wanes throughout the day like the phases of the moon. Accessing an individual by their predominant developmental or emotional state became a more reliable predictor of behavior than chronological age would typically indicate. A successful intervention relied upon accurately assessing when an individual operated from his or her infant, child, adolescent, and/or mature emotional state.

Emotional maturity evolves naturally and organically until stress activates immature subparts of our personality, which regress into a stress response. Some people operate from an infant stress response most of their adult life. Severe borderline and/or bipolar personality disorders, as well as abuse victims, can easily regress into an agitated infant or childlike emotional response when stressed. The brain's ability to think abstractly develops slowly and completes by the ages of twelve to fifteen. Children usually do not understand the source of their emotions as a result, but this is not age specific because many adults struggle similarly. Volatility, lethargy, and/or passivity may occur when traumatic memories resurface. Narcissistic behaviors and survival-of-the-fittest strategies are common for stressed-out individuals who struggle with personality disorders, psychoses, and/or severe symptoms related to unresolved PTSD. When emotional hot spots resurface, they may cause our brains to fight/flight/freeze and regress emotionally into an infant, child, or adolescent stress response.

Paradoxically, we have all seen small children act in a very tender and emotionally mature way, for example, when parents regress into a primitive state due to stress or suffering. Many neuroscientists believe that automatic imitation is possible due to the mirror neuron system that occurs between brains.[12] Children often mirror a nurturing model and intuitively know what to do or say. By reversing the traditional parent/child role, a child can help the family restore its equanimity. However, children typically are not solving family mysteries or mentoring but simply mirroring modeled forms of love, grace, and equanimity witnessed previously. How many adults do you know that are just as clueless as a child about their emotional motivations? Emotional maturity is unrelated to chronological age. The form of illusion mirrors both wisdom and immaturity as starting points for us to sort out the difference, as Aristotle brilliantly stated.

Maintaining the equanimity, balance, and wisdom to progress through each maturational milestone is a herculean task. While our brain prefers harmony, repetitive setbacks, regressions, and stagnations are grist for the mill within the form of equanimity. Jumping back and forth from one emotional state to another throughout the course of a day is normal for most people. Next, I will share the four stress responses (infant, child, adolescent, and mature adult) that reflect the emotional states humans possess from moment to moment.

It takes two mature people to negotiate a good, long-lasting resolution. Adversaries who are regressed and embroiled in immature stress will argue endlessly, and agreements unravel quickly. Healthy resolutions need emotionally mature partners who negotiate in good faith. In my practice, I quickly access the maturity level and stress responses clients employ and adjust my approach accordingly, which provides more successful outcomes than assuming emotional maturity is related to their chronological age. These stress responses are directly correlated to our reptilian, emotional, and higher brains.

INFANT STRESS RESPONSE

> "Can't you give me brains?" asked the Scarecrow.
> "You don't need them. You are learning something every day. A baby has brains, but it doesn't know much. Experience is the only thing that brings knowledge, and the longer you are on earth the more experience you are sure to get."[13]

I believe when the soul arrives in a physical body, our direct awareness of the divine and intimate connection to divinity sever. Birth requires separation, and this event activates reptilian-based primal fear and the mistaken belief inherent in all humans that "I am alone." Separation from our divine source is our primary abandonment template and has historically terrorized the reptilian brain with its frightening illusions and agonizing emotions. Note that when an infant wakes up alone, she will either coo happily or scream with separation anxiety. From our beginnings as infants, fear of abandonment dulls our experience of love and light, which confuses the human brain—but not our soul.

Newborns believe the world revolves around them and are totally dependent upon others to survive. Babies possess global awareness of the surrounding emotional milieu and respond to the happy, silly, and sad faces of caretakers. Infants possess no real understanding of their emotions but make dialectic discoveries through trial and error. Operating primarily from her primitive reptilian brain, an infant is unable to distinguish if her emotions come from self or another stimulus—the infant feels and responds, period. Newborns live in an undifferentiated state of henosis with a central primal focus on "I need an outside power to satisfy my needs and ensure my survival."

Object constancy is a psychological term used to describe an infant's ability or inability to remember if his or her parents continue to exist when they leave the room or play peek-a-boo. Infants lose their bearings and forget they are loved all the time. Stuffed bears or monkeys serve as surrogate parents or symbolize aspects of self and soothe the infant when they feel alone. Nurturing parents feel empathy and compassion fills their hearts when they hold their crying baby close. The infant being held remembers she is loved so her pain subsides.

Occasionally, an extraordinarily empathic infant will unknowingly absorb a family member's pain or belief system like a sponge and create a lifelong assumption that the pain she feels is only her own. This is a complicated concept to prove, but perhaps the principle of nonlocality within quantum theory and the phenomenon of mirror neurons trigger the neighboring infants to cry sympathetically in hospital nurseries when one is hungry or wets her diaper and starts to wail.[14] Human infant research data suggests that a mirror neuron system develops within the first twelve months of life.[15] Babies react to everything that happens around them, so witnessing another baby crying may trigger contagious empathy. Who hasn't felt the pain of another? Infants have labile moods and yet may be mimicking the family's angst without knowing why they feel bad. (That dynamic is a corrupted form of intuition, which will be discussed in more detail later.)

Narcissistically inclined individuals, people with personality disorders, and trauma survivors with untreated terrorized infant personality aspects often regress into the emotional state of infancy in adulthood. When our reptilian brain dominates our adult personality without the emotional awareness and the calming effects of our higher brain, interpersonal relationships suffer. When we consider our emotional responses in relationships with these insights, the phrases echoed time and again by lovers—"Don't be such a baby!" or "Don't be so sensitive!"—take on new meaning.

A heated-up reptilian brain loaded with undifferentiated passion can override the higher brain's ability to calm or sort things out in stressful situations. The higher brain in an infant has yet to mature, which is why babies need soothing from another to help settle down—they can't do it alone. Adults who operate primarily from their reptilian brain and respond to stress like an infant will struggle to self-soothe when under duress. Everyone has personality aspects and/or stress responses that make them moody and emotionally labile. Emotionally charged events create stress and can activate archaeological memories, which can cause our mood to fluctuate like the weather. To simplify this discussion and make our caged emotions sound more endearing, going forward I will call those aspects of our personality, which retain our unresolved or unconscious emotional material, our *monkeys*.

When stress activates a number of our monkeys with their pictures hanging on our brain's wall, we can become overwhelmed with the collective mood of our monkey clan, which can trigger an infant stress response. "Time-outs" help because removing threatening stimuli creates breathing room. Stressed-out monkeys get swept up into infant-like, emotional frenzies and rattle their cages to warn us of danger until the emotional needs of each monkey are addressed with love, wisdom, and equanimity. This is a deliberate emotional maturation process that avoids the now hardwired reptilian shutdown or the emotional fight/flight/freeze response. Losing equilibrium always makes matters worse. Family members, friends, therapists, or mentors can serve as a temporary exterior higher brain for those struggling in an infant stress response by providing a peaceful presence. When someone patiently listens to our screeching monkeys without flying off the handle, stress diminishes and solutions take hold. Emotional equilibrium returns when the infant stress response subsides and we have the emotional maturity of our higher brain. Since these emotions are very difficult to manage, I am including in this chapter several simple, helpful techniques I have shared with my clients to use and restore emotional equanimity.

VISUALIZATION: SMOOTHED BY THE HEART OF MOTHER

Before starting this visualization, it may be useful to reread the form of cherish from chapter 4 and/or use the Camel Wave Meditation with the form from appendix A to deepen your experience of giving and receiving emotional support. Set an intention to cherish, center your mind, and embrace every emotion within your heart. Use the following visualization to soothe every monkey in your mind that is frightened, sad, and/or angry and to help him or her feel safe and secure.

Suffering and sorrow are emotional states that need soothing, reassurance, and to be cherished. Spooked monkeys have stress responses, which are designed to protect us or frighten off anything perceived as harmful; they represent the valuable aspects within us overwhelmed with emotions. Like abandoned infants, monkeys need soothing and heartfelt reassurance from a loving mother or father. To start this visualization, go to a quiet place and invite every spooked monkey rattling its cage in your mind to join you.

As you sit or lie down on the ground, visualize taking these little monkeys into the nurturing heart of Mother Earth. After your arrival, let your sorrow and pain be embraced by Mother's heart like a crying baby being soothed by a loving parent.

Allow the all-encompassing love from Mother Earth and the hearts from every soul who previously recovered from a similar experience cherish you and provide compassion. Allow your heart to be soothed by this union.

Cry, laugh, or play; stay in this emotional space for as long as you like. Allow the love to wash over your suffering like waves from the ocean. Don't try to control your experience because feelings surge and ebb like the tides; stay in the flow until your pain drains and subsides.

Let your monkeys revitalize you and stay with this visualization until you feel reenergized. Feel the love pulsate and weave into your being— let the love you sense find its home. As your heart fills, let the love become your own experience of wholeness. When you feel cherished and all the monkeys are calm, take a deep breath and conclude the visualiza-tion. [16]

CHILD STRESS RESPONSE

Children are impulsive and immature and learn through trial and error. When a child realizes the consequences of his or her actions, experience is gained and lessons are learned about self and the world at large. Children express emotions through their behavior (active or passive), and the feedback received from other people and the environment is educational. Children usually struggle to discuss or express what causes their emotional states because abstract thinking and left-hemispheric analysis doesn't kick in until ages twelve to fifteen. Overwhelming emotion can trigger a shutdown response of the reptilian brain or the fight/flight/freeze response of the emotional brain and offers another explanation for why children are frequently clueless about their own emotions.

Adults and children pass emotions back and forth to one another like a ball in a ping-pong match. Perhaps the previously mentioned mirror neurons, which exist between humans, facilitate this game of *tag-you're-it*. The ineffable way all humans are inexorably linked shows the pitfalls of oneness because children frequently absorb the emotional garbage from the family like lint traps on dryers. That lint may become a lifelong affliction or a primary love template. The intuitive child can experience wide mood swings due to their ability to access and process the emotions of others. [17] Children express their emotions through their behavior, and the emotions an adult feels while in the presence of a child provide clues to the child's internal experience. To the trained eye, a child's behavior is a good indicator of their emotions. On the other hand, adults can guess what the child is feeling by the body language of a child (avoiding eye contact, big smile, turning red in the face, pursed lips, etc.) and the emotional reaction the adult feels internally in response to the child's behavior.

Overcontrolling, abusive, or neglectful authority figures create an emotional dynamic in children where pain is repressed through dissociation. Burying suffering is a brilliant survival strategy, but it also shuts down expressions of both pain and joy, which stifles emotional maturity.

166CHAPTER 7

Repressed emotional energy can remain dormant temporarily but not forever, which means that childhood stress responses can carry over into adolescence and beyond but will need to be addressed eventually as an adult. Fear, sadness, and anger exist on a continuum and move in unison with joy, love, and happiness. Curtailing negative feelings will automatically reduce our ability to experience the full range of positive emotions accordingly. Running away from pain never creates happiness in the long term because love and our ability to cherish can transform what we consider negative emotion.

Unresolved and unexpressed emotion can morph into depression, oppositional behavior, and anxiety-related syndromes, to name a few. Until we release, resolve, or unhook our emotional baggage and the associated illusions buried within our reptilian, emotional, and higher brains, they will continue to rule our behaviors and recycle unproductive primary love templates, personal paradigms of suffering, and/or victim/perpetrator dramas. If the child stress response persists into adulthood, it may take the form of a mother-son marriage dynamic, where both the husband and wife fail to create an egalitarian, mature adult relationship based upon self-responsibility and mutual sovereignty. Father-daughter emotional marriages occur, but four out of five of this type of immature romantic relationships, in my experience, are the mother-son variety. The parental spouse never feels emotionally safe enough to be vulnerable as an equal while the emotional child spouse never grows up much like Peter Pan. Both spouses want to please the partner but suffer in the long run because, like a child, they fail to meet their own emotional needs.

Firm boundaries create psychological safety for the child struggling with inappropriate behavior, impulsiveness, and periodic emotional regression. Believe it or not, children and immature adults in the midst of a child stress response need external controls and will eventually respond favorably to a caring adult who provides the structure they are unable to provide for themselves.

Our higher brain is the access point for the emotionally mature adult aspect of our personality. This aspect of self can learn how to talk to and soothe our inner child when we, as adults, are in the middle of a stress response. The following dialectic discovery can be used not only to help an actual child gain more insight into emotional life but also a regressed child aspect of our adult personality embroiled in a stress response.

Loving presence and acceptance also create safety and provide an opportunity for our inner child to explore his or her emotional needs and positive intentions that initiated an unproductive behavior.

THINK-FEEL-DO THREE-LEGGED STOOL EXERCISE

Anchoring your passion or a dream in the physical world is accomplished by synchronizing your mind, heart, and behavior into a stable unity, like a three-legged stool. Mental focus, emotional desire, and dedicated action, when grounded with awareness and integrity, create the opportunity to materialize our wants and needs. This think-feel-do balancing session is useful not only with someone embroiled in a child stress response, but with anyone you know who wants to learn how thought, emotion, and action create self- discipline.

Before beginning this self-guided personal discovery session, center yourself and set your intentions. The task ahead is about discovering how to unify your mental, emotional, and behavioral "legs" into a stable, sound stool able to launch your desire. Illusions block dreams, so do your best to find which leg is destabilizing your desire during this dialogue. You can start by integrating the mental, emotional, and behavioral aspects of your personality and developing more internal consistency. Choosing to reread the form of illusion from chapter 2 or using the Camel Wave Meditation in appendix A with the intention to find your illusions before this session is wise because it is useful to know which aspect of your personality creates your reality.

Stressed-out aspects (aka caged monkeys) of the human brain are separate entities with different mental perspectives, emotional agendas, and behavior strategies. Let your emotionally mature adult ask the following questions of the most vocal aspect to find out what it thinks it needs, emotionally desires, and is trying to accomplish by its actions. Allowing each immature aspect to draw, journal, or conversationally explore its perspective, agenda, and strategy in a safe environment helps you discover needs, express feelings, and link behavior with intention. Healthy communication gives our mature adult aspect the space and motivation to integrate stress responses into wholeness.

- *Ask yourself: What do you THINK about an event?*

- When you run out of words, ask: How do you FEEL about the event?
- Ask questions and gently probe for feelings. Then ask: What did you DO or want to DO next?
- If/when you run out of words and have explored your motivations, move to one of the other two theme questions.

Since there are three areas of questioning, you can always circle back to a feeling question once you or the monkey aspect embroiled in the stress response feels comfortable with the conversational flow.

Emotions are the nerve endings of our being that sense what feels good or not. We grow and mature when we have productive strategies to meet our needs, are aware of our emotions, and are highly motivated to consistently do the work necessary to overcome our illusions. Ministering to stressed monkeys that dominate our proverbial microphone requires love, compassion, and communication. Once our three-legged stool is balanced, we can attract our heart's desire and actualize dreams. Intellectual integrity, emotional honesty, and dedicated action are essential elements to create unity, which activates our soul and henosis on earth.

Unlike the three wise monkeys in Japanese culture, who see no evil, hear no evil, speak no evil to model equanimity, this think-feel-do three-legged stool exercise encourages communication, self-awareness, and self-realization. Once you have a better grasp of how thoughts and emotions influence behavior, it may be useful to consider practicing the Wise and Loving Inner Voice Meditation described in appendix B to help you evaluate the wisdom of your inner voice to make better decisions in the future. The line of questioning within this dialectic discovery is useful for helping others to understand how actions, emotions, and thoughts work together.

ADOLESCENT STRESS RESPONSE

Autonomy and self-determination are the primary drivers of adolescents, whose primary developmental task is to launch into the world with a healthy identity and the ability to make productive, autonomous choices. Opposition, resistance, and outright rebellion are traditional tools used by adolescents to express youthful idealism, personal opin- ions, and self-guided solutions. Adolescents sometimes struggle with low self-esteem or a tenuous sense of self and may become locked into a self-imposed level of hell of stagnated growth due to persistent resis- tance. Saying no to authority figures feels empowering initially and is a necessary step toward the adolescent's individualization, but if we are still locked into this method at the age of thirty, we likely are suffering from the repercussions. Exercising our voice and saying yes or no based on self-governing principles is critical in this stage of emotional devel- opment to prepare for future life challenges.

Adolescents with fiery dispositions judge authority figures merciless- ly if those authority figures engage in hypocrisy. Adolescents often thrive in environments with behavioral, emotional, and intellectual hon- esty or integrity. Oppositional behavior is frightening to some adults, so a threatening teen who acts out publicly gets more attention than the depressed young man or woman who internalizes suffering or buries problems. Adolescents frequently feel dismissed by adults and become squeaky wheels to draw attention to their issue or problems within the family system.

Some adolescents instinctively say no to any request, never mature emotionally, and tend to struggle with relationships requiring collabora- tion and compromise as an adult. The ability of the higher brain to calm down the other two stress responses (infant and child) matures during this stage of human development. When as an adolescent we accept our intuitive abilities and create clear emotional boundaries with others, our spiritual connection to all of creation vastly improves.

Healthy young women instinctively gravitate toward interconnection and emotional closeness and openly communicate feelings with girl- friends. Friends respect the girl who shows genuine concern for others and shares her emotional life with her community. Girls tend to gather in egalitarian groups while guys are more hierarchical. Troubled teen- age girls typically act in toward themselves through depression, suicidal gestures, or unwanted pregnancies. Times are changing, however; some of the gender expectations are blending and becoming more egalitarian.

Troubled young men typically act out their emotional issues through substance abuse, violence, and criminal activities. Healthy young men seek independence, and buddies respect them for their talents or skill sets. For young males, sharing emotions is not a priority. Adolescent males don't know much about emotions and experience the moods of girlfriends as something to fix. Young women freely share emotions with boyfriends in an attempt to connect and vent. Immature males often feel smothered or controlled by emotion and often run away from emotional connection like Peter Pan, the boy who wouldn't grow up.

Wholeness includes *fixing* emotional problems with action (masculine expression) as well as *venting* emotion to allow hearts to connect with one another (feminine expression). Both styles are needed, but unfortunately each gender frequently misunderstands the other's perspective around this issue. A healthy balance of *fixing* and *venting* is good for every loving relationship in the long term. The following short-term versus enduring solution discussion is useful to help adolescents begin to think, respond, and understand love like mature adults. Teenagers, internal adolescents, or adults with the emotional maturity of an adolescent are impulsive, think in the short term, and sincerely believe they've got all the answers. The natural idealism possessed by adolescents coupled with minimal experience frequently means their dialectic theories fall short in creating the love they want in the physical world.

SHORT-TERM VERSUS ENDURING SOLUTIONS DISCUSSION

Adolescents abhor hypocrisy and notice the mistakes their elders make; they seek autonomy and resist authority. Idealistic and passionate but lacking the practical knowledge gained from hard-earned experience, adolescents frequently succumb to a shortsighted notion that opposition and idealism create sovereignty. Mature, loving wisdom requires discernment between shortsighted illusions versus enduring solutions. The purest forms of love transcend illusion and have access to henosis and the quantum field.

This discussion is useful not only with someone embroiled in an adolescent stress response, but with anyone you know who wants to evolve from shortsighted illusions to enduring, enlightened solutions.

Growth is accomplished through trial and awareness, so begin this discussion by centering your thoughts and heart on the goal to develop the equilibrium and discernment to accurately assess if your perspectives, agendas, and strategies contain loving and enduring wisdom. Let your emotionally mature adult ask the following questions of your adolescent aspect or stressed monkey to find out what need, want, or desire he or she is addressing. Carefully explore their master plan and any contingency strategies. You may choose to reread the form of love from chapter 3 or use it with the Camel Wave Meditation from appendix A, especially if you need assistance shifting your focus from judging short-sighted autonomy to mature equilibrium and presenting enduring solutions.

Instruct your own adolescent aspect to explore, journal, or communicate its rationale, emotional agenda, and/or behavior strategies in the following safe format. This process can assist in the development of an understanding of subliminal motivations and encourage long-range perspectives. When practiced on yourself, this dialectic discovery engages your mature adult or a similar wise aspect of your personality so you can integrate loving wisdom to modify any unproductive adolescent stress responses to return to wholeness. Adolescent aspects (monkeys) tend to think in the short term, lack the proverbial wisdom others glean from actual experience, and often do not know what it takes or have the patience to consider guidance from mature, incorruptible models. Let the adolescent aspect reveal his or her wants, needs, and desires and action plan first. Compliment them if they found an enduring, loving solution. Since the goal is love, explain why it would be in their self-interest to listen to another perspective if they planned an ill-advised adventure. By listening carefully to their rationale, you can prepare a well-crafted argument using examples from their presentation to support your attempt to teach them about an enduring, loving, and mature perspective.

- *First, encourage the adolescent (monkey) aspect to present their rationale, emotional agendas, and motivational strategies for their behavior.*
- *Listen carefully, gently ask questions, and get a complete grasp of their positive intentions without interrupting, correcting, or judging.*
- *Gain a complete comprehension of the depth of their reasoning before letting your mature adult take his or her turn.*
- *Compare the pitfalls of an adolescent short-term rationale to the incorruptible wisdom of an enduring, loving solution.*

- *Consequences for adolescent aspects for missing love's mark are inappropriate. They can be offered, however, to an actual teenager from an authority figure only as an incentive to get their attention.*

Once you have a better grasp of how your shortsighted attempt toward autonomy failed to become an enduring solution, it may be useful to consider the Wise and Loving Inner Voice Meditation described in appendix B to help you weigh the wisdom of your inner voice to help you make better decisions in the future.

THE EMOTIONALLY MATURE ADULT

Mastering the challenges of the previous developmental stages requires maturing until a willingness to say yes to life is developed. Effort and enthusiasm are needed to pursue a dream. Character, commitments, and careers need tender loving care. Self-responsibility is required to become whole. Heart-felt connection to others is attractive to a healthy adult. Commitment to heal our delusions about love to achieve this union is primary. Regression needs to be recognized and illusions identified as we gain the ability to objectively self-monitor our actions. The emotionally mature adult makes the effort to self-correct. In order to meet our own needs with equanimity, a healthy adult will respond very differently than someone with an infant, child, or adolescent stress response. When our sense of self is strong, our heart can love, takes responsibility, and has integrity. An incorruptible heart can merge with someone else without falling into his or her hell—if that is what our beloved is experiencing.

I believe we are divine beings living in human form. The ability to construct our dream into a *tangible*, earthly form is physically created by our actions and generated by the masculine nature of every human. The *invisible* world, which includes our emotions, thoughts, intuition, and spiritual connection, comprises the feminine nature of every human. Our feminine nature can dream, communicate with our soul, and experience henosis. Self- esteem (feminine) and self-responsibility (masculine) embody the power and strength of our divine expression in the physical world. Creativity, love, and emotional connection are aspects of our total being that embrace unity empathically and logically. Healthy adults combine masculine and feminine natures by uniting the desires of the heart with dedicated action. For example, to create is a feminine (invisible) expression and to embody is masculine (tangible). Both are necessary to create . . . even a mousetrap, for example. It's the feminine creative side that invents the new mousetrap, gets inspired, and imagines the new design. Our masculine side draws the dimensions, gathers the physical materials (wood, wire, bait, etc.), and builds the mousetrap.

The emotionally mature adult has both a logical and an intuitive left/ right hemispheric awareness of the various perspectives from reptilian, emotional, and higher brain stress responses. When our words, emotional expressions, and actions are congruent, our three-legged stool stabilizes and dreams realize. Possessing a good connection to our higher brain lets us use its enduring wisdom wisely. Accessing our intuitive abilities allows us to assist others while we maintain appropriate emotional boundaries and dispose of unnecessary, useless emotional garbage. Our higher brain and a mature heart are what a healthy adult uses to spiritually connect to wholeness or henosis. A good relationship with self, others, and the divine stems from a mature relationship with our monkeys and the behavioral, emotional, and intellectual aspects of our being.

Certain situations will cause even an emotionally mature individual to regress and exhibit infant, child, or adolescent stress responses. Tracking the source of our reactions provides clues about a primary love template and/or dysfunctional personal paradigm to prevent childhood triggers from creating havoc in our lives. Environmental stress, unexamined emotions, and unresolved historical debris cause aspects of our personality to screech like frightened or angry monkeys rattling a cage. Though painful and unpleasant, a stress response backs us into a proverbial corner, reveals a current emotional weather pattern, and pinpoints a primal wound with the precision of a laser beam.

Accumulated unexamined or unexpressed emotion can trigger a primitive stress response regression in the same way an electrical surge blows a fuse in a house. Stressed-out monkeys fray our nerves and create short circuits to reveal something valuable. In short, if our reaction is larger than the "crime" committed, the inflated emotions can throw a monkey wrench into our aspiration. Our task is to learn what each monkey wants and why they want it, which dignifies their emotional imperative and soothes the monkey. The Empathy Round Table that follows is designed to access our mature adult, replace blown fuses, and get the lights back on, but unfortunately it doesn't rewire our traumatized monkeys. The Empathy Round Table ferrets out external stimuli from unconscious, underdeveloped, or frozen aspects of our personality locked into primary love templates, dysfunctional personal paradigms, and/or victim/perpetrator dramas. Terrorized infant, overwhelmed child, and stressed-out adolescent aspects of our personality can cause our emotionally mature adult to temporarily regress in extreme emotional situations. When we carefully listen to each monkey, learn what it wants, and give it love, understanding, and empathy, we reduce our regressed stress responses.

Stress responses can be broken down into component stressors to identify an individual monkey's reaction to a precipitating event, such as criticism, jealousy, betrayal, or indifference. For example, criticism from an employer, self-criticism, and/or critical parent trauma often become screeching monkeys triggered when our spouse criticizes us, even if the criticism is delivered in a loving way. Recognizing the emotional imperative behind each aspect of our personality (such as the monkey that reacts to criticism) calms down our reptilian and emotional brains and gives the higher brain an opportunity to have a more productive conversation with the person that triggered us. Conflict is best resolved with two emotionally mature adults, as opposed to a scenario with two screeching, immature monkeys age regressed to infant, child, or adolescent stress.

THE EMPATHY ROUND TABLE

Before starting this exercise, it may be useful to reread the form of equanimity from chapter 6 or use it with the Camel Wave Meditation from appendix A to regain your balance and maturity. The Wise Lover, Wounded Beloved Reconciliation from chapter 3 describes relevant information about self-soothing. The goal of this exercise is not to heal each monkey but instead to have a compassionate internal dialogue to help us identify, dignify, and recognize the concerns of each monkey so we can respond to life in a healthy manner and in real time. The deeper wants, needs, and desires of each monkey may be addressed later for resolution in an even more loving and thorough way.

- *On a scale from zero to ten, consider the number society would rate the situation (crime) you are experiencing. Now, using that same scale, access your brain's logical left hemisphere to give your current experience a number.*
- *If your number is larger or smaller than the "crime" the general public would perceive, your right hemisphere and a stressed monkey are skewing your reaction. When society and the other person thinks he or she deserves a level two response, defensiveness occurs if we unleash our emotions at a level eight. (For example, if society's number for the crime of parking in a handicap spot is a two and your emotional reaction is an eight, the extra six points represent the degree of your historical conscious and subconscious sensitivity to the situation that is activated . . . not the actual number of related archaeological events that I'm calling monkeys.)*
- *It is important to listen with an open heart to calm down our hysterical and/or hurt monkeys when they are in the middle of an infant, child, and/or adolescent stress reaction. Unleashing them onto others, while angry at a level eight rather than two, produces poor results. By giving our emotional monkeys space to express themselves without placating them in the safe presence of our higher brain, they settle down. After reaching a state of equanimity appropriate to the level of the "crime," then address the issue at hand with maturity. This approach tends to provide positive results.*
- *Upset monkeys need respect, empathy, and heartfelt recognition before they will achieve a sustainable level of calm or embrace an enlightened solution. Getting to middle ground as a centered, calm, and balanced negotiator requires moving from level eight to at least level two intensity. Addressing the situation with the other person at an appropriate level two recognized by polite society is the goal. When our monkeys experience compassion, they pass it on to others. Discharging extraneous emotion based upon archaeological events and overheated associations, which are unrelated to the current problem, creates defensiveness, conflict, and victim/perpetrator dramas.*

- *Now, in your mind, see a round table. Imagine your higher brain sitting at the head of the table alongside your soul. Invite every monkey from your reptilian, emotional, and even higher brain that has an opinion about the situation to take a seat at the table. Let your stressed-out infant, child, and adolescent take their place at your Empathy Round Table.*

- *Listen carefully and respectfully to what each monkey needs or desires so your higher brain with help from your soul can create a plan to address these issues. Sometimes empathy, acknowledgment, and embracing the emotions within your heart are enough. The goal of this exercise is to achieve dignity, equanimity, and consensus, not healing.*

- *Once you have created a solution and every monkey accepts the plan, you should sense that everyone has calmed down to a level two or less. This is a good time to address the situation with the person you are angry or upset with at this time because you can do so with the balance and equanimity of an emotionally mature adult.*

- *Final notes: These monkeys have great purpose; they exist to show us where we are blocked or broken. Our unresolved, unconscious issues will remain in our mind and create havoc and suffering until they are addressed. The monkeys will return to their cage or run free once we recognize their valuable input. They settle down when we make a commitment to address concerns in the future. When we restore peace in our emotional brain, the maturity of our adult higher brain comes back online.*

The Empathy Round Table balances our brain's hemispheres by calming our personal monkeys so they won't contaminate a current problem or create more stress reactions in others. Interpersonal relationships will frequently activate any unresolved, dormant monkeys of both participants. Life is like a funhouse of mirrors reflecting distorted illusion. Use the Wise and Loving Inner Voice Meditation described in appendix B whenever you get dazed and confused because it will help sort out your delusions from good decisions. A monkey accomplishes his or her mission when we recognize that our sorrows are merely leading us to wisdom on how to love ourselves and others more completely. This is accomplished when we welcome every aspect of our personality into *our heart. When we respond to our monkeys with respect, the merry-go-round stops and wholeness returns. When we become one inside ourselves, henosis blooms on the outside.*

THE ONENESS PARADOX

We are all one, yet humans are polarized in their views and speak many different languages. When something triggers us, uniting our brain's three functions and responding with a mature adult stress response is challenging. Wholeness is complicated simplicity—and the yellow brick road to unity often seems convoluted or paradoxical, just like it did to Dorothy in Oz. Meeting a wizard, a witch, or a stranger, for example, is difficult because diversity (e.g., an adversary or strangeness) requires reconciliation. It is a formidable task to reconcile our triggers to look past inhumanity and cherish adversaries. Maintaining an adult stress response, while reconciling our reptilian, emotional, and higher brains to the paradox of oneness, necessitates resisting illusion and producing incorruptible solutions.

It is extremely challenging to witness violence and resist the temptation to fall into a similar hell beside those lost in the illusion. Monitoring our stress responses, searching for wisdom, and embodying love while declining the invitation to react similarly is the essence of incorruptibility. Philosophers and wise elders have been guiding lights about the paradox of oneness. It takes steadfast principles and self-discipline to actually use the forms in this book in our everyday life experiences, especially due to the confusing aspects of paradox. Solving my problems with bullies by calmly admitting to them that I stuttered was my first introduction to the mystery of a paradoxical solution outside the familiar victim/perpetrator paradigm during my youth. The suggestions offered by my parents, priests, and speech therapists were not nearly as effective as my own. My sense of self would have collapsed if the verbal attacks had continued and the form of grace hadn't entered my life to provide a resolution. Autonomy blossoms and matures in those with a secure reptilian brain, emotional boundaries, and an incorruptible higher brain with access to intuitive solutions and spontaneous innovation. An emotionally mature adult coordinates their left/right hemispheres and masters their infant, child, or adolescent stress responses, which paradoxically work together but have diverse agendas. Initially, we align the different needs and perspectives of our physical, emotional, and intellectual aspects of our body until we become adapted to the paradoxes of life.

How we respond to the stress from our most seductive paradox—that to the same degree we are separate or different but also one—is the challenge of *noticing how similar others are to us, not focusing on the differences*. Paradox stretches our mind and pries it open to novel solutions. The word *paradoxon* in ancient Greek described a concept contrary to expectations or a perceived belief. Shortened to "paradox" today, it's currently defined as a statement or proposition that, despite sound (or apparently sound) reasoning from acceptable premises, leads to a conclusion that seems senseless, logically unacceptable, or self-contradictory.

We are all one is an important paradox of being human. Macrocosms are often best implemented as a collection of microcosms, similarly to how our behavioral, emotional, and mental aspects congeal and synchronize into wholeness. Inner peace is attained when we develop mature stress responses; unify the diverse voices within our reptilian, emotional, and higher brain; and listen to our monkeys. Illusion is the testing ground for us to withstand all the challenges as we learn how to become mindful. Adversity and diversity liberate us from the suffering affecting us all and are a central paradox for love to unravel. The great Chinese philosopher Laozi explained the promise of wholeness in the following way: "A great nation is like a great man: when he makes a mistake, he realizes it. Having realized it, he admits it. Having admitted it, he corrects it. He considers those who point out his faults as his most benevolent teachers. He thinks of his enemy as the shadow that he himself casts."[18]

8

THE EMPATHY PARADOX

Prior to conception, our soul existed in a sea of oneness and individualized to achieve the ultimate: to experience oneness as a human. Before we leave our human form and our soul returns to its divine origins, solving the paradox of oneness within diversity is one of our most significant challenges. Love and empathy are beautiful qualities, but the negativity on earth can pour a mountain of salt on a delicious meal. How to become sovereign and connected to all without accidently absorbing someone else's illusions and emotional debris can be a mystery. This chapter provides an empathy assessment tool and effective solutions to help the casual traveler discern empathy from emotional contagions originating from other people.

Considered a virtue by the major religions of the world, heartfelt concern for the well-being of others and the intention to alleviate suffering is commonly called compassion. Sorrow for human misfortune is called sympathy. Understanding and viscerally experiencing the feelings of another is a skill called empathy. Auspicious in its origins, the word "empathy" actually birthed from philosophers. Its roots evolved from the Greek words *empatheia* (passion, state of emotion) and *pathos* (feeling). In 1873, the German philosopher Vischer adapted these words and coined the term *Einfühlung* (from *ein* "in" + *Fühlung* "feeling").[1] Thirty-five years later, the philosopher Titchener translated "feeling in" into English and gave us the word "empathy."[2]

When we sense suffering and feel compassion, we are using our natural instinct to empathize. Empathy includes not only the willingness to understand but actually co-experiencing the pain of another, which is why people cringe or divert their eyes when witnessing others suffer. Instinctively, we feel another's pain due to our innate ability to feel compassion unless circumstances lead us to deaden our heart connection. Humans are born naturally empathic and must be trained to behave otherwise. Empathy is how the human heart tracks another's emotions, and the *mirror neurons* introduced in chapter 2 might be one of the mechanisms helping us experience what others feel.

Neuroscientists, psychologists, and social scientists have studied mirror neurons since 1990, and the debate about empathy and its development continues to this day. Psychotherapists and mind/body/spirit practitioners recognize that emotions move between people and teach their clients about effective boundaries. Cognitive strategies are frequently used in the field of psychology but were unproductive with my highly empathic clients because unwanted energies and emotions from others continued to stick to them like lint on Velcro. Without clear boundaries and a way to discern if the emotions we feel are our own or originate from others or the surrounding environment, every emotion we experience will be processed as our own. When discernment tools and cleansing strategies are lacking, the emotional milieu from others can stick to us. Mood swings, psychological imbalances, and emotional storage problems can occur due to permeable boundaries. Unfortunately, when we suffer, self-criticism follows; then judgments from others complicate matters.

After experiencing success helping numerous clients, including many suffering from immune disorders, I developed the *Somatic Empathy Theory*. Highly empathic people are often misdiagnosed with mental illness, but they have something important to teach us about human connection. Boundary awareness, emotional cleansing, and discernment strategies are fixes people can do at home without professional assistance. Prior to discussing my personal observations, suggestions, and conclusions about empathy, I will summarize the four most popular areas of study currently being examined by neuroscientists and psychologists.

THE FORM(S) OF EMPATHY

Empathy is the cognitive, emotional, and/or physical ability to identify with another's felt experience and correspond with sensitivity, sympathy, and compassion.

This definition provides my foundational belief about empathy, which describes how humans sense what others feel and respond accordingly. Empathy includes not only cognitive understanding but also our emotional and/or physical connection to the felt experience of another. For example, some of us are visceral responders, which may include fainting at the sight of blood or experiencing our stomach convulse when someone upchucks nearby. Instinctively, most of us feel another's pain unless circumstances lead us to deaden our heart connection. Humans are born naturally empathic and must be trained to behave otherwise.

Since the discovery of *mirror neurons* in 1990, neuropsychologists and the scientific community have taken great interest in how empathy develops within humans. For example, research now suggests that the presence of the hormone/neuropeptide oxytocin increases empathy.[3] However, discovering how empathy, bonding, and attachment generate from our innate mirroring capacity dominates the research landscape. Tracking the emotions of others is important for our safety, security, and sanity. The mirror neurons within our brain mentioned in chapter 2 help us experience what others feel and determine what actions to take.

Toddlers sometimes attempt to comfort those suffering, and this impulse may be a rudimentary form of empathy. When infants and toddlers cry spontaneously in the presence of a sobbing adult, some researchers call it empathy, while others such as Doris Bischof-Kohler examine efforts toward consolation. In Dr. Bischof-Kohler's study with children and toddlers, she defined empathy as the capacity to experience emotional connection and respond with helpful actions. However, the ability to understand and co-experience the feelings of another without physically reaching out to help is called empathy by other researchers. Empathy research is ongoing, and I will summarize some of their findings before presenting the Somatic Empathy Theory.

EMOTIONAL CONTAGIONS

An emotion we experience that originates from others is considered an emotional contagion. Neuropsychologists have discovered, when someone smiles at us or moves in a certain way, the neural pathways associated with those identical activities are simulated similarly in the brain of the observer. This phenomenon, as previously mentioned, is likely caused by mirror neurons and may explain how we co-experience what others feel in our own body. Researchers now recognize contagious emotions and have been debating on how empathy develops within humans. Current research focuses upon observable visual cues and MRI results, but I wonder if mirror neurons might actually be a physical door to unity consciousness. My clinical experience suggests that invisible emotional contagions affect highly empathic people greatly and stick to some of us like lint on Velcro.

Contagious emotions include the previously mentioned infant, who cries without a discernible reason when others cry. From my clinical experience, everyone experiences emotional contagions, when we spontaneously feel what others feel without words being spoken. An empathic transmission occurs, and our brain interprets what is going on based upon our personal history, emotional maturity, and familial/cultural background. Without awareness, we can become an energetic sponge absorbing emotional contagions from others due to permeable boundaries. Detective work to discern the true origin of our felt experience and taking corrective actions are recommended. Otherwise compassion fatigue, emotional burnout, and intimacy avoidance may follow.

Contagious emotions need to be addressed immediately, which requires accuracy, emotional regulation, and boundary awareness. Emotional accuracy is the ability to read the emotions, thoughts, and intentions of others and distinguish them from our own.[4] Emotional regulation combines self-awareness with equanimity in the presence of powerful mood swings originating from others.[5] Boundary awareness includes an intimate knowledge about incoming and outgoing emotional interactions between people.[6] The ability to walk in another's shoes or take his or her perspective is another aspect of empathy. Practical suggestions to access our empathy accuracy and regulation will be discussed later in this chapter.

COGNITIVE EMPATHY

Cognitive empathy is the ability to understand someone else's felt experience without actually feeling any emotion yourself. However, holding a mental picture and imagining what others are going through and appreciating their frame of reference is an important ability. Empathic understanding increases sympathy and compassion. Without the ability to relate to another's suffering, perpetrators will traumatize victims with indifference, and politicians, for example, will ignore human rights violations. Many people have blunted emotional responses, such as trauma survivors, conduct-disordered individuals, and those born within the autism spectrum.

Like so many aspects of life, empathy lies on a continuum. Some people are intellectually aware but just don't care, while a highly empathic individual can access the emotional milieu in their surroundings and might mistakenly think the emotional deluge they experience is his or her own. Cognitive and affective (emotional) empathy research is ongoing, and consensus lies in the future. Clinically, my observations suggest emotions are contagious and empathy is a cognitive, emotional, and/or full body experience. In ancient times, playwrights knew how contagious emotions were and fostered empathy cognitively by means of a Greek chorus.

A Greek chorus (*khoros*) consisted of between twelve and fifty homogeneous actors dancing, singing, or speaking in unison, commenting in a singular voice on the dramatic action of a play. The chorus offered perspectives and insights individual actors could not say, served as the characters' alter egos, and/or provided thought bubbles, which represented collective consciousness. The chorus effectively taught ancient audiences how to empathize with the universal aspects of the human drama. Cognitive empathy deepened audience connection. Drama opened the door to heartfelt empathy and eventually a universal experience.

EMOTIONAL (AFFECTIVE) EMPATHY

Educating the mind without educating the heart is no education at all.—Aristotle

Emotional empathy is the ability to resonate with the felt experience of another and the willingness to co-experience their emotions physically in our body. Researchers currently examine the neural pathways associated with facial cues, which trigger mirrored emotions between people. The visual and physical parameters of how mirror neurons interact between people are scientifically important areas of study, but I believe our ability to be emotionally empathic is also intuitive and organic and transcends what modern science knows about oneness. In addition to their contribution to cognitive empathy, the Greeks also had something to say about emotional empathy.

In ancient times, the Greek word *pathos*, when used as an adjective, literally meant *experience suffering*. When Aristotle wrote *Rhetoric*, his treatise about the art of persuasion, he recognized how pathos influenced an audience.[7] *Katharsis*, now commonly spelled "catharsis," follows pathos and is the modern term for emotional release, which also meant purification or cleansing in antiquity. Greek choruses would enflame emotion, create sympathy or pathos, and offer insightful perspectives to the unfolding tragedy as an overview. Ancient playwrights fostered empathic connections to trigger an audience to experience a private emotional reaction to the tragic spectacle and release it publicly through catharsis. Pathos purges and catharsis cleanses human emotion. Plotinus concluded that empathy and cathartic release evoked an innate desire for spiritual and intellectual clarification.

Today we use the terms "affective empathy" or "emotional empathy" to describe not only pathos but also the enjoyable feelings we co-experience with others. Current brain research suggests that our right hemisphere manages affect and interprets the meaning behind our emotional reactions, which are based upon previous experiences. Stored emotional memories and the decisions we made about life are filed in our right hippocampus.[8] Since our right hemisphere perceives stimuli before the left, intense reactions out of proportion to the actual incident often occur.[9] Immature emotional stress responses based upon trauma co-exist with our executive abilities. Principles about empathy, ethics, and pro-social instincts stem from our right brain.[10] Creating a novel solution to a problem is an extremely important right-brain activity for when physical sensations flood our whole body.

SOMATIC EMPATHY

"Somatic" comes from the Greek word *somatikos*, which means concerning or affecting the body. Somatic empathy includes the absorption of contagious emotional energy, cognitions, and felt sensations of others in our body. When crucial sensory information from an outside source fails to activate the cognitive or emotional legs of the previously mentioned metaphorical three-legged stool, our physical leg will register it with or without our awareness. Tracking the ambient mood in our surroundings is often accomplished with body awareness, which explains why children complain about tummy aches after family disruptions. Like lint accumulating on Velcro, highly empathic individuals process their emotional milieu viscerally in their body.

Steven Porges, in his polyvagal theory, describes how the ventral and dorsal vagus nerve processes external sensations from our five senses and informs our somatic experiences. Our brain stores our beliefs, assumptions, and neuroceptions, which interpret sensory input for safety and security considerations. Since 80 percent of our vagal neural pathways send information from the body to our brain stem, tracking our physical, emotional, and mental reactions to our surroundings is crucial. The polyvagal theory describes how *neural arousal* affects each hemisphere and the previously mentioned stress responses within our higher, emotional, and reptilian brains.[11] Coordinating stress responses optimizes our coping strategies, but unexamined and accumulated trauma can cause emotional regression and physically short-circuit our access to right-hemisphere higher brain innovation. Healing traumatic memory starts with differentiating past from present and converting previous decisions into current reasonable solutions.

We all are interconnected and have empathic connections with others, unless something blocks our compassion. Internal awareness is a visceral experience, while external awareness is sensing the emotions from others inside your body. Covert awareness without knowing how you know what you know is called intuition. Sensory input is registered as physical symptoms for those of us who process unconscious emotional material through body awareness. Somatic empathy and our visceral sensations let us sense and access transcendent wisdom to avoid the mental and emotional traps set by illusion. Body-based intuition helps us determine what lies beneath confusing presentations and helps us discover the unconscious motivations of others.

SOMATIC EMPATHY THEORY

> I must go beyond the dark world of sense information to the clear brilliance of the sunlight of the outside world. Once done, it becomes my duty to go back to the cave in order to illuminate the minds of those imprisoned in the "darkness" of sensory knowledge.—Plato

An ongoing, honest communication between our mental and emotional reactions to the *darkness of sensory knowledge* is often solved by somatic awareness. Our body is a reliable source of accurate information from the outer world. Bessel Van Der Kolk recognized this phenomenon when he named his groundbreaking book about trauma *The Body Keeps Score*. Accurate information about the subjective nature of our inner reality and outer world is crucial for survival. Discerning fact from fiction is often felt as a visceral gut reaction. Physical sensations are often more reliable sources of information than our emotional reactions and cognitive explanations. A collaborative relationship exists among our mind, emotions, body, and spirit, which energize the wheels of creation through empathic connection. When each leg of our three-legged stool embodies our higher purpose and principles, our soul lends us a hand.

Moment-to-moment recognition of our personal reactions and subtle changes within each leg of our stool is desirable. Donald Kalsched in his book *Trauma and the Soul* mentioned how ancient societies recognized and now modern psychology recommends that we have one eye looking inward and the other outward.[12] Our outward eye examines the hard edges of external reality and expectations, while our inner eye mines our invisible, subjective experiences for truth. Transforming illusion and transcendence requires binocular vision in life and, of course, in fairy tales.

In the original book *The Wonderful Wizard of Oz*, the Wicked Witch of the West had one eye, "as powerful as a telescope," keeping her abreast of the activities of Dorothy and her companions. Unfortunately, her blind eye apparently never looked inward because she lacked empathy and, like a bully, victimized others. Glinda the Good, on the other hand, embodied compassion for her people. Perhaps through inner work, she maintained clear emotional boundaries, did not rescue Dorothy, and modeled heightened human potential. Binocular vision allows the creation of a living *third potential*, which allows our human and spiritual nature to unify once we discern the subtle emotional shifts between self and other. To this pursuit, Plotinus aptly said: "We must not run after it, but we must fit ourselves for the vision and then wait tranquilly for it, as the eye waits on the rising of the Sun which in its own time appears above the horizon and gives itself to our sight."[13] Toward this effort, I have created the following theory about how emotional energy moves between people and is registered as somatic empathy.

Somatic Empathy Theory states that emotional energy moves between people and attaches to us like lint on Velcro. When we scan the environment for accurate information for safety and security considerations, ambient emotional energy is absorbed into our physical body. These transfers occur with or without our awareness due to mirror neurons and the universal nature of our human empathic abilities. Everyone is born empathically connected to another's felt experience unless circumstances interfere with or enhance our somatic empathy.

As a species, humans need to develop more empathy for one another. But first, we need to get our own house in order before we can re-create henosis collectively. Like the sun evaporating the morning mist at dawn, inner peace, mindfulness, and love burn away illusion. However, our newfound equanimity can be fleeting if our empathy is boundless and we inadvertently vacuum the suffering of others into our body. Henosis, oneness, and love are fearless medics and often rush to human suffering to offer aid and assistance. Unfortunately, without awareness, emotional debris will attach to us. Balancing all the forms and challenges described in this book often resembles a nonstop Whack-a-Mole game, where mastery just leads to additional challenges and more complexity. The Somatic Empathy Theory provides an opportunity to balance love and illusion with appropriate self-esteem, emotional hygiene, and clear boundaries.

Our immature stress responses need loving compassion and somatic empathy strategies to distinguish external origins from internal information. Criticizing our unexplained mood swings and the contagious emotions we attract from external sources invites the form of illusion into our life.

CONNECTING, NOT ATTACHING

Everyone is born intuitive, but heightened forms of empathy, which sense the emotional states in others accurately or energetic shifts over great distances, occur regularly. Unfortunately, sensory reception does not necessarily lead to mental detection or appropriate action. Most people are rational and question gut reactions, while animals are more instinctual. For example, when the Indonesian tsunami hit on December 26, 2004, most people did not run for safety until the wave arrived, but prior to visual confirmation, elephants screamed and then ran for the safety of higher ground.[14] Intuition is a sixth-sense sensing ability and a heightened form of empathy, which every human possesses to varying degrees. Emotional contagions, which include cognitive, emotional, and somatic information, inundate our senses every day. Discerning *intuition versus reason*, *fact from fiction*, and *mine or yours* is not an easy proposition, a challenge Plotinus addressed during contemplation (called meditation today). Plotinus suggested we access our intuitive/spiritual abilities in the following way: "You must close the eyes and call instead upon another vision which is to be waked within you, a vision, the birth-right of all, which few turn to use."[15]

The challenges facing a highly empathic child without boundary awareness had powerful implications early in my life. As a stutterer and a highly empathic child from an alcoholic family, reading moods came easy and was a necessity. After a group of boys ridiculed me in kindergarten for hammering my words, perpetrators and victimization became a paradigm I endured for years. Confounded by the unconscious behavior from bullies and family, I was a target for disassociated anger and absorbed dysfunction. Unable to discern *mine from theirs*, fear, anger, and hopelessness ricocheted within my brain and body like pinballs in an arcade game. After watching and wondering about unconscious empathy since then, here are some of my discoveries.

Over time I've learned that we access the emotional tone around us naturally by extending our awareness into our surroundings. These scans obtain useful information allowing us to feel safe and secure. Our innate ability to sense our environment is remarkable, and its accuracy can be spooky. For example, children of dysfunctional families empathically sense the mood of Mom and Dad so they can know whether to hide, avoid, or interact.

Many highly empathic individuals don't realize we gather information this way, and for most people, it is an unconscious process. Like a 360-degree vacuum cleaner, we suck odds and ends from the environment into our five senses for review. Trace amounts of the positive or negative moods of others or the ambient emotional energy from our surroundings are absorbed physically in our body from these scans. Some of the emotional material will come from others or the environment, and unfortunately, most of us mistakenly believe the deluge we feel is our own. When things "feel off," we assume the negativity originates within and neuroceptions are created to explain what's going on. Our brain will come up with reasons why we feel the way we do, but this assessment will be inaccurate on occasion . . . adding to our stress. Life has enough challenges without innocently adding the dilemmas of other people to our own. Absorbing emotions and moods for assessment purposes and misdiagnosing mine from yours are significant problems for highly empathic people and can cause chronic imbalances. Emotional information travels between people like static electricity. Our trusty sensing mechanism acts like a pair of shoes shuffled on a wool carpet. Serious shocks develop when we are unaware that our assessment tool attracts stray emotion like a lightning rod attracts electricity. People become ill and wonder why their moods vacillate back and forth.

Maintaining a state of wholeness while sensing everyone's emotional soup is a very challenging skill to master. The challenge is to experience our feelings, assess the emotional milieu, and release the residue originating from others. We also have to deal with a slew of cultural trainings teaching us that it is noble to take pain away from someone else. Lovers frequently want to take the pain of a beloved away with attitudes like "I would die for you" and endure the death or pain themselves. There are many reasons why people suffer, but absorbing another's pain is not the answer to cure suffering. It actually *doubles* the pain, creates an entangled mess, and misses the altruistic mark.

Henosis is oneness with all, but the complexities of balancing oneness with our highly refined forms of intuition and empathy require equanimity. Understanding why we feel terrible when *we are all supposed to be one* is a significant challenge as our awareness and sensitivity increases. Why would I want to be one with someone else's pain and suffering? This question is difficult to answer with a one-size-fits-all solution because the answer requires accessing the full situation and responding to only the issue at hand. Balancing our physical and divine nature creates the *internal boundaries necessary to experience external oneness with equanimity and without corruption.*

In *The Wonderful Wizard of Oz*, Glinda the Good had special intuitive tools, which included empathy and compassion. The Great Book of Records allowed her to know everything that was happening in Oz instantaneously, which sounds suspiciously like heightened sensing abilities. In the center of Oz, she created the Forbidden Fountain and filled it with the cleansing Waters of Oblivion, which redeemed those with cruel intentions. When invading armies drank from its waters, they forgot their evil plans. Water was used symbolically in this fairy tale as a strategy to purify emotions, inspire reason, and cleanse debilitating illusions. Glinda's objectivity allowed everyone in Oz to explore his or her enchantments and provided water to wash away what Plotinus called mud on a perfectly good statue. My story about the splattered mud, which prompted me to develop somatic assessment skills and seek the cleansing Waters of Oblivion, follows.

IGNORANCE ABOUT EMPATHIC VELCRO

> Being is desirable because it is identical with Beauty, and Beauty is loved because it is Being. We ourselves possess Beauty when we are true to our own being; ugliness is in going over to another order; knowing ourselves, we are beautiful; in self-ignorance, we are ugly.— Plotinus[16]

Around twenty years ago, I was introduced to a variation of the Tibetan Buddhist meditation practice of Tonglen. Traditional practitioners of this meditation intentionally inhale the suffering of another person into their heart and compassionately exhale a heartfelt intention for the recipient to find happiness and mastery. Advanced forms of intention and somatic empathy practitioners need skill, mindfulness, and distinct personal boundaries to master this practice. The masters of this practice know divine assistance is required to transform inhaled suffering. The practitioner calls on the divine to take away the recipient's problem with the knowledge the practitioner will get ill if they try to heal others without divine assistance. A number of years ago, a member of our group had a trauma she wanted to heal, so we tried a Tonglen-type healing circle to remove her negative emotional baggage. With deep sincerity, I held the intention to receive her suffering and asked the divine to transform her trauma. She felt great afterward and reported a significant improvement in her mood in the months to come. My experience took a different path as I drove home that day. Prior to that session, I had enjoyed good health and a strong spine. When I arrived home, I had to crawl to my front door on my hands and knees due to back pain. Later, when I began studying energetic healing methods in 1994, my empathic Velcro-related problems escalated. Thankfully, I met other highly empathic people like myself and compared notes. My symptoms were a mystery because people I treated usually improved, but I was frequently exhausted and emotionally drained after the session. This sticky, entangled emotional energy dynamic continued for over a year.

The culprit causing my problems finally surfaced during a critical moment while working with another trauma survivor. I heard myself silently whispering to my client's terrorized inner child, "Give me your pain; I'll take care of it." Once I found and recognized my unconscious intention to heal her trauma by myself—without divine assistance—I started remembering how many times I had jumped in the middle of my parents' fights and absorbed the suffering of others throughout my life. Future sessions revealed my primary love template and Velcro tendencies related to my unconscious somatic empathy. I had empathically absorbed my mother's chronic anger and encoded both of my parents' self-sabotaging tendencies. As I matured, I treated myself similarly.

A young child's divine connection is initially fearless, and each of us creates primary love templates, which attach to our caregivers' or parents' positive and negative patterns as early as in utero. Finding and reevaluating every mental imprint without awareness of having done so is a tough task to unravel. Talk-based therapies struggle with in-utero and early infant decisions, due to an overreliance on adult memories. Grace occurred when I heard my unconscious belief corrupting my

Tonglen practice during session. Reconciling my recycled familial attachments allowed me to join with the collective strength of the divine rather than trying to remove the mountains of suffering all by myself.

People are born with varying degrees of empathic ability, and if I were to venture a guess, about one in five people possesses heightened sensing skills. The empathic child naturally assumes everyone has these talents and shares those experiences with parents. If friends and family don't understand the empathic gift, the child will stop relying upon an innate sensitive nature when criticized for being too emotional. Unfortunately, when our intuitive skills are not supported, we may fail to understand this beautiful gift or become critical of our awareness in order to blend in with those around us. Many empathic children use their perceptive ability to process the emotional debris from parents to protect the self or assist friends and family. It's an attempt to make the world more predictable and safe, but there is an inherent problem associated with these attachment strategies. Love becomes linked with helping others, and the child often fails to recognize his or her own needs or know how to meet them. Emotionally sensitive people frequently rush to rescue others, overlook their own plight, and sometimes become scapegoats.

In family systems theory, scapegoat dynamics develop within families, when members dissociate from suffering and blame others for their problems. Minority groups have been scapegoats for perpetrators throughout history for similar reasons. Throughout my career, I have seen how the scapegoat absorbs pain from others. One time an adolescent told me during his psychiatric hospitalization for a suicide attempt that he would always drop a glass on the floor when his parents were arguing. He hated conflict and preferred to have his parents yell at him instead. And interestingly, his parents independently reported that they would go through a case of glassware every holiday season. Family systems and scapegoat theories provide the most consistently viable reasons for the symptoms I will describe shortly.

Heightened empathy is a paradox with obstacles to overcome but also the capacity to produce profound gifts. I did not know about the empathic challenges children face or understand my own sensitive nature when my daughter was young. Emotions are expressed either passively or actively, but a family becomes empathically entangled in the moods of each member, assuming every emotion experienced is their own. Mirroring distorted reflections of one another's homespun emotional debris clouds perception and lets confusion reign. Highly sensitive people may even develop physical ailments from accumulated emotions that overload the body, heart, and mind. Privately, unexamined somatic empathy can cause sensitive individuals to absorb every criticism and judge self mercilessly as a survival method.

To understand the dynamic further, my daughter has kindly shared her personal perspective on this complex subject.

A PERSONAL ACCOUNT FROM AN EMPATHIC CHILD

My earliest memory is a dream. I was three years old and standing on the armrest of a couch, eagerly trying to fly. However, the more forcefully I tried to break gravity's hold on me, the stronger it became. As my frustration pulled me deeper into defeat, I sensed another force vying for my attention. Unlike the cold heaviness pulling me down, there was a feeling of warmth subtly raising me up. I closed my eyes to embrace it, and in that moment I began to float. Empowered, I flew back and forth between each armrest until gravity became a memory.

Flying dreams were so common throughout my childhood; they became a consistent source of freedom and escape. Accordingly, the more unbalanced my life became, the more I struggled to fly. There are limited happy memories from my childhood outside of these dreams, the likely outcome of my focus at the time. I'm told I was an inquisitive, quiet child, but exceedingly skeptical and angry at home. I remember being sad, though, not angry. I remember holding more pain inside me than I knew what to do with, rejecting the notion that I should accept it, and I desperately sought love and understanding. It seemed clear that this was the one obstacle to my happiness, and I was set on overcoming it.

At first, I saw pain as my enemy and blamed those who gave it to me. I vividly remember sensing pain in my parents and feeling that it was undoubtedly an attack on me. All the pain must be for me. Unfortunately, that belief became a self-fulfilling prophecy. When I shined a spotlight on the pain I felt, hoping to eliminate it, I'd receive more. I was overwhelmingly confident in the belief that if my parents loved me, I could simply tell them that their anger hurt me, and they would stop.

Despite my efforts to communicate this, cyclical fights continued, and in my exhaustion, I concluded that my parents just pretended to love me. I couldn't understand how so much anger targeted at me could coexist with love.

After repeatedly seeing the same hopeful actions create the same painful results, I began to believe I didn't deserve love and inevitably sought support elsewhere. As my frustration grew, so did my weight. I vacillated emotionally from unguarded excitement and bursts of energy to black holes of blame and self-sabotage. There was a dichotomy to my life that I was unable to balance. As children do, I developed my sense of self through how others perceived me. In my external world, I was talented and intelligent, liked by my peers, and successful in sports. Internally, I carried a self-destructive filter through which I interpreted the world around me, informing me I was unwanted and unloved. Any pain I felt validated this damaged sense of self and was further strengthened when my family knowingly caused more.

By the age of ten, I had decided that negative emotions were the real adversary. I determined that pain was just the result of self-destructive emotions that controlled their owner. My extreme devotion to eliminating pain led me to realize that my own targeted anger hurt others, just as theirs did me. Without knowing how to change this, I blamed myself and felt increasingly burdened by causing the problem I was desperately trying to solve. The pattern was clear. The more I blamed, the more anger I received. Expressing sadness or anger only seemed to create more of it, exponentially strengthening and spreading those emotions despite other intentions. Upon this realization, I couldn't fathom why anyone would choose to have these emotions and I decided to simply stop feeling them.

Inhibiting these feelings and thoughts was easier than I imagined, quickly improving my focus and temperament. Eventually, however, I became so disconnected from my environment that I didn't feel much of anything. Even my flying dreams, which until then had been a peaceful escape, became irregular and painful. The majority of the dream was spent battling to leave the ground in order to evade an imminent collision. Ignoring negative emotions failed to provide the control I desired. I became less able to perceive all emotions, including happiness, the very thing I had been in search of. The resulting emptiness blurred my ability to see my future self but ultimately taught me the first component of control. By dialing down the volume of my internal dialogue, I learned how to break the connection between my thoughts and actions.

I had gained the ability to separate my thoughts from my "self," which allowed me to contemplate both their origin and consequences before acting. But I only saw one path in front of me—I only knew how to blame. Being intimately aware of the damage that path caused, I stood rooted in fear staring at a "wrong way" sign. Looking ahead at that solitary path, knowing where it led, I felt helpless. I had no experience successfully overcoming negativism in myself or others. Without knowing how to direct my thoughts and actions toward a desired outcome, I could not determine which direction to safely step. Listening inward, I could weigh the validity of my passing thoughts but was unable to weigh their priority. Immensely cautious of acting on loud thoughts, I struggled to forecast the consequences of acting on the quiet ones. I yearned to know which thoughts led to long-term happiness. With a predisposition toward self-criticism, I accepted this as my second failed attempt to achieve happiness and opened the floodgates to feeling again.

At age thirteen, I had more self-criticism than pride. The gap between who I wanted to be and who I had become overwhelmed me. I identified with the pain I felt and blamed myself for it, a belief justified by my failed attempts to resolve it. I had fought for love and fought against negativism, but it was not until I stopped fighting altogether that I began to navigate toward happiness. My instinct had been to blame those who didn't seem to see that I was worthy of love, but I had been doing the same thing to myself. I had unwittingly invited in the very thing I had been fighting to keep out. Upon this realization, the problem finally felt manageable. I needed to offer myself the support I had been expecting from others. Then I could see if what I had been seeking was possible and, if so, learn how to offer it to others.

By learning to control my flow of passing thoughts before acting upon them, I learned to listen. When I focused on feelings of worthlessness and self-blame, they easily drowned out my intellectual pitches for self-love. This occurred until I realized I was confusing familiarity with purpose. My path of accepting self-blame was familiar, not purposeful. Without attention directing actions, familiar paths stand out simply because they are worn in. I was accustomed to letting pain in simply because at a young age I had decided that it wasn't going to leave. It was my first attempt at understanding the world, but it would not be my last. I knew I would not be able to release my tendency toward self-blame until I uprooted the reasoning for it.

Familiarity felt similar to necessity, as if it were a part of me. Despite this predisposition, once I began separating my negative thoughts from their source, something broke its hold on me. It was suddenly clear that I no longer needed the pain, nor to protect myself from it, because I no longer had reason to identify with it. I was not my pain, nor did it ever protect me. In fact, by holding it inside, I was only inviting more. To release it as it came, I simply needed to understand why it was there and intently direct each future step with the lesson it provided. I remember a weightlessness take over me that I had only ever felt in my dreams. By releasing the deafening voice of negativity, I abruptly sensed warmth from within that I knew had been there all along. For as long as I can remember, I had sought for others to release a burden from my shoulders that I had to do myself. I broke the negative filter from which I saw the world, freeing me to choose how I wanted to perceive and act on each moment to come.

Self-love easily emerged from my understanding that I was not my thoughts or my memories. I was what I chose to do about them. I identified only with the lessons I had gained from these experiences and was determined my future actions be purposeful. There was still a worn path in front of me, but I was not afraid to step off. I could forge a new path knowing that I would be purposeful with each step and learn from every stumble and fall.

By fifteen, my childhood dreams returned to me. I felt awakened, as if I had come across a support system with no detrimental side effects. No longer held back from becoming the person I wanted to be, I listed the desirable qualities of my future self and lived each coming day as she would. The need to protect myself from pain was gone because feeling became an essential tool to my success. It became clear that emotions were motivators, able to take control of a passive owner but rarely ever achieving their intended goal. Understanding their source empowered me to retain stability in each step.

I constructed a world for myself I couldn't previously envision. Negativity seemed to have no lasting effect on me anymore. I learned to find comfort in the uncomfortable. New obstacles became mentors and the resulting lesson, a part of me. I exercised twice a day, used food as fuel, and experienced a new level of physical and mental clarity. Just as my weight gain was a manifestation of negative intention, my positive intention created a seventy-pound weight loss throughout the following summer. Successes poured into every avenue of my life, strengthening my transformed belief system. Hopeful for reward from risk, I accepted a merit scholarship to a Division I university across the country that was more than slightly out of budget and, despite having no experience, joined the university's rowing team.

Despite injuries and inexperience, I learned to balance academics and year-round two-a-day practices, with constant physical and mental challenges. By my second year, I was a scholarship athlete fighting for a seat among Olympic hopefuls but was often drained from waves of anxiety. I knew, however, that not all of what I sensed was my own. Over time, I required exceedingly less intention to understand my emotions. It became effortless, allowing me to offer more attention and compassion to others. This shift in focus to helping others, although immensely rewarding and beneficial to the relationships in my life, led me to unknowingly let others' pain in again. When I began losing healthy boundaries protecting my empathic nature, new obstacles surfaced echoing my childhood battles. As a typical empathetic child with a developing self-identity, I perceived all emotions I sensed as mine and I was still learning to overcome this tendency. When alone, I was at ease, but among teammates and friends, waves of negativity resurfaced. The more I cared for someone, the more challenging it became to avoid absorbing their pain.

As much as I sought to aid others in achieving clarity, I knew this would never actually help. Fear and anger serve vital and visible roles for self-preservation, purposefully abrasive and loud. In contrast, love is not as easily detected. By offering others what I used to long for, it became apparent that they sought the same things: understanding, appreciation, and inevitably love from those closest to them. Without offering these actions and emotions to oneself, it is a struggle to feel them from someone else. Negativity exists in the absence of positivity, and those who are on the path must find the power and will to choose to step off. I began to recognize how many people in my life struggled with the same battle I did. I thought, if others were unknowingly absorbing the negativity of those around them, perhaps they would absorb positivity too.

To find a way to remain constant through this fog, I visualized a column of light surrounding me and sent it outward. This tool anchored my focus and offered support to others without draining me in return. In rowing, team success requires moving in complete unison. The change in my attention had a positive effect on others and led me toward personal success as stroke seat of the top boat. Unable to see my teammates behind me, I led our pace by focusing on the boat moving as one entity. With my rank, experience, and growing emotional stability, more teammates came to me for support. My role became that of a mentor, guiding attention to their goals instead of their obstacles.

As a child, I thought my purpose was to conquer problems. Empathically taking on the pain of others was my way of loving. It was only after I looked inward and learned how to take responsibility without blame that I could love myself and offer that love to others. That insight uprooted the filter from which I perceived my world, allowing for self-creation and adaptability based upon my desired future self. I learned that negativity will only breed more negativity, just as focusing on what weighs us down will only strengthen its hold on us. Similarly, positivity amplifies that which raises us up, a lesson mirrored in my childhood dreams. This is as true for our internal dialogue as it is external, when we communicate in groups and communities. With each thought, we feed the belief system we choose to listen to. Even though it may seem personal, every choice we make is capable of weighing down or lifting up everyone we encounter.

SOMATIC EMPATHY WITHIN FAMILIES

Confucius said, "What the superior man seeks, is in himself; what the ordinary man seeks, is in others."[17] Without empathy awareness, maturity, and clear boundaries, life can be a roller coaster of highs and lows for those with heightened sensory abilities. Families laugh and cry together and hopefully transform challenges and thrive together as one stable entity. Emotional bonds create the sense of togetherness that can mirror heaven or hell but usually mirror both.

Initially, most people compensate for the emotional debris of a beloved by processing their disowned mood, either internally or by expressing their excess emotion externally. Others dissociate from turmoil, which creates imbalances that can activate stress responses, primary templates, and/or personal paradigms. Dissociating from emotion or processing what we attach to ourselves from others are misguided attempts to create homeostatic balance and sacrifice our health for loved ones. My mother, who was also very intuitive and a childhood scapegoat, became a family lightning rod when she expressed the repressed anger that my father numbed with alcohol. Mom had untreated childhood trauma, but her unconscious empathic nature was certainly a factor.

Later in life, through Murray Bowen's family systems theory, I learned how family members often carry the unexpressed emotions of others, which is how triangulation creates scapegoats.[18] Both my wife and I tended to bury our anger when we were young, which activated similar familial scapegoat patterns within our daughter. The empathic and determined nature of our child absorbed, internalized, and expressed some of our disowned emotions. One day, for example, as a young teenager, my daughter wanted me to choose between two tops she wanted to wear while I was on the phone fighting with my brother. When I quickly waved her off, preferring to focus my rage elsewhere, she turned on her heels and left in an angry flourish. Today we both recognize how her empathic nature was working in a negative way—she sucked in my rage and activated an unconscious personal victim/perpetrator paradigm. Scapegoats provide a target for others to discharge their unconscious projections, disowned impulses, and unwanted emotional material. Unconscious primary love templates, personal paradigms, and empathic Velcro tendencies can devastate in the long term, so education and awareness are needed to find loving solutions.

Since highly empathic individuals tend to have the courage of a lion, absorb negativity like the Tin Man, and have an irresistible urge to help others like the Scarecrow, we gravitate to the healing arts due to our compassionate hearts and extraordinary talents. With earnest intentions, we can haphazardly fall into a pit of despair, a primary love template, or a personal paradigm unless we learn how to discern *yours from mine*. Transmutation skills follow boundary awareness. And yet, on the flip side, the benefits of being empathic are amazing when we reach a state of incorruptibility, which we will cover in chapter 9. With my daughter in college, her ability to sense the moment anyone on the rowing team was off stroke allowed her to immediately absorb another's imbalance to benefit all. Suffering through back pain to benefit the team or, at the extreme, actually fracturing a rib from exertion (which she did once while racing) were small prices to pay because her boat moved as one and *walked on water*.

Empathic people benefit groups in countless ways due to their tireless dedication to the whole. My best competitive swimming performances as a high school and collegiate All-American were on relays. We have immediate access to the negative and/or positive emotions in our surroundings. Athletes and allies dig deeper for friends and family. Highly sensitive individuals readily embrace suffering that is not their own, thus allowing them to connect deeply to anything or anyone with compassion. Poor energetic boundaries can corrupt us physically by allowing extraneous emotional energy to enter our body. Wide mood swings and misguided neuroceptions often result. Emotional contagions and unconscious Velcro tendencies compromise our emotional wellness in the following ways:

- Like a spreading pathogen, our emotional hygiene becomes contaminated.
- Permeable boundaries attract emotional debris, if unmonitored; symptoms generally associated with mental illness can develop.
- Problems occur when we are unable to protect or cleanse ourselves from emotional contagions. Chronically owning the emotions of others will affect our physical health.

Emotional garbage from our surroundings will affect our mood, which is a recipe for somatic disturbances over time. Highly empathic individuals frequently become awash in the emotional debris of others and are often unaware of why their moods fluctuate wildly. Criticized for appearing flaky or histrionic during a crisis since their youth, some highly sensitive individuals have a very self-critical primary love template. Their emotionality frequently elicits their greatest nightmare: more negativity and judgment from the external world. Some are deemed unreliable or too emotional to make effective decisions due to wide mood swings. Others become depressed, hate their emotionality, or get into addictive behaviors to numb out the constant influx of energy they can't effectively store or process constructively. In my professional career, I've seen a significant number of health-care professionals, healers, and openhearted individuals present with somatic empathy–related boundary issues.

After learning about empathic Velcro and firming up my boundaries, the first person I treated who modeled a corrupted form of somatic empathy was a client whose symptomatology included:

- wide mood swings,
- frequent crying spells,
- emotional explosions, and
- crisis-to-crisis existence.

The medical community diagnosed her as having affective disorder and labeled her histrionic; a psychiatrist prescribed anxiety medication and antidepressants. When I discovered that her amazing empathic abilities, self-critical nature, and lack of emotional boundaries were causing her erratic mood swings, we went to work. Once she learned protection strategies, cleansing methods, and boundary awareness solutions (shared later in this chapter), her self-esteem improved, and she reduced and eventually stopped her meds with her physician's approval. When she learned to embrace her highly empathic nature and developed appropriate energetic boundaries, her personal and professional life immediately took off in a positive direction.

Men are intuitive, and some men are highly empathic. Since tradition favors stoicism, many males tend to hide their sensitivity. As an anxious child with a significant stuttering problem, I always judged my emotionality as weakness, hid it publicly, and tried to numb it. Since many cultures equate stiff upper lips with strength, this leads empathic men to wonder if something is wrong with them. When highly sensitive men try to control their moods and lean into reason over intuition, many men privately feel like wimps during an emotional storm.

When we are all one, my experiences become yours and vice versa. Cutting oneself off from society removes a valuable resource to access wholeness; the life of an enlightened hermit is not the answer anymore. Healing humanity one person at a time by absorbing their suffering is equally unproductive. How do we become one, feel it all, and then let it go? Incorruptible power does reside within the collective. Tonglen meditation works when we are whole and intimately connected with the divine in the state of henosis.

Highly sensitive individuals can immediately sense suffering during a major disaster and can absorb global trauma even if they don't see it on the news. Unfortunately, becoming inundated and overwhelmed with pain or problems is an occupational hazard for the individual with this innate gift. Visualizing physical, emotional, and spiritual growth geared for the good of others works best. We can send support if we wish to without attaching the pain onto our body or righting the world's wrongs all by ourselves.

When somatic empathy is corrupted, we are often unaware that the source of our physical and emotional stress occurred when we scanned the angst of another person into our body. This dynamic frequently leads to a difficult life full of self-doubt, blame, and shame, criticizing self, judging our emotionality, and engaging in self-destructive behaviors. The importance of accurate assessments, mood regulation, and cleansing strategies for foreign emotional contagions cannot be overstated. With my clients with autoimmune disorders or with chronic central nervous system sensitization issues, the following symptoms repeatedly surfaced:

- chronic stress and depression;
- poor emotional boundaries;
- problems from storing accumulated emotion from outside sources;
- self-criticism and unattainable, unconscious expectations; and
- rigid primary love templates and personal paradigms.

Unlike the Wicked Witch of the West, who only had one eye, you can use both of your metaphorical eyes to assess your empathic nature. Let one eye scan the horizon but dedicate the other eye toward self-examination. The Somatic Empathy Self-Test listed below asks you to rate your neutral emotional baseline from zero to ten and then assess if your number changes in the presence of emotional contagions. This self-test is designed to help you determine if environmental contagions add undue stress. Hopefully, the Somatic Empathy Solutions that follow this assessment will help you return to your baseline stress level.

SOMATIC EMPATHY SELF-TEST

There are many ways to experience wholeness *without* taking on the confusing and complicated emotions of another. Oneness means we experience the pleasures and pains of all, while making sure we are protected, safe, and secure. It is a good practice to have one eye looking inward to get accurate assessments in each moment. Determining when something is *yours or not* reduces stress responses. The following self-test can help you determine if your emotions originate from outside sources:

- **Maintain baseline emotional awareness.** Rate your average baseline mood on a scale from zero to ten and watch it with one eye like a barometer. Choose any number that feels accurate. Any significant numerical change can be assessed for empathy Velcro and addressed immediately.
- **Scan the horizon.** For example, let's say your baseline mood at a restaurant was a five before a couple started an argument in a nearby booth. If your mood jumped up to a seven and returned to five after they left, your empathic awareness may have tapped into the couple's conflict and their emotional contagions.
- **Notice your mood changes.** In that moment, you can ascertain if the internal change is personal/psychological or has external origins. Hold the following intention for the issue, "If it's mine, let it stay, and if not, let it go." Then visualize a waterfall cleansing your body and/or a large drain underneath you removing emotional residue.
- **Assess what emotion moves or remains.** Assess if your waterfall helped you return to your original mood or stress level. If your emotional baseline remains elevated, make a commitment to address your stress response or unresolved monkey. A quick physiological and psychological self-examination can help determine the origin of discrepancies.[19]

This somatic empathy self-test can help you rule out or realize how often another's anxiety or a chaotic environment affects your emotional stability. Check how often your emotional state fluctuates throughout the day and try to determine why. Here is a list of possible somatic empathic reactions to emotional contagions adapted from Caitlin Matthews's book *Psychic Shield*:

- sudden depression, impending dread, or groundless fear;
- vitality depletion, anxiety from unknown sources, or soul disquiet;
- feeling overwhelmed, empty, or hollowed out;
- ache in the solar plexus as if being sucked dry;
- wide mood swings or a lack of interest in your daily routine; and
- a succession of low-grade illnesses, which never clear up.[20]

Watch your brain come up with reasons for these symptoms, which may or may not prove true. Assessing your empathic nature is the first step. If you deem it appropriate, implementing the suggested solutions and visualizations provided below is the second step.

SOMATIC EMPATHY SOLUTIONS

In the fantasy-comedy motion picture *Groundhog Day* (1993), the protagonist relives the same day until he stops replaying his dysfunctional dramas, templates, and paradigms. Predictable outcomes occur when he manipulates others to manufacture immature pleasures. When deception rules, he wakes up and relives the same twenty-four-hour period until he can truly give and receive love throughout one full day. Once this feat is accomplished, the protagonist wakes up and literally experiences a new day. By cherishing himself and loving others, he is cherished and receives the love he desperately craves.

Endearing stories like *Groundhog Day* portray how love overpowers illusion. Somatic empathy issues can resolve as simply as they do in the movies. Emotions move between people as naturally as wind, water, and weather but can stick like Velcro. Misunderstood sixth-sense empathy has simple remedies, which include visualization, intention, and appropriate boundaries. Scientific evidence or awareness about how energy travels between people is not necessary to achieve success. Energy travels between people with or without our active participation. The solutions listed below can be evaluated if they produce results (dialectic discovery). Perhaps a new day will dawn for you just like the protagonist discovered in *Groundhog Day*, when he found an enlightened solution.

- **Visualize protection.** We can visualize a protective shield surrounding us and providing protection from extraneous environmental, emotional debris. For example, simply surround yourself with a sturdy transparent eggshell for protection. But be aware that a shield fades away without maintenance.
- **Narrow your attention.** Absorbing suffering from others can be bypassed and empathic Velcro reduced by narrowing your attention. Intention makes a difference so refocusing awareness to your immediate surroundings, no more than an arm's length away, helps to stop the cycle. Powerful focused intention can pump toxic emotions between individuals like an umbilical cord. When you cannot stop thinking about someone, a cord may have developed between both of you. Release cords with loving awareness and reestablish sovereign boundaries.
- **Find tangible solutions.** Showers, walks in nature, sunlight, and physical exercise (yoga, tai chi, and chi gong, for example) move energy/emotions. Music, chanting, EFT tapping points, essential oils (tea tree oil), and incense remove stress. Soaking your feet in salted hot water and tiger balm provide healing. In dire circumstances, attaching an antistatic computer wristband to your wrist and grounding yourself like a lightning rod may provide benefit.
- **Stabilize and ground.** When flooded with emotion, imagine, for example, an anchor attached to your backbone being dropped through to the core of the earth. Then allow the emotions and stress to drain down this anchor line into Mother Earth until you feel stable. Taking an actual shower, grounding emotion through your feet, or fantasizing that you are under a cleansing waterfall also clears extraneous emotion. For groups with heightened emotion, visualize a huge drainpipe in the middle of the room with the ability to drain everyone's extraneous emotion.
- **Which emotion belongs to whom?** You can identify when your mood is related to another person in any situation by holding the following intention and saying, "If it's mine, let it stay, and if it's theirs, let it go." If an infantile, childish, or adolescent stress re-

sponse gets activated, refer to the Wise Lover, Wounded Beloved Reconciliation (chapter 3) for ideas on ways to calm down.

- **Cleanse your body.** Breathe in divine white light into your lungs and watch love transform into cleansing bubbles in your blood. Allow your heart to circulate the bubbles within your blood to any area of discomfort and notice as the determined bubbles scrub and wash away illusion. Exhale the spent bubbles with appreciation and continue breathing in the divine and exhaling illusion until you glow.
- **Pray.** As you attempt to clear your energetic field, which is an arm-length around your body, ask for assistance from the divine and your spiritual advocates. During conflict, imagine peaceful coexistence and reconciliation birthing from the sacred-self in everyone.
- **Affirm and clear with intention.** Say the following affirmation to stabilize, increase protection, and release any illusions that do not belong:

I am the light
The light lives within me
The light surrounds me
The light protects me
I can discern light from illusion
Release what does not belong to me
I AM the light[21]

- **Unwind.** Sympathetic resonance with your internal experience releases emotional suffering. Attune to what feels foreign inside and use sound and movement and/or express dormant emotion with compassion. Accept lessons with acceptance; then remove any excess emotion with awareness.
- **Use every tool at your disposal.** When your friends, family, or humanity suffer, you can access the form of empathy (described below) and use it with the Camel Wave Meditation (appendix A). You can be like Glinda the Good, and instead of fixing, vacuuming, or attaching, you can send love and peace to their heart and soul through intention, while visualizing suffering diminishing and engaging your trust in the divine will.

- **Visualize a column of protective light.** When emotional contagions become overwhelming, imagine standing in a shimmering column of radiant light anchored in earth and connected to the divine above. Commune with the divine in this space completely protected, while you fearlessly engage with others.

The column of protective light meditation just mentioned creates an impenetrable boundary to emotional maelstroms from outside sources. As a divine being in a physical body, we can embody an incorruptible form of empathy when we are connected to heaven and earth in a state of wholeness. *Somatic Empathy Self-Tests* and *Solutions* are very empowering as daily practices. When we access our divinity and protect our body, we can experience wholeness within diversity without Velcro-related symptoms. Highly empathic individuals are pathfinders who model for humanity how the positive and negative aspects of oneness can be reconciled to experience henosis. Don't succumb to the illusion that our intuitive tendencies are something to fear or a problem to overcome. Empathy is a gift, and learning how to use it productively creates an asset. The world will be in a better place when humanity is more empathic and cannot harm others without co-experiencing their agony. I firmly believe that love, empathy, and compassion are how we will solve the paradox of oneness within diversity and truly become one people on one planet.

Unfortunately, as energy chronically builds up in the cellular structures of the body, some people develop addictions, fibromyalgia, or chronic fatigue as our body stores the emotional overload. Being an empath without awareness can cause emotional storage problems and health issues. Henosis *is* oneness with the whole of humanity, but mindfulness is advised since many of the people on the planet are suffering. Becoming one with global suffering and then processing others' pain is not the promise of wholeness. This is why we need to take care of ourselves with accurate assessments and boundary awareness strategies. The following story describes how Ruth healed fibromyalgia using these techniques.

FIBROMYALGIA AS A FORM OF CORRUPTED SOMATIC EMPATHY

Ruth's father was a victim of the Holocaust and suffered from a bipolar disorder. Two of her aunts were Holocaust survivors, and Ruth grew up hearing horrific stories about suffering, survival, and heroism during family gatherings. Times were rough but got worse when her beloved sister began to demonstrate the same bipolar tendencies and behavior markers that troubled Ruth's father. Ruth bonded deeply with her mother, and the women supported each other during challenging times.

To know Ruth means you love her. She is the nicest, most sincere, and thoroughly good person you would ever want to meet. Even though she has fibromyalgia, she keeps her health issues to herself to avoid burdening anyone with her pain. She's a leader in her field and a loyal family member and courageously addresses every problem head on with complete dedication.

Ruth was overly responsible, prone to guilt paradigms, and struggled initially with permeable boundaries. She blamed herself for her suffering and boundless empathy. The family historian, she filed claims with the Claims Resolution Tribunal (CRT) for Dormant Accounts of victims of Nazi persecution in Switzerland and the Holocaust Era Restitution Taskforce (HEART), which "helps with restitution for property that was confiscated, looted or forcibly sold" during the Holocaust. Her fibromyalgia would flare up significantly during the debilitating task of documenting the victimization of her father, property confiscation, and bureaucratic harassment of her extended family during World War II.

An amazing acupuncturist, Ragani Buegel, and I worked with Ruth on a regular basis to assist her in developing self-nurturing instincts and creating appropriate emotional and familial boundaries. For Ruth, we initiated a plan that included psychotherapy, Western medicine, and also the ancient art of acupuncture. The acupuncture sessions that Ragani provided helped reset Ruth's natural energetic pathways, which stabilized her physical body. When emotional memories, repressed decisions, and dysfunctional primary love templates would surface, I helped Ruth renew with psychotherapy. The Wise Lover, Wounded Beloved Reconciliation (chapter 3) and some of the Somatic Empathy Solutions created stronger emotional boundaries. Due to the therapeutic safety that Ragani offered, Ruth also released emotional material through acupuncture and inner focusing techniques. When Ruth experienced the deep mental, physical, and emotional relaxation that acupuncture and psychotherapy offered, Ruth started to recognize, address, and then transform her most suppressed templates and emotional paradigms. Ruth shared what she discovered during each therapy session, which gave Ragani and me clues to take her healing further. [22]

Ragani's perspective follows:

> When working with physical symptoms, it is important to address the underlying energetic component that both creates and sustains those symptoms. In the process of true transformational healing, the "felt sense" behind these symptoms can provide a wealth of information on the underlying psychological and emotional patterns that underlie a physical malady. As these patterns emerge and are observed, a curious thing often happens: the symptoms themselves frequently subside, and often epiphanies and insights come to awareness. Throughout her treatment sessions, Ruth was an exceptional explorer; she was courageous in her inner journeys, and she listened to what her body wanted to share with her. She paid attention to how she felt, and she was willing to delve into the energetic levels of her physical issues. Over time she was able to observe a great deal of her energetic and emotional patterns, and this enabled her to begin reworking her habits of interaction with herself and the world around her. Importantly, she discovered her ability to define boundaries with others and to truly nurture herself.

During a deep self-guided Empathy Round Table Session, Ruth found that she had decided at a very young age to dedicate her life to removing any form of pain from the Jewish people. Ruth wept powerfully when she remembered the "never again" intention her little girl made and realized what she had done as a loyal, courageous daughter. Ruth had experienced the horrors of the Holocaust through the family's storytelling and had never consciously known that her unconsciousness decision, somatic empathy, and lack of boundaries were linked to her fibromyalgia. When she released her instinct to absorb the suffering of other people and learned appropriate emotional boundaries, the "fibro pain," as she calls it, as well as her widespread pain index (WPI) and symptom severity scale (SS) in her nineteen general body areas subsided. When both of her parents died within nine weeks of one another, she had a setback, which helped her anchor more appropriate boundaries with her bipolar sister. Her quality of life has improved, and her good health has returned.

Ruth showed me that when toxins are chronic, get stuck in our cells, and have nowhere to go, diseases tend to develop and, if allowed to fester with self-criticism, become toxic. Empathic individuals are spiritually open and possess extremely refined discernment gifts designed to sense, monitor the environment, and serve the *greater good* of a collective. On the positive side of the ledger, highly empathic people possess amazing abilities to connect, heal, and enjoy relationships; they will lift any group they join.

The courage of a highly empathic individual in a crisis situation is prodigious; they become fearlessly loving examples of henosis in action, despite their personal challenges. Compelled to tell the truth and be in our truth, we are emotional firefighters, energetic policemen, and trusty medics that rush toward the suffering of other people. We immediately sense what needs to be done with our extraordinary intuitive abilities. Significant mood shifts are recognized as signals to consider: *How much of what I feel is theirs or mine?*

Mood swings can originate from various psychological and physiological sources, such as immature stress responses, untreated trauma, and hormonal surges due to PMS (Premenstrual Syndrome) to name three. Psychotherapists are taught to consider or rule out physical causes for a presenting symptom prior to labeling someone mentally ill. Somatic empathy, if unconscious, is the act of physical absorbing emotions from others. Protection and cleansing strategies help avoid any Velcro-related emotional, physical, or psychological problems. Metaphorically speaking, it's simpler to take lint off Velcro than to simply think you're crazy. Better yet, preventing anything from sticking in the first place helps tremendously.

Oneness and diversity are dicey bedfellows. The personal shields my daughter used offered temporary relief from emotional debris, but "shields" require ongoing maintenance. Some people become afraid, rely on shields to block emotion, and become social hermits. Since fear begets fear, it's not a sustainable solution. Boundaryless empathy absorbs and internalizes everything—the love and the pain of others— thus creating the potential for overwhelming emotion, and unfortunately, this is how many experience oneness. Appropriate empathy says, "I feel you. When I feel whole, I know what belongs to me and what belongs elsewhere." We can create sturdy, yet pliable, interpersonal boundaries.

EMPATHY WITHOUT SUFFERING

Have you ever wondered why people cringe or avert their eyes when others suffer? Unless trauma disconnects our heart connection, the instinct to sense another's suffering and feel compassion is natural. Empathy is the willingness to embrace the pain of another *but not necessarily take it away*. Developing more empathy is not the primary problem for most people. The salient issue is reconciling our emotional blocks and increasing boundary awareness to determine which emotions are *yours or mine*. Since antiquity, empathy literally has described our ability to feel another's passion or suffering within our body.

"Sympathetic resonance" is another phrase describing the elegant process of two people experiencing the same emotion and healing each other with love. Paradoxically, perpetrators may abuse because they are disconnected from their own and a victim's suffering. Perhaps through the process of mirror neurons, witnessing another's suffering calms down the unhealed trauma too painful for the abuser to endure. Perpetrators need to access their own emotions and learn to empathize with their own dissociated pain to prevent their primitive instinct to lash out and traumatize victims who serve as mirrors.

The form of illusion lures us away from our original nature and reveals imbalance. Isolation and numbing cause disruption until an empathic connection to self and others is created. When pain activates a heartfelt loving response by another, we are reminded that humanity is intimately connected. Pain has a destiny, and the world will mirror our physical disassociations until we can objectively discern what separates our heart from love.

Today modern science has microscopes that reveal how heart tissue cells from different donors in nearby Petri dishes synchronize to beat together as one when they touch each other in the same dish.[23] Additionally, quantum entanglement theory has presented amazing evidence that may indicate how *all* of our hearts are connected through time and space, but ancient man already knew this.

Some of us are born with extraordinary empathic abilities, which are corrupted by Velcro tendencies. The resulting emotional volatility and self-judgment cause us to conclude we are unworthy. Like an oversalted meal, too much empathy can ruin any endeavor, and we are challenged to become empathically responsible and ultimately incorruptible to become whole. When we create healthy boundaries and truly believe in our worthiness, access to our unlimited potential within the unified quantum field can be realized and the forms explored in this book fully materialized. As love and wisdom fill the voids where dysfunctional paradigms, primary templates, and stress response monkeys once ruled, not only does our self-esteem transform but also our empathy, intuitive abilities, and a deep sense of interconnectedness toward *all* of humanity expand.

As a form of love, empathy needs to be mastered individually before humanity can learn how to become incorruptible to the collective illusions that continue to recycle victims and motivate perpetrators. Human connectedness and compassion make it difficult to bear witness to the suffering of others without becoming motivated to intervene. When we experience the pain of what the Greeks termed pathos and offer loving support, suffering diminishes because the *shared* experience reminds all parties of our divine home—where our soul came from. Hearts beating as one in unity with the divine is henosis.

Mind/body wisdom, medical/psychological research, and quantum entanglement theory recognize the profound interconnectedness of humanity. Psychologists, psychiatrists, and mental health counselors use system theory, which recognizes that individual members of a family or group will process the diverse emotions of their collective as one entity. For example, if both parents fail to address their anger appropriately, at least one child will carry the anger for the whole family.

For this reason, pets offer companionship when pain is experienced. Pets lend a heart, love, and resonate with our pain as a noble act of empathy. A tiny seed of love from the empathic heart of our beloved pet always washes some of the pain away. We respond because we are reminded of the collective sea of love called henosis. Empathy can make us whole. Laozi said, "The highest good is like water. Water gives life to the ten thousand things and does not strive. It flows in places people reject."[24] Empathic individuals model the essential traits for human connection, loving solutions, and eternal wisdom designed to benefit everyone.

I hope that the mind/body, medical/psychological community will be inspired to do further research into Somatic Empathy Theory. Empathy quickly heals others but can also mitigate the debilitating effects of emotional Velcro. The general public needs to learn about incorruptible empathy and empathic Velcro. My clinical experience has convinced me that some mental and immune disorders (like fibromyalgia and chronic fatigue) result from decades of accumulated somatic empathy storage problems, withering self-criticism, and "I'm on my own" primary love templates or personal paradigms that erode our physical, emotional, and mental health until our immune system eventually becomes compromised. After decades of misinformation, a mysterious disease manifests, which reflects the chronic emotional pain and accumulated suffering the person has endured.

Education about how a family processes its emotions as one entity, monitoring mood swings, and boundaries awareness is greatly needed. Addressing the deeper psychological reasons behind people's tendency to internalize the emotional pain from others is important for both the professional psychological community and individual healers. Many additional legitimate reasons exist for why people develop these diseases, but I hope that the Somatic Empathy Theory gets traction and becomes an additional possible explanation. In my opinion, our current approach for treating symptoms and ignoring alternative causes is similar to how doctors used leeches and bloodletting in the Middle Ages or lobotomies in the twentieth century. Health professionals can do more harm than good to a highly empathic individual by treating symptoms, giving prescriptions, and failing to address root causes, including somatic empathy. My fondest hope is that the ideas outlined in this chapter are considered and protocols instituted to treat highly empathic people more effectively rather than merely treating symptoms and creating pathology. In the following chapter, I will offer a panoramic view on the role empathy plays in terrorism. It is time to consider emotional contagions and somatic empathy from a fresh view so that we can change painful paradigms to mental illness *prevention*.

EMPATHY AWARENESS LIES ON A CONTINUUM

If cherish is a grammar school formula describing a form of puppy love, then the form empathy is a required course before writing your doctoral dissertation about the philosophy of oneness. The challenges associated with somatic empathy start when we learn to recognize our illusions buried within our primary love templates, stress responses, and victim/perpetrator paradigms. Equanimity exists beyond our immature stress responses once we take responsibility for our creations.

Unraveling illusions that became hardwired habits and replacing them with loving solutions is a challenging but accomplishable goal. Like any unrefined skill or talent, somatic empathy and expanded awareness can create spectacular opportunities but also Velcro-related catastrophes. Erosion of our self-esteem occurs if we are unaware of how we experience empathy. The form of empathy meditation that follows examines empathy to help you become incorruptible to its illusions. For now, consider your empathic nature and let the following ideas open up your awareness. Try reading this form meditation aloud to own the message, and then take a break for reflection. You may also explore more deeply by using the form of empathy with the Camel Wave Meditation (appendix A). The Wise and Loving Inner Voice Meditation (appendix B) will help you to discern the internal voices within your brain that provide both useful directions and/or problematic empathic complications. Explore the freedom of letting flow the ideas, the feelings, and the thoughts that the forms trigger. Then move onto the next section.

When you feel the need, you can return to the form meditation about empathy, reread it over and over, and practice the somatic empathy boundary strategies until you are incorruptible.

FORM MEDITATION: EMPATHY

While I coexist with billions of humans with diverse agendas, I can also embrace my soulful desire to incorporate oneness. The form of empathy integrates many paradoxes into a highly refined form of love that embraces all there is with equanimity. Separation and enmeshment anxiety can overwhelm me sometimes, and my task is to access divinity and my divine nature but also create appropriate boundaries. Incorruptible within this divine embrace, I can access the suffering of another in the unified field of love free from agenda. I can courageously have and choose to co-experience the agony and ecstasy of another person without somatically owning either emotion of that person. The promise of wholeness means that I have the ability to resist temptations to rescue, judge, or absorb others' suffering. I can intervene by simply feeling what exists in the totality of henosis with mine/yours awareness.

I am beginning to understand a little-known fact about human nature: everyone is born empathic. From birth, everyone is connected to everything on earth. Life's traumas, enchanting templates, or delusional paradigms may temporarily disconnect me through anti-empathy, but I may, in any moment, choose instead to embrace all that occurs even when I cannot comprehend what triggers my stress responses. Everyone and every part of me is worthy of compassion and the comfort of empathic connection. I feel better and notice my pain lift when someone simply holds my hand, walks beside me through a challenge, deeply listens, or comforts me. When waves of pain, suffering, and agony crash into my heart, it sometimes feels like a tsunami. Empathy in its incorruptible form is a powerful expression of love . . . stronger than any tempest. Humans mirror their illusions to one another but also reflect the loving embrace of the divine to each other. When I link my empathic heart with others, I soar into ecstasy by reflecting loving compassion to a heart in need of comfort.

Great spiritual teachers model wholeness, embody empathy, and offer heartfelt compassion while suffering. Empathy is an enigma, a paradox of the form of love that may invite suffering. Helping others is a noble purpose in life, but having the courage to embrace the pain of another without flinching, falling into a hole beside them, or confusing whose pain is whose is a hallmark of an incorruptible empathic connection. Embracing the pain of another requires that I personify an advanced level of mindfulness and boundary awareness—the suffering I experience happens if I rush into the agony of others without consciousness. Empathy is one of the most important expressions of love. But not harboring any somatic suffering, which remains after an empathic connection, is what keeps me whole and wholly functioning. Henosis is the human's natural state of connectedness and wholeness, yet I must also exude willingness on my part to be part of the whole, a separate sovereign being yet an integrated part of all that is.

But there is another paradox associated with empathy: if I remain connected to all of creation and divinity, my view of what suffering is diminishes. If I embrace the pain of another while mindful and whole, the suffering of each of us diminishes. Because more of the totality of humanity is carrying this load, perhaps through systems theory, collective suffering is also balanced in this shared experience of oneness. But the key is to let the waves of unity wash over me, cease clinging to suffering, and let that moment pass. Empathy in its incorruptible form means that I choose to NOT own that suffering forever.

When the light of divine empathy illuminates the shadows on my cave walls, love returns, illusions vanish, and I become whole—I am at one with all of my emotions and at one with all. Then I have instant access to divinity, and the inner peace, mindfulness, and love that lie within the paradox of duality rise up within me. Safe and secure within my fragility and sovereignty, I attain a state of equanimity and wholeness. Empathy and compassion seal up the voids occupied by illusion and allow me to experience individually and as part of the whole. An aspect of oneness includes me sensing the experiences of others as if the experience were my own through my perceptions. As my heart expands the boundaries of the physical body's awareness, I pick up more of the emotional information surrounding me. I start sensing others' emotions as my own, yet I can, at the same time, discern which emotion belongs to whom, thus improving my empathic ability.

Without boundary awareness, emotional accuracy, and mood regulation, my illusions and the emotions I attach to can accumulate and cause a variety of maladies. This is why I must truly recognize my own emotions and be mindful of my heightened sensory abilities to sense and feel the emotions of others. By modeling empathic elegance and releasing Velcro-like attachments to suffering, I gently remind my loved ones of their own divine connection and inspire others to do the same.

Empathy in its incorruptible form is an important milestone to master, for it is how humans can truly experience how oneness within diversity works without somatic disturbance. I choose to embrace my empathic nature with a delicate balance of joy, love, and somatic awareness because my heart is very sensitive and can get overburdened. Self-love, self-discipline, and somatic awareness strengthen my empathic na-

ture into an incorruptible form. When I feel strong through dedicated self- care, it becomes a joy to love, have compassion, and pass the elegant expression of empathy forward.

Empathy is the yellow brick road to a love that can become problematic. Empathy is also the vehicle that spreads love, the most vital word in the human language, and when the connections among the heart of humanity beat as one, that is the promise of wholeness.

9

HUMAN INCORRUPTIBILITY

While I worked at a psychiatric hospital, one out of three patients on my unit attempted suicide or seriously considered it. The answers to the following questions always had great meaning. I would ask, "Do you truly not want to exist tomorrow? Or is the pain you're experiencing so great that death is the only form of relief you can imagine?" For the few who truly wanted to exit, we attempted to find purpose and reasons for hope. Since most patients wanted relief from unbearable emotions and pointless optimism, the following observations I shared about suicidal ideation usually became our therapeutic goals. I would tell my suicidal clients, "Clinically, I've noticed something always needs to die, whenever someone has suicidal thoughts or attempts suicide. Something needs to die . . . but not you. Let's explore what needs to die in your life, and then we'll see what changes." By working with the human instinct to end suffering, incorruptible solutions gained footholds.

Pain creates passion for change, and love motivates replication. This pattern of how illusion leads to love reoccurs throughout human history. The fairy tale *The Wonderful Wizard of Oz* feels timeless because vulnerable, lovable characters endured repeated challenges to achieve what appeared impossible. Frank Baum illustrated this pattern brilliantly when Dorothy Gale and her companions failed, tried again, and eventually overcame terrifying obstacles during their ordeal. Willpower, steely resolve, and enduring love for one another enabled Dorothy and her companions to overcome every illusion Oz had to offer.

According to traditional Eastern and Greek philosophy, maintaining one's values and virtues during challenges demonstrated invulnerability, incorruptibility, and ultimately invincibility. And, like many of his predecessors, Plotinus saw the human condition existing on a light/darkness continuum (called love and illusion in this book) and did *not* consider darkness or evil as a devil to conquer. Negativity, adversity, and malicious illusions were never turned into deities or a malevolent being. Plotinus believed we create our circumstances, which can lead to wholeness or splattered mud on the face of a perfectly good human. Suffering recycles our miscalculations until the *forms of love and illusion* are truly understood. Opposition creates the required contrast, and self-responsibility liberates humans. A harsh teacher, suffering is simply the training program for resolving unconscious patterns to become immune to illusions like suicidal ideation.

THE FORM OF INCORRUPTIBILITY

Maintaining our principles in the midst of overwhelming suffering is quite challenging. Accountability and incorruptibility work in tandem to repeat daunting challenges and sacred wounds until we become immune to illusion. The word "incorruptible" originates from the word *incorruptibilis*, which in Latin means imperishable. However, for the purposes of this book, the Greek word *aptharsia* (which indicates indestructibility, immortality, and the inability to experience deterioration) more accurately captures the conceptual essence within the form of incorruptibility.

Today as it was in ancient times, the word "incorruptible" is often attributed to a deceased body that does not decompose. There are many examples of a deceased spiritual sage or saint from various religious traditions failing to decay for centuries after their death. For the purposes of this book, however, the Greek definition will be used. We are all on a hero/heroine's journey, and the love/illusion continuum helps us recognize corruption. Love transforms illusion, and incorruptible humans transcend their circumstances. Recycling primary love templates, stress responses, and victim/perpetrator paradigms does not create heaven nor actualize henosis. Refusing to run off a suicidal cliff with our fellow lemmings requires sovereignty and incorruptibility. Sovereignty requires a strong mind, sound heart, and hardened resolve. The form of incorruptibility builds upon the mastery of the six previous forms (illusion, love, cherish, grace, equanimity, and empathy) and can develop into a form of *aptharsia* prized by the ancient Greeks, which relies upon the inner strength and fortitude often found in remarkable people who overcome dire circumstances.

Incorruptibility includes the following qualities:

> The farther down the yellow brick road we go, the more we will be tested repeatedly and in epic proportions. As torchbearers seeking wholeness, we will be challenged to maintain our principles and values during significant adversity. The quintessential challenge associated with incorruptibility has to do with sustaining our principles and treating others accordingly without attaching to an outcome. Despite a solid spiritual connection and maintaining correct actions, the incorruptible challenge is to weave our principles into the fabric of our body and soul so completely that nothing, even death, will make us abandon what we know is love for a seductive illusion. Plotinus described the challenges incorruptibility offers as follows, "But being completely purified is a stripping of everything alien, and the good is different from that. . . . The good will be what is left after purification, not the purification itself."[1]

Incorporating our principles, values, and the forms into the fabric of our body and soul is a spectacular goal. Maintaining equanimity and being mindful after abject failure requires determination. Incorruptibility differs from the dark night of the soul, where the body and soul merge as we re-experience the agony associated with our original divine disconnection. Instead, incorruptibility challenges us to maintain our core principles and treat everyone with love and compassion, even while nothing we do seems to be working for what feels like an eternity. Adversity often activates victim/perpetrator paradigms, but a truly incorruptible soul consistently chooses love over illusion, while being stripped of everything alien to *good* during a difficult purifying process.

Unfortunately, the darkest illusion to grow out of the victim/perpetrator paradigm is terrorism. Terrorists claim to have incorruptible focus and steadfast principles and believe death is preferable to compromise. However, the sanctity of life is nonnegotiable, and terrorism twists the victim/perpetrator paradigm into what appears to be a per-

petual purification challenge. Incorruptible strategies are needed to
address terrorism's ability to strip us of our humanity. We are experiencing a modern-day plague of epic proportions, so terrorism and its
purification challenges will be explored throughout this chapter about
human incorruptibility.

Liberating people from terrorism and stripping away its corrupted
noble causes has proven to be a confounding proposition. Nick Chopper, the Tin Woodsman, begins our exploration into terrorism because
a familiar fairy tale can address the complex topic of incorruptibility and
terrorism without setting off our moral or cultural triggers about our
current perception about good and bad guys. By exploring fiction, we
have an opportunity to make the confounding more comprehensible.

TERROR IN OZ

In the original book *The Wonderful Wizard of Oz*, before the terrifying
flying monkeys took flight, Nick Chopper, the woodsman later called
the Tin Man, fell in love with a humble maidservant from Munchkin
Country named Nimmie Amee. When she returned his affections, Nick
happily went off into the woods and began chopping down trees for
their future home. Nimmie's lazy employer heard about their plans and
began plotting to keep her maidservant in her employ. The woman
bribed the Wicked Witch of the West, who enchanted the woodman's
axe to prevent Nick Chopper from marrying his sweetheart.

The witch's spell worked perfectly. Each time Nick felt love in his
heart for Nimmie, he lost his focus and the axe would slip and chop off
one of his arms or legs—eventually he lost his whole body. Unaware of
the spell, Nick hired the local tinsmith to replace his missing body parts
with prosthetic limbs and organs made out of tin. Nick persevered and
returned to the forest, chopped wood, and continued to create a home
for the love of his life. Grief stricken, one day Nick Chopper succumbed to his mounting losses and completed the spell when his tears
rusted his iron joints shut. Locals called him the Tin Man, and for a
year, he remained frozen in the woods with plenty of time to think.
Since his love for Nimmie had waned during his long ordeal, Nick
assumed the tinsmith had failed to replace his heart. Once Nick lost his
love, one could say he became a Tin Man frozen in thought until Doro-

thy Gale found him and provided hope, love, and kindness. When Dorothy arrived with the Scarecrow, her gentle heart, empathy, and generous oilcan freed Nick to start his journey to heal his heart. Eternally grateful for their help, Nick's core values returned and he became a loyal companion.

> It was a terrible thing to undergo, but during the year I stood there, I had time to think that the greatest loss I had known was the loss of my heart. While I was in love I was the happiest man on earth; but no one can love who has not a heart, and so I am resolved to ask Oz to give me one.—The Tin Woodsman[2]

In the tradition of the philosophers, Dorothy, the Scarecrow, and the Tin Man debated the relative benefits and liabilities of having a heart versus brain, without a conclusion—similar to our philosophical debates that continue to this day. However, the Tin Man's heart remained incorruptible even though he thought his heart was lost. Fortunately for the Tin Man, the deluge of attacks failed to deter him because the tin, which replaced his skin after prior trauma, protected him. A very emotional man, he cried often, and Dorothy always oiled his joints when his tears rusted them shut. At the conclusion of the book, the Wizard awarded the Tin Man with what modern doctors would call a placebo: a velvet heart filled with sawdust. But as we know, he had a heart all along, which was aptly demonstrated by his sensitive and loving nature.

GOOD INTENTIONS, CORRUPTED SOLUTIONS

The Tin Man offers us a fairy tale example of how our heart connection wavers when we mourn our beloved or experience significant losses. Dorothy Gale's oilcan symbolizes the love and empathy we all need until we reopen our heart to love after being victimized. This secret elixir produced from the reflective mirrors of love is easily seen by imagining a child scraping his knee and running to his mother in tears. When Mother compassionately and lovingly holds him, the child remembers he is loved, the pain diminishes, and tears dry as henosis facilitates his healing. At one time or another our heart will break, just like the Tin Man's, and love gets it going again.

Another mother may *go* on crusade on behalf of all children with scraped knees to punish a group of people or someone she blames for her child's suffering. Heartfelt passion, a loving intention, or an empathic connection can trigger an appropriate protection or an immature stress response that can motivate a person, clan, or country to demand *retribution or revenge*. *Twisted activism based upon retaliation and/or corrupted* protection can grow from a victim's misfortune to a corrupted solution, which creates perpetrators, terrorists, and even martyrs.

Good intentions, unconscious emotions, and unexamined motivations can twist a hardwired reptilian need for security into a heat-seeking need for scapegoats and victims. Knowing when to stand our ground, hold someone accountable, or accept adversity with equanimity is often a mystery. Some, like the lazy employer and the Wicked Witch of the West, terrorize while others are victimized like Nimmie Amee and Nick Copper. However, in this fairy tale, love healed the Tin Man's heart and provided seeds to an enlightened solution to the victim/perpetrator paradigm.

Similar to how the *road to hell* is paved with positive intentions, perpetrators and victims recycle *corrupted solutions*. Justified retaliation, retribution, and righteous indignation are timeless catalysts, which have fueled human conflict from primeval times to the modern day. Now, we see what terrorizes humans around the world virtually the instant it occurs, and the victim/perpetrator paradigm has grown into a purifying epidemic of epic proportions. The global suffering has fueled the ponderous illusion that we must push back. Paying back the evil villain as a noble endeavor never seems to fall out of style.

That said, both the lazy, wealthy woman and the Wicked Witch of the West had to close off their hearts to lose the ability to empathize or sympathize with another person's suffering to accomplish their hedonistic goals. The employer's indifference to Nick and Nimmie's agony in order to serve her personal agenda resembles the calculated tactics used by perpetrators, including terrorists . . . past or present. To a corrupted heart, the pain of others is a small price to pay for hedonistic pleasure or actualizing a political agenda. When a victimized world leader or a martyr has a corrupted heart, they can make believable claims about "divine retribution." Good intentions to end suffering and corrupted solutions are what justifies and rationalizes murder for the "greater good."

Infant, child, and adolescent stress responses are attracted to quick fixes and fail to consider long-term ramifications. Chronic suffering and unconscious anger want immediate results. In frustration, people abandon their values and principles when loving solutions seem to fail and feel time-consuming. The intention to stop a perceived perpetrator often feels good and noble, even though their impulsive solution may terrorize innocents. What is often misunderstood is that terrorism *is a form of love*, but it is love *in a corrupted form* that chops off our heart connection like a heartless, enchanted axe.

THE NEVER-ENDING STORY OF SUFFERING

Now I know I've got a heart because it is breaking.—The Tin Man[3]

Society often believes criminals, terrorists, and (in our fairy tales) witches are born wicked. But I have seen firsthand in my practice that these people usually were victims themselves before they began to victimize. Clans and communities create cultural storylines of "us versus them," which the form of illusion corrupts, transforming people into adversaries to overcome. Some people transcend trauma while others unfortunately recycle the modeled templates of abuse and neglect they previously experienced.

Suffering can, like it did with the Tin Man, increase our sensitivity and empathy. Dissociation and addictive behaviors can numb pain temporarily but eventually create more suffering over time. Blaming friends, family, and adversaries for causing our troubles is simply a dysfunctional stress response, which momentarily pushes pain onto scapegoats. Truthfully told, victimization can induce self-destructive tendencies or payback fantasies. Self-love, social awareness, personal responsibility, and the willingness to look behind the curtain concealing our illusions ensure our connection to humanity and divinity. The angst from victimization never separated the Tin Man from his divine essence. During his year frozen in thought, he never lost his principles, while everything he once perceived as loving, good, and beautiful faded. Trauma may create a terrorist, but resisting illusion and maintaining values during a purification challenge is transcendence.

In Oz, the Tin Man's trauma ultimately led to his destiny—Nick discovered his uncorrupted heart. When trauma strips away our identity, incorruptibility leads us to our destiny. Mastering this purification process leads to transcendence. We do not need to see the Wizard (a perceived god or holy man) or a tinsmith (a therapist or healer) to heal our heart. When we are secure and self-aware and take responsibility for our responses to a tragedy, we can heal and be mindful like the Tin Man. After his tragedy, he walked very carefully, with his eyes on the road, and when he saw a tiny ant toiling by, he would step over it, so as not to harm it. The Tin Woodman thought he had no heart, so he never was cruel or unkind to others. "You people with hearts," he said, "have something to guide you, and need never do wrong; but I have no heart, and so I must be very careful. When Oz gives me a heart of course I needn't mind so much."[4]

Dorothy and her companions were relatable characters who achieved liberation; however, Glinda's storyline is critical in regard to the purification process associated with sovereignty. An empowered witch, she had the power to stop the tragedy, but she chose to witness, embody henosis, and let everyone solve their own problems. As Dorothy Gale and her companions solved their problems themselves, they became stronger and eventually resisted the Wicked Witch's enchantments without a wizard.

Mastering illusion is empowering and leads to transformation, incorruptibility, and transcendence. Disempowered people resort to control like the Wicked Witch of the West and unfortunately produce more of the terror that lies dormant within their heart. Is it possible that Baum used the character of Glinda to demonstrate how principles and values, when woven into the fabric of our body and soul, instilled incorruptibility? Did Glinda honor the Tin Man and resist the urge to rescue, which allowed the Tin Man to rediscover the *good* in his heart on his own?

Would it have been nobler of Glinda to prevent wrongdoings or punish the evildoers? Or did she already know terror begets terror? Why does evil exist and why does the divine, who has the power to intervene, not rescue humanity? Perhaps personal growth of an incorruptible heart is what Baum wanted readers to consider.

THE TERRORIST CONTINUUM

We are not separated from spirit, we are in it.—Plotinus[5]

Terrorism is the most insidious illusion existing today. At this point in *The Promise of Wholeness*, we have the necessary background to explore how corrupted empathy can become a dangerous teething ring, which can twist people into terrorism. When innocents are violated, we naturally feel empathy for those harmed. Victimization awakens a zealous fury to protect loved ones and virulent forms of righteous indignation. But the ancient and still popular knee-jerk war cry "an eye for an eye" to avenge wrongdoings corrupts our well-intended empathy the very moment we use violence against perpetrators and/or innocent bystanders to stop violence. Self- defense is appropriate for protection, but indiscriminate retaliatory responses create more victims and more people wanting to right wrongs.

Sadly though, "fighting fire with fire" merely awakens the beast of inhumanity in a corrupted form of empathy, which subsequently creates more wrongs to right as victims and perpetrators trade places. The allure of honoring a martyr is a very persuasive battle cry to convince others to pick sides to avenge a wrongdoing. Pain and suffering tug at the heartstrings of humanity and produce compassion, which is employed by victims to win sympathy and the war of public opinion. Polarization inspires propaganda to solidify the story of "us versus them" or rhetoric that justifies retaliatory measures and harsh retribution to right wrongs.

Terror is not new. The term "terrorism" was first coined during the French Revolution. The roots of terrorism go back two thousand years, when the Jewish "dagger men" assassinated Roman occupational forces. The passion and zeal they exuded earned them the title *zealots*. From the late thirteenth to the seventeenth centuries, an Islamic sect in northern Iran introduced suicidal terror to the world when they sent what became known as the assassins to murder rival leaders in their palaces. The task to protect or preserve a beloved way of life is potent for it evokes powerful passions, which have birthed philosophies such as *the end justifies the means, might makes right, an eye for an eye,* and *we are God's chosen people* that still motivate people today.

While immersed in shadows and darkness, life on earth is often perceived as separate from love and kindness. The form of illusion reveals and puts us through a purification process until we take responsibility for our actions. Stripping away what is alien to good lets us discover which actions actually work. Negative consequences are alarm signals that indicate we have missed our mark. Light takes many forms—even darkness or what some people deem evil—for the purposes of love. Strengthening our incorruptibility muscles may cultivate virtue in a wounded heart contemplating retaliation. The question becomes, where do we find the inner peace, mindfulness, and love that humanity seeks? On this subject, Laozi wrote:

> Cultivate Virtue in yourself, and Virtue will be real. Cultivate it in the family, and Virtue will abound.
> Cultivate it in the village, and Virtue will grow. Cultivate it in the nation, and Virtue will be abundant.
> Cultivate it in the universe, and Virtue will be everywhere.[6]

EVIL IS IN THE EYE OF THE BEHOLDER

Two thousand years ago, according to the linguistic scholar Dr. Neil Douglas-Klotz, the Aramaic word for good meant ripe, evil meant unripe or corrupt, and sin implied that one had missed the mark or made a mistake. In Douglas-Klotz's book *The Hidden Gospel*, he states that in ancient times, the English translation for forgiveness included to *set free, let go, loosen, leave out,* or *omit* what was unripe.[7] Nowadays, malevolence, damnation, and frightening devils lurking in the dark are instantly associated with evil. The word "evil" has gone through a curious makeover, and I wonder if we are better off with this darker interpretation. Terrorism or the inhumanity of man to his fellow man certainly does miss the mark and leads to endless debates. Like beauty, evil lives in the eye of the beholder.

What emerges when you consider the following questions?

1. How do you define darkness or evil? Does that definition include terrorism?
2. Why do illusions exist and can good (light) exist without evil (dark)?

3. Do you feel victimized by life's difficult challenges or recognize their role in making you incorruptible?

4. Why did wicked witches exist in Oz? Why are the terrorists plaguing our world today allowed free reign to torture others? Why doesn't the divine intervene?

5. Why does the divine permit victims and perpetrators to recycle endless trauma?

6. What is the relationship between illusion, purification, and incorruptibility?

7. Do good intentions and innocence protect us from darkness? Or do we even need to be protected from darkness?

8. If my immature stress responses harm others, am I evil?

9. If love begets love and anger begets anger, what does terrorism beget? Can wholeness actually beget itself? Carefully note what your body, heart, and mind have to say when you review these questions and gauge how your answers compare to what others have told you.

10. Now, are your answers similar or are there discrepancies?

Dogma attempts to organize people into manageable herds. Frequently, our answers to these questions are rooted in something we were told, not something we intuitively ascertained to be true. One-size-fits-all explanations and rigid beliefs have led humanity to recycle dreadful illusions endlessly. Incorruptibility, in my opinion, includes self-awareness, clear boundaries, and a dedication to expressing our principles and virtues *externally* in the outside world. Self-objectivity, incorruptible integrity, and self-responsibility motivate us to actualize our principles and virtues *internally*. Dogma tells us what is beautiful or evil and discourages personal interpretation. Sovereignty, self-actualization, and self-realization are reliable maps for unique solutions—not dogma designed by people with one-size-fits-all agendas. Our heart and soul provide reliable guidance and intuitive wisdom when we make decisions designed to help everyone around us.

The eternal debate about good and evil occurs in virtually every civilization. Some argue that we are genetically *ripe* or *unripe* at birth, while others are convinced childhood models and our environment affect our emotional stress responses. Genetics and temperament are important factors, but every child interprets his or her experiences uniquely. Natures versus nurture discussions continue to this day, but I believe the debate is irrelevant because our response to our circumstances is what matters. In the Greek-influenced European culture, notions of good and evil were compartmentalized conceptually and linguistically, which led to the polarizing, black-and-white thinking commonly associated with Western religious thought. Middle Eastern philosophy and Semitic scholars took a different path by conceptualizing good and evil as opposing poles on a continuum. Corruption and illusion were recognized as necessary aspects of life teaching humans how light and darkness have a reciprocal relationship to help us grow.

Scientists today recognize that everything in the universe has its unique frequency. *Shem* was the Aramaic word to describe the vibration of an item or person two thousand years ago. Since meanings of words vary contextually in the Aramaic language, *shem* could mean light, word, sound, reputation, name, or the surrounding atmosphere depending upon the intent of the speaker. *Alaha* meant Sacred Unity, Oneness, the All, the One without opposite in Aramaic. According to Neil Douglas-Klotz, the Hebrew-Aramaic word for universe or cosmos combined the words *shem and alaha* to produce *shemaya*. This indicates that the ancients believed that the divine-light vibration resided within every particle of the universe. This provides an ancient perspective as to why the divine created darkness and allows darkness to continue because of a contradictory consideration that in fact evil is an aspect of divinity.

We exist on this light/darkness continuum, which is why we can access our soul, divinity, and wholeness. Goodness and light beget each other, and evil, darkness, and illusion beget each other to create matching bookends. When primordial fears are activated, they can subsequently trigger a fight/flight/freeze stress response based upon trauma, religious dogma, or illusion. Questions about the purpose of suffering and the nature of evil often result. Without the calming influence of the higher brain and the unifying concept of a benign divine-light continuum, the purifying nature of darkness can become overwhelming.

A snake is a beautiful reptile to some people and to others the devil himself in the form of an evil serpent that tempted Adam and Eve in the Garden of Eden. Emotionality and vulnerability alter our perception of what is real and can make anything we fear dark, dangerous, and seemingly evil. Most people appreciate the emotional clarity and internal consistency, but occasionally a primitive stress response will close off a traumatized heart for protection purposes. Dissociation is an intellectual form of self-defense to keep trauma at bay, but fragile walls do not last forever because life always reveals illusion. When dissociated emotions are suddenly freed, we may get overwhelmed with the newfound honesty.

For example, two of my former clients with a significant amount of unresolved trauma taught me a profound lesson about the perception of evil and what can happen when dissociated emotion breaks free. Accustomed to numbing, denying, or blaming others for their troubles, raw emotion terrified these clients and they shut down any healthy resolution. Hours after my clients' hearts softened, tears finally flowed and true self-connection occurred. After this initial success, though, both clients ultimately disconnected from that initial connection and rejected any form of support completely.

Raw emotion can act like a defibrillator to resuscitate an overburdened heart. Unfortunately for both of the clients just mentioned, each recycled a familiar primary love template by running away from their vulnerability and rejecting a new possibility. A frightened emotional brain will use its fight/flight/freeze response to protect itself if the higher brain fails to intercede. Serious trauma blocked emotion and trust within these two individuals, thus blocking the healing elixir of love. The moment of experiencing emotional release and possible reconciliation was ultimately lost. Peace was followed by pain in their past, so they closed their hearts and ended our connection. They returned to the comfort of their own personal shadows rather than moving through the trauma and exploring the other side of their angst. I was saddened to learn later that tragically, both died violently within the year.

Do you remember how the Cowardly Lion, before he met Dorothy, attacked others to appear to be courageous? Lacking emotional maturity and equanimity, his unmonitored fight/flight/freeze response preferred to elicit terror in his victims rather than addressing his own demons (i.e., emotions). The unexamined emotions exploding within my clients were too frightening to them to endure. Sometimes people are terrorized, when their heart suddenly opens, fearing more agony will follow. Burying the terror, abandoning their pain, and running away feels preferable. Inspirational ideas, revolutionary concepts, and uniquely pure perspectives threaten the sedentary nature of the primitive mind. Foreign feelings challenge the internal sanctuary of our reptilian and emotional brains and activate the infant, child, or adolescent stress responses that may panic, push back, or conclude that something diabolical is at play. Darkness leads to light and vice versa. Victims and perpetrators will flip-flop roles or move into the light for good.

VICTIMS AND TERRORISTS FLIP-FLOP ROLES

Victims and terrorists have a reciprocal relationship within the victim/perpetrator paradigm. Terrorists, for example, accept murder and mayhem as necessary activities, which require victims for noble causes. In order to create agony and/or punish an adversary, terrorists must develop a singular, myopic focus and close off their hearts to the suffering of their perceived enemy. A terrorist may honestly believe victimization is justified, will benefit mankind, and consider themselves loyal friends and dedicated compatriots. Much of what a terrorist internally experiences is sincere love and heartfelt compassion, which is why terrorism is such an intertwined, insidious, self-perpetuating cancer.

When a victim retaliates with violence, many feel absolved of any repercussions because they never threw the first punch. This is an important factor that motivates victims and perpetrators to take turns and trade places. Most of us are taught that murder is morally wrong and illegal, and consequences occur if we take someone's life. It is perplexing to our heart and soul to be told that we are all *one* but murder is somehow noble when sanctioned by war. What makes terrorism so tenacious is that violence is motivated by heartfelt loving intentions. No matter how many times a good guy attempts to right wrongs, even with noble force, ostensibly for self-defense, the risk is becoming, in effect, a perpetrator or de facto terrorist.

A sedentary mind full of unexamined beliefs perceives the world in black-and-white absolutes similar to the ways authoritarian leaders use fear-based tactics and religious dogma to control people. Immature individuals with unexamined child stress responses tend to follow authority figures who promote *safety* and promise to meet their *security* requirements. Frightened people herd like lemmings and gravitate toward authoritarian leaders and dogmatic certainty to soothe the security needs of *reptilian* mindsets. Panic, anxiety, or intense pain activates the safety and security considerations of our reptilian/emotional brain.

Most of us dissociate from pain and suffering. The resulting abandoned emotional material, which I called *monkeys* in chapter 7, holds our infant, child, and adolescent stress responses. Monkeys were created for defense, when we were powerless. Frozen at the actual age when we dissociated our trauma, monkeys tend to be immature and disempowered and will recycle the illusions we possessed when our suffering began. Healing our monkeys, seeking wisdom from divergent sources, or considering unique solutions that could succeed in the long term require our higher brain's involvement. Incorruptible solutions require intellectual curiosity, toleration of uncertainty, and the courage to follow our convictions.

Strangers, spouses, or society periodically enrage and frighten us all. Like children fearful of malevolent creatures lurking under beds, we all have monkeys living in our brain trying to protect us from real and imagined suffering. Compassion allows us to notice the pain of our "enemy" beating within our heart. Then we can recognize our reflection mirrored to us by strangers, family, and society. Love and equanimity help us perceive oneness mirrored throughout humanity.

My initial encounter with a hardened, conduct-disordered, terrorist personality type was with a teenager placed on my unit at a residential treatment center forty years ago. I was an eager young healer fresh out of college when my coworker found one of our residents hanging upside-down, suspended from a tree in the woods nearby with cigarette burns covering his arms. We were an open-door facility, and the perpetrator lived right down the hall from the victim. Following a few more episodes of extreme cruelty and numerous failed attempts to unlock his heart, no staff member other than myself would take the perpetrator out on pass. Naïve and a headstrong optimist, I took a small group off campus for an authorized fishing trip only to have this teenager break into my car and destroy my treasured stereo.

The perpetrator was very effective at pushing love away. He could walk into a room, and a chilling silence would replace laughing without a word being spoken. In treatment, we never broke through the protective wall covering his heart. He eventually was placed in a lockdown facility to protect society after he almost killed someone with a bicycle chain. Psychologists would have labeled him a psychopath or sociopath in earlier decades, but a series of traumatic experiences and identification with the perpetrator paradigm motivated him to terrorize. His heart remained closed so it would never hurt again. Looking back, I believe he tortured others to witness their pain, which gave him temporary relief from his own dissociated, untouched trauma. He taught me about the limits of good intentions and the need for protection.

A perpetrator's reptilian brain can successfully shut down compassion and heart connection and throw away the key. In fact, conduct-disordered individuals, the label used nowadays, are generally so disassociated from their emotions they can pass a lie detector test (which is the reason why these tests are not admissible in court). Though I haven't worked directly with international terrorists, I surmise through my clinical experience that some terrorists are conduct disordered. By employing political, religious, or military propaganda, terrorists rally others to their "cause" to regain lost power and in some cases unleash unconscious rage.

I believe the majority of terrorists, however, are similar to a Vietnam veteran I treated who had committed wartime atrocities with his platoon in a village in Vietnam. Unable to sleep due to flashbacks and nightmares, he used marijuana and alcohol to numb the memories haunting him from twenty years prior. Before the war, he was a red-blooded, All-American teenager who loved his country, followed all the rules, and believed it was his patriotic duty to protect and serve his country in Vietnam. Through months of experiencing the horrors of war, his platoon developed deep bonds, and my client felt he owed his life to them. One day they discovered the disemboweled remains of several comrades strung up in trees outside a village. Enraged, his entire platoon snapped and unleashed their agony on the suspected villagers. In his horrified grief, my client became a perpetrator after his friends were victimized and sought relief by creating similar suffering. Unfortunately, terror begot terror that day. His buddies urged him to commit atrocities as justified retaliation, and he succumbed. Empathic and loving in nature, his traumatized heart turned into tin for the next twenty years—frozen and rusted shut.

The drinking and the nightmares ended when my client finally realized he wasn't a monster. He forgave himself when he re-accessed his frozen emotional material deep within his right hemisphere and resuscitated his traumatized monkey reliving the horrific events each night.

Remembering that he acted out of love and loyalty for his friends, while overwhelmed with terrifying grief himself, he recognized how he had succumbed to the retaliation, retribution, and payback his comrades encouraged. He wept profusely as the frozen agony left his body when he remembered his intentions, and through self-forgiveness, he was finally free to love himself and others again.

War begins with terror, and the haze of war creates more terror, pain, and suffering, which pushes people deeper into the victim/perpetrator paradigm and the purification processes within the darkness/light continuum. This Vietnam vet was loyal and empathic, which triggered the urge to right wrongs through retaliation. I believe terrorists are also subjected to overwhelming oppression and take on noble causes to regain control by overpowering a perceived adversary. Resisting authority, blind loyalty, and fierce autonomy are the hallmarks of the adolescent stress response. A terrorist may want his people's *pain to end* and retaliates to stop the suffering but unfortunately just recycles the victim/perpetrator paradigm.

Fundamentally, the logic justifying the actions of terrorism is fundamentally flawed. Murder, mayhem, and victimization ignore the fact that we are all aspects of divinity. Bessel Van der Kolk, a leading PTSD researcher, mentioned during a presentation I attended that *40 percent* of all combatants and civilians engaged in war will suffer from symptoms consistent with post-traumatic stress disorder. Statistics from a July 2016 VA publication state that twenty U.S. military veterans commit suicide every day.[8] This statistic has been consistent for the past twenty years and is twice as high as the general population in the United States. In his book *The Body Keeps the Score*, Van der Kolk encourages better treatment protocols and recognition of the true cost of war. This leads us into powerful questions:

1. Does the world need repairing? Should I right perceived wrongs, when God doesn't?
2. Can enduring love result from terrorism, martyrdom, and/or victimization?
3. Is the blood of innocents worth the price of a noble cause?
4. Are my principles incorruptible to the sirens of war and retaliatory responses to terrorism?

Some people believe the end justifies the means, but a corrupted means will desecrate a noble end. Terrorism is an illusion, which promises peace but recycles agony. Genocide, homicide, and/or suicide do not honor a beloved martyr or the divine. The divine is love and nothing else. Terrorism and victimization, in any form, demonstrate a fundamental separation from our divine lineage. It takes our mind, heart, and soul to access an incorruptible empathic connection to another's pain. Man's inhumanity to man demonstrates the "sin" of missing the mark. When we resist the illusions associated with retribution and possess incorruptible principles, we can say *yes* to loving actions, even if we feel disloyal to our companions by *not* lashing out in our agony. Henosis is attained through incorruptible principles and regaining our original state of wholeness, which happens to be a possible solution for stopping the recycled rage buried within the victim/perpetrator paradigm and acts of terrorism. Every spiritual master that inspired a major religion was immune to illusion and provided solutions to terrorism. Incorruptible principles can lead to transcendence in dire circumstances as evidenced by the following story.

THE FREEDOM TO CHOOSE ALWAYS REMAINS

On a philosophical note, let's explore what Viktor Frankl (1905–1997), after surviving the Holocaust, wrote in his book *Man's Search for Meaning*: "If there is meaning in life at all, then there must be meaning in suffering."[9] That meaning is found when we reach a state of incorruptible equanimity beyond the trenches of reciprocal chaos and divine retribution. A pragmatic man, Frankl believed that humanity needed to recognize that the ultimate purpose for our suffering would always remain a mystery. The choices made in the aftermath of a tragedy, the meaning of our existence, and the principles we use to guide our life is what he thought mattered most. The freedom to choose how we respond or react to victimization and terrorism always rests within. Frankl's observations about human nature when people are subjected to inhumane treatment are timeless and eternal. Like those of Plato, Plotinus, and the great philosophers throughout history, his wisdom still inspires.

Incorruptible people are fierce and powerful . . . undeterred by darkness. Illusion is transformed and transcended because their heart accesses love and its unlimited potential. When our body, heart, and mind align with a soulful purpose to serve something greater, mountains move. When circumstances are unmovable, the freedom to choose our response always remains. According to Frankl, Dostoevsky once said, "There is only one thing I dread: not to be worthy of my sufferings." Frankl went on to say, "These words frequently came to my mind after I became acquainted with those martyrs whose behavior in the concentration camp, whose suffering and death, bore witness to the fact that the last inner freedom cannot be lost. It can be said that they were worthy of their sufferings—the way they bore their suffering was a genuine inner achievement. It is this spiritual freedom—which cannot be taken away—that makes life meaningful and purposeful."[10]

Only one person out of twenty-eight inmates survived the World War II Nazi concentration camps.[11] Frankl noticed that the people with a higher chance of survival were future-oriented and had a higher purpose for life other than self-gratification. Principles retained meaning, personal goals remained important, and dreams of reunification with loved ones kept them alive. Those lost in grief, who allowed their purpose for living to slip away, succumbed quickly. Hopelessness, born from suffering and loss, often led to suicide, so Frankl and his fellow inmates helped these hopeless prisoners find reasons to live. They noticed that once someone found out why they should live, the question of how wasn't as difficult to answer.

The following passage from *Man's Search for Meaning* demonstrates how Frankl used these principles to survive:

> We stumbled on in the darkness, over big stones and through large puddles, along the one road leading from the camp. The accompanying guards kept shouting at us and driving us with the butts of their rifles. Anyone with very sore feet supported himself on his neighbor's arm. Hardly a word was spoken; the icy wind did not encourage talk. Hiding his mouth behind his upturned collar, the man marching next to me whispered suddenly: "If our wives could see us now! I do hope they are better off in their camps and don't know what is happening to us."
>
> That brought thoughts of my own wife to mind. And as we stumbled on for miles, slipping on icy spots, supporting each other time and

again, dragging one another up and onward, nothing was said, but we both knew: each of us was thinking of his wife. Occasionally I looked at the sky, where the stars were fading and the pink light of the morning was beginning to spread behind a dark bank of clouds. But my mind clung to my wife's image, imagining it with an uncanny acuteness. I heard her answering me, saw her smile, her frank and encouraging look. Real or not, her look was then more luminous than the sun, which was beginning to rise.

A thought transfixed me: for the first time in my life I saw the truth as it is set into song by so many poets, proclaimed as the final wisdom by so many thinkers. The truth—that love is the ultimate and the highest goal to which Man can aspire. Then I grasped the meaning of the greatest secret that human poetry and human thought and belief have to impart: The salvation of Man is through love and in love. I understood how a man who has nothing left in this world still may know bliss, be it only for a brief moment, in the contemplation of his beloved. In a position of utter desolation, when Man cannot express himself in positive action, when his only achievement may consist in enduring his sufferings in the right way—an honorable way—in such a position Man can, through loving contemplation of the image he carries of his beloved, achieve fulfillment. For the first time in my life I was able to understand the meaning of the words, "The angels are lost in perpetual contemplation of an infinite glory."[12]

Perhaps incorruptibility is what Frankl described when he said, "What is to give light must endure burning."[13] Good is what remains after burning and may be the ultimate destiny for humanity, but for now, wars rage and people suffer mightily within a perpetual victim/perpetrator paradigm. Within the confines of the concentration camps, Frankl discovered in all classes, ethnicities, and groups that there are only two types of men: the decent and the unprincipled. Some acted like animals and forgot their dignity, while others maintained morality and meaning . . . connected with humanity. Retaining their full inner liberty and internal values added purpose to their lives. Those men and women became living proof that principles, values, and inner strength are more powerful than any outer fate. Viktor Frankl survived the Holocaust and taught us how to survive ours. He was a beacon of light in the darkness . . . a decent man . . . incorruptible and worthy of his suffering.

WAR AND PEACE

Viktor Frankl modeled incorruptibility at an important time in history and, like Plotinus, considered unity humanity's only solution. The notion that genocide, terror, and war create peace continues today. Philosophers, theologians, and politicians have always had different notions about oneness. Some promote peace and cooperation, while others jam guns and damnation down people's throats. We battle over territory, philosophy, religion, and politics, convinced that dominating an adversary makes us noble and brave. The rhetoric changes each year, but the ancient axioms about *winning being the only thing* remain the same. War is a misuse of power and force and has yet to create lasting peace.

Overrunning another individual, group, or country engages a collective victim/perpetrator paradigm. When a powerful person, a contentious clan, or a country dominates others, the oppressed gather together as victims to garner sympathy and compassion. Empathy is a powerful unifier, and the world mourns slain martyrs. Heart-wrenching videos of carnage and suffering family members motivate noble causes. Passive forms of anger, like claiming victimhood status, enable the weak to feel empowered and gain access to the strength of a collective. Supporters then implore friends to rise up with noble intentions and righteous indignation to "right the wrongs" perpetrated against them. Unfortunately, this scenario attracts more martyrs who sacrifice themselves for the same cause that just produced the death, pain, and suffering of their deceased comrades.

A confusing, confounding aspect of terrorism occurs when love, gentleness, and forgiveness are promoted as solutions. To someone deeply infected with the victim/perpetrator virus, peaceful solutions seem ridiculous and disempowering. The spiritual masters who inspired the religions many terrorists and victims claim to represent would address the people's economic, spiritual, and human rights inequities with loving intent and matching behavior. Unfortunately, I suspect those spiritual masters also would be seen as ignorant, spineless jellyfish.

Illusion is the cancer within the victim/perpetrator paradigm, when people dissociate from suffering and fail to address their areas of responsibility. In order to take the life of another, suicide bombers, drone operators, and supporters must disassociate from the price adversaries and innocent bystanders pay. Oneness fades into darkness when combatants enjoy the process of making adversaries suffer. Just like the boy at the residential treatment center who tortured others with cigarettes and my schoolyard bullies—watching a victim suffer makes perpetrators feel better. Others, like the Vietnam veteran I treated, can lose touch with their own humanity and lash out to release internal agony. Dissociation, like the faces of the victim/perpetrator paradigm and terrorism, can take many forms.

Many around the world believe that fighting fire with fire signifies strength and is the only way to deal with terrorists. After 9/11, it would have been interesting if America had resisted declaring war and replied in a revolutionary way. The paradox after victimization is in resisting the temptation to retaliate and take our turn as a perpetrator. After a tragedy, every one of us has this same opportunity. As Viktor Frankl previously mentioned, the freedom to choose our response to any circumstance always remains with us. We learn what does or does not work by experiencing the results of our actions in real time. Illusion challenges us to become incorruptible to our circumstances. Dorothy was free to click those ruby red slippers to go home, but first she went on a journey, had an adventure, met extraordinary people, gained wisdom, and defeated her nemesis, and then she realized she already had the freedom and the power to choose.

TURNING THE OTHER CHEEK

When our leaders fail to model core principles such as human rights, mindfulness, and/or compassion, the door to the victim/perpetrator paradigm opens. Payback philosophies signify strength and power to many. When the Babylonian king Hammurabi, who reigned from 1792 to 1750 BCE, introduced one of the earliest comprehensive legal codes, his famous phrase *an eye for an eye and a tooth for a tooth* was a spectacular improvement over the retaliatory justice practiced by mobs. Situational mores and relative justice established safety for his subjects.

Retribution and punishment have been woven into theology and notions of justice for a very long time. The Christian Bible and Jewish Torah, for example, state that Adam and Eve are thrown out of the Garden of Eden for violating a command from God. The disobedient and wicked deserve retribution in the Quran. Irresponsible actions result in retribution in the Buddhist Dhammapada. Bad behavior creates bad karma according to the Hindu Bhagavad Gita. "What humans do has consequences" seems to be the logical takeaway, which echoes when the Bible says, "Whatever a man soweth, that shall he also reap." The efficacy of punishment as a motivating philosophy by a governing entity or a deity has and always will be subject to rigorous philosophical debate, but interestingly the messages seem unified.

The challenge before humanity is to be responsible and incorruptible to adverse circumstances. *Might makes right* is another philosophy that offers a solution and still has proponents today. The original idea that many scholars believe inspired the popular phrase is attributed to the Greek historian Thucydides (436/435–404 BCE), who wrote in the *History of the Peloponnesian War*, "Right, as the world goes, is only in question between equals in power, while the strong do what they can and the weak suffer what they must."[14]

Under extreme stress, the human emotional brain responds with the urge to fight/flight/freeze. The challenge is to find solutions that are not binary in nature, like power or control, so we can create enlightened possibilities. Power and control are tempting illusions, and religious intolerance, punishment, and retribution are still very prevalent today. Love as a solution takes more time, is more passive, and is perceived as a sign of weakness. When the phrases *turn the other cheek* and *go the extra (second) mile* were suggested two thousand years ago, an enlightened response was offered to the oppressed that were subject to people in power. Those phrases were spoken by Jesus Christ at the Sermon on the Mount, and he also added a third phrase, *give them your cloak as well*, which went far beyond Hammurabi's *an eye for an eye and a tooth for a tooth* law. Many well-intended theologians have misinterpreted this profound philosophy as a recipe for pacifism.

In my youth, we were taught to turn the other cheek in my parochial school, and I unsuccessfully attempted to apply the concept of passivity to the bullies attacking me. Praying for them did not take away the internal rage, terror, and anger accumulating within me daily. When I gave up my passive plan of acquiescence and started punching them like my father suggested, my *eye-for-an-eye* response gave me the opportunity to experience both sides of the victim/perpetrator paradigm. For more than two thousand years, just like me, millions of people have misinterpreted what *turn the other cheek* originally meant.

When I stumbled upon a third option, which including standing up to the bullies without malice or fear in my heart and admitting my stuttering problem, the abuse stopped. Empowered, I discovered a method to achieve an incorruptible solution to my stuttering problem and never engaged the victim/perpetrator paradigm with those bullies again. In his groundbreaking book *Engaging the Powers*, the Biblical scholar and theologian Walter Wink (1935–2012) provided a definitive explanation about what Jesus recommended as an enlightened response to Roman oppression in his Sermon on the Mount, which denies the oppressor the opportunity to continue to humiliate and bully his or her victims.[15] Here is the quote in the Bible that Wink addresses:

> You have heard that it was said, "An eye for an eye and a tooth for a tooth." But I say to you, Do not resist an evildoer. But if anyone strikes you on the right cheek, turn the other also; and if anyone wants to sue you and take your coat, give your cloak as well; and if anyone forces you to go one mile, go also the second mile. (Matt. 5:38–41; see also Luke 6:29)

My summary of Walter Wink's understanding of first-century Roman law and social mores as they applied to each phrase follows:

1. "But if anyone strikes you on the right cheek, turn the other also."
    Superiors in the ancient world would backhand an inferior with the right hand, striking the victim's right cheek, since the left hand was reserved for unseemly personal hygienic uses. Equals in the Roman Empire fought with both hands, so a superior would never strike an inferior with his left hand. Turning the other cheek would prohibit the superior from striking a second blow, since using their left hand elevated the inferior to an equal status. Romans would loathe treating an inferior as an equal. Thus turning the other cheeck was an act of sovereignty, resistance, and salvaged dignity.
2. "And if anyone wants to sue you and take your coat, give your cloak as well."
    Imperial occupational policy taxed heavily and charged exorbitant interest rates, so indebtedness plagued a conquered society. Roman law prohibited the forced removal of possessions from the home of a citizen, but the debtor was required to hand over their

coat each day to the debt holder and essentially work in their underwear (cloak). People wore only two garments in the first century, so handing over both meant they were naked. Nudity was considered more humiliating to the one watching or causing it than to the naked person in that moment of history. This unique advice tipped the scales of power and helped restore the dignity of the debtor.

3. "If someone forces you to go one mile, go also the second mile."

A Roman soldier in the first century, by law, could force anyone to carry his pack, which weighed between sixty-five and eighty pounds, for only one mile. The soldiers would be disciplined by superiors if one mile became two. Offering to go the extra mile in this case forced the Roman to experience the paradoxical dilemma of asking to have his pack returned or he risked retribution by his superior. Thus walking the extra mile was an act of empowerment for the oppressed.

In another of his books, *The Powers That Be: Theology for a New Millennium*, Walter Wink said that the Greek word for "resist" mentioned in Matt. 5:39 is *antistenai*, which literally means stand against like an adversary would during warfare.[16] In 1611, King James explicitly commissioned his then new translation of the Bible to remove what he regarded as "seditious . . . dangerous and trayterous [traitorous]" tendencies, which included any endorsements where subjects could disobey a tyrant. His subjects were encouraged to acquiesce to but not to *stand against* tyranny.

Initially, I acquiesced to bullies in my youth. Feeling disempowered, I fell into the victim/perpetrator paradigm and called in my passive strategy . . . my Jesus plan. I can only guess that King James would have approved. When I stood strong, looked the bully in the eye, and became emotionally immune to my stuttering and violence fears, the bullying stopped. Self-control, self-responsibility, and incorruptibility helped me resist the default victim/perpetrator paradigm. The "heathens" in my world helped me discover what Jesus Christ really meant when he said "turn the other cheek." When I showed restraint and became immune to the hatred pointed in my direction, I learned to love myself with my whole heart and nothing the bullies did mattered.

It takes principles and willpower to remain calm when lashing out at a perpetrator is our entrained knee-jerk reaction. Turning the other cheek, redefined by Walter Wink and his insights into what was actually happening to a conquered people during the time of Jesus Christ, offers critical insights that many of us have missed. Fortunately, Mahatma Gandhi and Martin Luther King Jr. actually understood what Jesus had meant almost two thousand years earlier. Similarly oppressed by Imperial British rule, Mahatma Gandhi employed a novel alternative to war using a nonviolent strategy in India of civil disobedience, which worked—this strategy enabled his nation to regain its sovereignty without armed insurrection. Dr. Martin Luther King Jr. credited both Mahatma Gandhi and Jesus Christ for inspiring his method of nonviolent resistance in the following quote: "Christ gave us the goals and Mahatma Gandhi the tactics."[17] Both men had witnessed corrupted, inhumane treatment of humanity, which inspired the actions that Gandhi and Dr. King took to establish political and racial equality.

Humanity reverts to domination paradigms and *might makes right* philosophies when illusion rules. The concepts of oneness and *turning the other cheek* to stand our ground are beacons in the wilderness. Darkness and light appear to be adversaries but lie on a continuum. Obstacles force us to make choices, and illusion is the alternative to love. We are divine beings inhabiting a physical body attempting to express love amid illusion to engage henosis on earth. Remembering our absolute, eternal roots in the midst of a formidable crisis can enable unique solutions to terrorism. Incorporating enduring principles and reviewing the forms within this book might be worth considering.

REHABILITATION AND DE-RADICALIZATION

From 1948 to 1951, America provided financial, economic, and technical assistance to sixteen countries in Western Europe. Widely recognized as crucial to Europe's recovery after World War II, the Marshall Plan asked countries to cede some sovereignty for greater unity. In exchange for reducing trade and currency barriers, grants, loans, and employment opportunities were provided by the United States to a devastated continent. When the Marshall Plan ended, the economy of Western Europe had increased on the average of 35 percent from 1938 to 1951.[18] Historians cite additional reasons for Europe's recovery but always acknowledge the Marshall Plan's economic wisdom and how it curtailed the spread of communism. At a crucial moment in history, compassion, rehabilitation, and generosity stimulated growth after Nazism terrorized the world.

Today, ethnic violence, immigration crises, and religious intolerance dominate the news, while malicious forms of terrorism spread. Massive resources are spent on homeland security, cyber-protection, and military interventions. Greed, injustice, and radical interpretations of scripture challenge our fundamental principles of equality, ethnic/religious tolerance, and compassion. Equality, economic opportunity, and egalitarian policies create unity. Opening our hearts to entrenched victims and perpetrators requires patience, inscrutable presence, and mastery of every form in this book.

De-radicalization programs attempt to rehabilitate potential terrorists, and about forty programs exist throughout Europe and the Middle East as I write this book. Reliable protocols are in their infancy, and the ageless debate about efficacy, security, and recidivism rates are being applied to terrorism de-radicalization. Education, vocational training, family involvement, religious dialogue, mentoring, and post-release monitoring are the most popular interventions.

From my clinical experience, lasting change occurs when perpetrators and victims reopen their hearts, release their emotional trauma, and change behavior. Closed hearts are hard to heal, but I have seen many people accomplish this feat throughout my career. Some hearts never open, and society will always need protection. *Rehumanizing* from extremism and the seven deadly illusions takes the courage of a superhero. Maintaining a loving place for an "adversary" and remaining incorruptible while exploring new ways to respond to terrorism will open the door for innovation to enter the hearts and minds of both perpetrators and victims, both individually and collectively.

Equanimity creates the space to honestly respect the sovereignty of others. From this place, perhaps the collective heart of humanity can tackle terrorism and shun its eye-for-an-eye philosophy. We empower ourselves when we use the forms and remain incorruptible in the midst of illusion's purification challenges. Carl Jung considered the journey of human transformation, which he called individuation, and concluded that reintegrating different parts of self and synthesizing one's spiritual nature created an integrated whole being. My hope is that when the principles and values of each form are woven into the fabric of enough souls, rehumanizing will become the norm rather than an extraordinary exception.

Horror movies have captured a universal phenomenon of recidivism repeatedly. Just when the perpetrator looks like he or she is about to succumb, the villain rises up more frightening than before. The deeper spiritual truth is thus revealed because obstacles exist, adversaries assist, and even terrorists are part of our purification challenge. Mastering our emotional reaction and maintaining a consistent state of equanimity means darkness can't bully us or be considered an adversary anymore. Enlightened like Dorothy and her companions who embodied their principles and modeled incorruptibility, we too can realize that we possess everything we needed all along.

When Plotinus merged with "The One," perception of lightness and darkness irrevocably changed. In that moment, when his principles and values were incorruptible and woven into his soul, in my opinion, Plotinus saw the light. Peace, presence, and a deep sense of wholeness spontaneously result. To Plotinus, the experience of oneness was beyond conceptual, but due to the limitations of the Greek and Romance languages, subject and object were seen as distinct entities. Thankfully, having studied in India, Plotinus understood the following perspective familiar in the East: transcendence demands that we overcome the distinction among the knower, known, and knowledge. A thousand years later, Rumi described his sense of incorruptibility eloquently in the following way: "Beyond our ideas of right-doing and wrong-doing, there is a field. I'll meet you there. When the soul lies down in that grass, the world is too full to talk about. Ideas, language, even the phrase 'each other' doesn't make sense anymore."[19]

Inspiring words from philosophers like Rumi, fairy tales, and eternal stories from brilliant men such as Viktor Frankl teach us how to transcend our circumstances in any situation. It's almost impossible to imagine what it took for Frankl to become incorruptible during the Holocaust. Holding onto our principles and moral compass while imprisoned in a victim/perpetrator hell requires a herculean effort. Embodying the forms outlined in this book may help release the dross of duality to experience henosis and therefore pure unity. When Dorothy Gale truly was incorruptible, she returned to Kansas without a wizard.

She had possessed everything she needed all along, just like the rest of us. Plotinus described the process of realizing The One in the following way:

> There, our Self-seeing is a communion with the self, restored to purity. No doubt we should not speak of "seeing," but, instead of [speaking of] "seen" and "seer," speak boldly of simple unity. For in this seeing we neither see, nor distinguish, nor are there, two. The man is changed, no longer himself nor belonging to himself; he is merged with the Supreme, sunken into It, one with It; it is only in separation that duality exists. This is why the version baffles telling; for how could a man bring back tidings of the Supreme as something separate from himself when he has seen It as one with himself?[20]

My family experienced traumas, tragedies, addiction, and spectacular beauty like most families. Throughout my career, I've seen hearts open in people's homes, on carpets in residential treatment centers, during psychiatric hospitalizations, and at my private practice office. This much I know. Hearts can open or will remain closed, but they often need assistance. Suffering seals hearts, so prying them open with more pain and punishment will not work. When hearts freeze, love heals and suffering thaws. When the dam breaks and emotions flow, love's delicate nature is all that's needed. It doesn't matter what actually happened or who was involved, *hearts heal with love*.

This observation may sound trite and simplistic at first reading, but let me explain the powerful truth behind how love heals. We are divine beings in sovereign form and possess the power to release every illusion earth offers. As mentioned previously, love is like water and embraces everything, even the low places. When we accept the beautiful but also our suffering, an important mystery about love is revealed. Physical pain and emotional suffering transform with mindfulness and compassion. Love opens hearts and transcends illusion, when our healthy adult feels compassion for an infantile, childish, or adolescent monkey in the middle of a stress response.

Parents, lovers, and mentors can model love and embrace our hearts, but people are divine beings and remain in control. Rejoice when a heart reopens, honor the journey, and never take credit. On the other hand, shut-down hearts can become dangerous and society needs protection from hard-core perpetrators and terrorists. There are terrorist and perpetrator rehabilitation centers around the world for criminals of all kinds. Having worked at residential treatment centers with violent offenders, I saw far more hearts reopen than those that remained closed during my tenure.

Debating whether treatment or lockup helps more people is a useless discussion in my opinion. Locking up people without an attempt at rehabilitation shuts down solutions like a heartless terrorist axe. After all the successes and failures I've witnessed and experienced, I know that love is the most powerful force in the universe. Humanity is diminished and our options limited if we shut down our hearts and just lock people up. When we employ the same tunnel vision with terrorists and suicidal clients with unbearable pain and few prospects, something needs to die . . . let it be illusion, not love.

CREATING INCORRUPTIBILITY

When we are lost in the dark and reeling in agony, mastering the forms of illusion, love, cherish, grace, equanimity, and empathy provides the platform that allows us to see our location and eventual destination within our very own innate moral compass. Transforming the darkness that is terrorism requires an incorruptible alignment with henosis to find the ultimate solution. In the midst of life's most formidable challenges, the form of incorruptibility prepares us and ensures our readiness to express our divinity *to do just that.*

Use the following form meditation to explore the many facets of incorruptibility. It is important to remember we only have control over our reactions to life's challenges. For now, just read the meditation and let the ideas take you beyond suffering to incorruptible principles and values. Try reading this form aloud to own the message. I also suggest taking a break after reading this and any other form meditation. You can strengthen this form through intention and breath using the Camel Wave Meditation (appendix A) by inhaling the form of incorruptibility and exhaling your intention to become incorruptible. The Wise and Loving Inner Voice Meditation (appendix B) can help you discern which internal voice within your brain provides useful directions or merely delusions. Explore the freedom of letting flow the ideas, the feelings, and the thoughts that the form meditations trigger. Let the wisdom simmer and the illusions become dimmer before moving onto the next section. When you feel the need, you can return and reread it over and over.

FORM MEDITATION: INCORRUPTIBILITY

Unifying my body, heart, and soul while nothing seems to be working is a great task requiring discipline and fortitude. Surrendering to divine timing and cherishing whatever happens while not falling into the victim/perpetrator paradigm enhances my incorruptibility. My trials and tribulations grind away the rough edges of my divinity like sharpening stones, molding and honing with the subtlety of rough sandpaper every one of my beloved delusions I hold dear. When the edges are smoothed, I can begin to develop immunities to the proverbial fires of human suffering through the use of the forms of love, empathy, and equanimity—and when all the forms combine to become my default loving response, I am still whole while I am in the midst of both observing and experiencing suffering.

Suffering forces the most stubborn aspects of my personality to examine my personal paradigms, stress responses, and primary templates. Acts of cruelty may enrage or overwhelm me, but I understand stress responses and perceptions based on previous trauma become monkeys I must soothe with mindfulness. If I try to take control or succumb to the conclusion that chaos, self-sabotage, or a punishing deity creates the suffering, I risk falling into the illusion that I am being victimized and accidently may become a perpetrator. When I justify hopelessness or believe in a divine right to demand retribution or retaliation, I know now I am recycling pain and suffering, which perpetuates my personal victim/perpetrator paradigm.

A critical step toward transcendence is accomplished when I recognize pain's purpose and realize my response to suffering enhances my incorruptibility. Suffering shows me if I am disconnected from my soul and reveals my misguided notions about sovereignty. Making a deliberate choice to evolve from my default knee-jerk reactions and surrender to an unknown incorruptible solution requires all the strength and trust I can muster. Suffering is not my preferred state of being, but I am beginning to recognize how pain shows me where my personal para-

digms and primary templates still have a hold on me. Suffering is a powerful milestone because pain motivates me to merge my body and soul into the richness of the omniscient, where the collective pain and peace experienced by the totality of humanity exists in each moment. My challenge is to experience the peace that is henosis without becoming corrupted by the illusion there is anything wrong to be righted.

When I choose to transcend the ancient good/evil dynamic of victims becoming persecutors and martyrs becoming terrorists, I enter the quiet in the eye of the chaos and acknowledge everything is already perfect. I build my awareness of the absolute perfection each time I experience even a momentary flash of the tranquility contained within this form. Incorruptibility is designed to guide me and teach me how to surrender. Yes, I'm stubborn sometimes and know my suffering will intensify until my body, heart, and mind unify with my soul to establish incorruptible responses. It takes all my courage to ask for appropriate assistance and access to the internal strength to accept guidance when I feel broken. Becoming one with the divine and developing a reciprocal relationship, even when I feel all that is divine has vanished, is tough, but this quintessential act of valor is essential to weather every storm on the horizon to become incorruptible.

The form of incorruptibility is a loyal companion and requires a similar mastery brilliantly demonstrated by the characters in Oz. After those characters endured the many trials and tribulations during their journey, they eventually realized that they already possessed the power, courage, heart, and wisdom to overcome every obstacle during their ordeal without a wizard. Inspirational stories are similar to forms because they show me roadmaps on how to overcome obstacles down my own yellow brick road. No matter how strange or difficult my circumstances, if I retain my principles and values no matter what happens, I can return to Kansas or henosis, heaven, home, anytime I choose.

Incorruptibility may appear passive to the uninformed, for it requires a significant amount of self-esteem to resist the popular eye-for-an-eye philosophies. Surrendering to the divine, if I have no answers or even when the answers I know to be true oppose the accepted dogma of my peers, requires a significant amount of courage. It takes an unwavering heart, which trusts the universe as a benign, loving place. The commitment to live impeccably even while suffering and when nothing I do works without understanding why creates mastery of this form.

I am an active participant in a divine plan I do not have to understand. I desire to express every form (cherish, grace, and love in a balanced state of empathy and equanimity), no matter how much pain or suffering or the form of illusion challenges my weaknesses, principles, and values. I choose now to exit the cave of shadows, claim sovereignty, and become incorruptible to every illusion thrown at me.

Embodying incorruptibility requires strength, willpower, and an unshakable usage of the forms. My full intention and soulful dedication is also required. During a tragedy of epic proportions where nothing is working, my principles and values become the indestructible foundation to feel whole. When I am feeling lost and alone, I can contemplate the following forms to remind myself about wholeness and use them as my yellow brick road to return home:

ILLUSION—*Am I aware of my tenacious beliefs, the ones that sabotage my dreams?*

LOVE—*Can I transform my suffering into love, while remaining true to me?*

CHERISH—*Can I love others without expectation or manipulation while embracing whatever happens as perfection?*

GRACE—*Can I be an active participant in what is occurring while radiating divine love?*

EQUANIMITY—*When I am hurt, can I remain mindful, fair, and balanced while maintaining the dignity of everyone, especially myself?*

EMPATHY—*Can I create emotional boundaries to discern my experience from the suffering of another?*

INCORRUPTIBILITY—*Are my principles, intentions, and actions truly incorruptible, even when nothing seems to be working?*

Incorruptible means I cannot be shaken; undeterred I will remain resolute and grateful for all the ugly and blissful experiences that lead me to merge and become one with each of these forms. I peacefully release my illusions and maintain principles no matter what happens in order to experience wholeness. If the world condemns me or I feel abandoned by the divine, I know that this is merely another illusion to overcome to weave my principles and values into the fabric of my soul. Therefore I can remain courageous, discerning, steadfast, and incorruptible because

I am acutely aware of my actions and reactions—I choose to experience the omega of suffering and become the alpha of tranquility.

10

THE PROMISE OF WHOLENESS

Birth hides a soul inside the human body—in other words, our divine nature co-exists with mortality. From birth, we are challenged to deal with a barrage of conflicting emotions, confusing advice, and twisted messages from friends, adversaries, and family. Accepting both the good and bad as forms of love feels normal and becomes primary love templates or what we sense as "natural." Sorting out why we react to the world the way we do is a journey of self-discovery and sovereignty. The forms outlined in this book provide guidelines toward love, incorruptibility, and eventually wholeness. As mentioned previously, our monkeys hold the emotional residue and the resulting belief systems from previous trauma. Illusion enchants with seductive songs of woe until we develop the discernment and wisdom conveyed in the timeless Allegory of the Cave by Plato, Chretien de Troyes's *Perceval, the Story of the Grail,* and the Wachowski siblings' contemporary example of Neo in *The Matrix* trilogy.

Many theologians and philosophers say they know the way home, but those prescriptive maps are often only as reliable as the scattered breadcrumbs dropped by Hansel and Gretel. Illusion pushes dogma, which knocks humans off course like a Kansas twister until enduring wisdom and our internal gyroscope help us recover. Similarly orphaned like Dorothy and deposited on earth, we have the perfect playground with an unlimited supply of friendly and antagonistic playmates. Developing the navigational skills to see through illusion requires the emotional maturity to love despite circumstances and accept antagonists as teachers. Then we no longer need pain to point us to our destiny.

We, like Dorothy, already have a homing instinct to return to henosis. As in Oz, our antagonists and protagonists help us along the way. When we truly understand the love/illusion continuum, incorruptibility appears on the horizon and then the promise of wholeness eventually rises like the sun. Unfortunately, the ability to love our circumstances waxes and wanes like the ocean tides. Our moods are affected by others and vary like the weather and lunar phases. Henosis is a fleeting awareness; therefore we are challenged to return there again and again. Here is the crucial point: no matter how many times we miss the mark, moving back to wholeness is how humans become incorruptible. *Failure* shows us where we missed the mark and highlights the need for alternative strategies. If we feel whole just once, then, at the very least, we can create a primary love template about the experience. Then we know, at least for a moment, that those ugly shadows and shackles are not real.

Ironically, the repetition required for true mastery is depicted brilliantly in our horror movies. Once the hero/heroine thinks their antagonist is slain, that demon usually jumps back to life and in more frightening form before the final resolution. Adversaries and personal monkeys help us become incorruptible to illusion so we can embody wholeness ourselves. Dorothy's mantra—"There's no place like home"—is everyone's mantra.

THE FORM OF WHOLENESS

Of course, Plotinus weighed in on the paradoxes and purpose of human existence. I was fascinated to find out that Plotinus concluded, through deductive reasoning, dialectic discovery, and mystical union with The One, that the characteristic common throughout the universe was unity. He observed that everyone and everything depends on unity; thus unity is the universal goal of life. Reunification with the divine is why the soul exists, and this concept was central in his writings. *Henosis* was the word Plotinus used to describe the soul's journey of reunification with the divine while on earth. A good life would entail an internal journey where we move from solely addressing our physical needs to embodying henosis on earth. Both Plotinus and Plato thought that our soul rejoices when we align with *The One/Goodness* and embody principles that help the whole.

The promise of wholeness and real transcendence can be likened to a butterfly in flight that suddenly appears and quickly vanishes. We *know* butterflies exist by the awe, wonder, and beauty we momentarily experience in their presence and the sadness felt when that magnificent creature leaves. People enjoy butterflies, but most of us expect they will leave, and the challenge is to not get hooked on trapping the butterfly. Similarly, peak experiences are almost impossible to maintain, and our task is not regretting the fact we were happy for an instant before it disappeared. Similarly, satisfaction and hunger pangs will return and leave, return and leave like the air we breathe. Interestingly, the Greek word for soul and breath in ancient times was *psyche*, but *psyche* was also their name for a butterfly. Butterflies transform themselves from an egg, larva, and cocoon stage until they fly away in a symbolic act of total freedom. The rebirth and resurrection of the human soul reminded the ancient Greeks of the courageous path of the gentle butterfly emerging from the cocoon with beautiful wings to fly with the gods. Thus, the soul and the butterfly shared the same name.

Emotions are mercurial like fireflies, appearing suddenly and disappearing just as unexpectedly. Similarly, henosis is initially experienced briefly, vanishes, and repeats. The more we become immune to illusion, the more whole we will feel in our future. Sunlight creates shadows, and similarly, love flushes out our illusions that keep us small. Light activates darkness, which arises spontaneously to inspire transformation, transcendence, and/or the promise of wholeness.

Agony and ecstasy are powerful motivators and are poignant reminders of the paradoxes within human existence. St. John of the Cross, who wrote the poem *The Dark Night of the Soul*, described the physical agony a human experiences before the ecstatic reunion with our soul. Many of us wonder why life works this way. Knowledge about the love/ illusion continuum helps us learn from our experiences without shame. The complementary roles agony and ecstasy play to enhance our incorruptibility are an enigma. Agony motivates us to look at our illusions in order to experience ecstasy.

MILESTONES FEELING LIKE MILLSTONES

Similarly to the sense of abandonment that accompanies a dark night of the soul, the milling process that creates incorruptible humans is very challenging. Maintaining any sense of self-esteem without a soul connection is quite difficult when nothing seems to be working. Previously, in chapter 6, a metaphor about a human three-legged stool was offered to describe the necessary role our intellectual, emotional, and behavioral "legs" play on the physical plane to actualize our dreams. Wanting something from the bottom of our heart, mindfulness practices, and wholesome principles create a unified purpose, which may activate grace and synchronicity. When we become truly sovereign, we resist illusion and understand how "grinding stones" enhance incorruptibility.

When one leg is longer than the rest, a three-legged stool teeter-totters. This is essentially what happens when various aspects of our personality work at cross-purposes. If, for example, our intellect always dominates, empathy and the stabilizing effects of equanimity are minimized. Wobbling will sabotage any goal, especially if our sole intention is to become whole. Mental focus, passion, and dedicated actions toward an uplifting goal, while remaining in a state of mindfulness and equanimity, are powerful practices. Plotinus experienced oneness and lectured on his experiences as have countless other sages and enlightened individuals throughout human history. From my perspective, the collective rhetoric of all those brave souls who exited Plato's cave of shadows offers valuable suggestions to humanity about how to build a sovereign stool.

Positive intentions, principled actions, and self-responsibility instill personal sovereignty. The oneness we experience invites miracles to occur, but paradoxically, an unexpected cascade of challenges occasionally follow if our stool wobbles. Maintaining healthy habits, removing emotional debris, and clearing mental blocks heighten our experience of divinity. After our purpose is truly unified and our metaphorical stool stabilized, every buried illusion keeping us small will rise to the surface and demand our awareness for the purpose of revealing our remaining templates, paradigms, and personal monkeys. The yellow brick road has "milestones," which function like millstones grinding away at our illusions to help us return home whole. Patience is required while problems occur in an endless stream of Job-like challenges that mysteriously appear, plaguing us after a little taste of success. The millstones increase their speed to smooth out any remaining rough edges. When success activates immature stress responses such as hubris, narcissism, or entitlement issues, milling often ensues. If we do everything right and nothing is working, hidden expectations and/or perfectionism fatigue become grist for the grinding stones. This is how our principles are tempered into hardened steel.

The characters in Oz remind us that the power to transcend suffering and remain tranquil lies within mastering the form of incorruptibility. Inner peace, mindfulness, and love will activate our internal monkeys like lights attract moths on a hot summer night. Millstones grind away to ensure our three-legged stool is stable and incorruptible. The finished product is an unshakable ability to retain our principles, values, and sovereignty so completely that nothing can exile us from wholeness. One of the last and most important milestones on the yellow brick road is the millstone that produces incorruptibility.

Here are some of the main points we have covered in the book, which propel us toward the promise of wholeness:

Understanding the role of illusion in facilitating growth can lead us to rich personal and/or collective experiences of unity.

- *Love* and *illusion* are often labeled as "good" and "bad" but occupy opposing ends of a unified continuum.
- Inner peace, mindfulness, and love are milestones that activate illusion's grinding stones to make us whole.
- Recognizing how *illusion* aligns our human nature with our soul and the greater whole, we achieve a level of tranquility not previously possible.
- The forms of *illusion* and *equanimity* stabilize our new reactions, responses, and behaviors.

Maintaining a loving heart, mindfulness, and sovereignty.

- When we *cherish*, we feel worthy and will reconcile every personal paradigm or primary love template recycling our suffering.
- Our subsequent responses and dialectic discoveries use *grace*, *mindfulness*, and *love* to transform illusion into wisdom.
- The forms of *cherish*, *grace*, and *love* help solidify new perspectives to strengthen our incorruptible foundation.

Positive and negative experiences make us incorruptible.

- Syncing the intellectual, scientific, and psychological knowledge about the brain and how our emotional stress responses affect us creates self-sufficiency, sovereignty, and self-awareness.
- The experience of wholeness requires emotional maturity and empathic boundaries to deal with the expanded awareness within the greater whole.
- The forms of empathy and incorruptibility strengthen our reunification goal.

My intention as a writer is to offer a comprehensive ontology about human experience with insights expanded by standing on the shoulders of many wise and revered philosophers. Realizations and the discoveries garnered from fighting my own flying monkeys and a lifetime of service to thousands of people provide prospective. Wrestling side-by-side with clients as they tackle their illusions has offered opportunities for me to notice what works and what doesn't. I am compelled to share my insights, philosophies, and knowledge about "monkey holds, rescues, and rehab strategies" because I want everyone to climb out of their cave of shadows.

Each person has a role within society, and when we realize that all the roles called "good" or "bad" are integral parts of divinity, humanity may understand why diversity exists. When henosis becomes our personal and collective destiny, relieving human suffering will become a priority. In *The Wizard of Oz*, a Kansas twister, flying monkeys, and the Wicked Witch of the West served as millstones and improved the Wizard and Dorothy's destiny. Let's review because I believe if it happened in Oz, it can happen in our world as well.

SOMETHING DIES INSIDE WHEN WE BELIEVE OUR LIES

Magicians, ventriloquists, and illusionists have delighted audiences and enchanted people with deceptive tricks since antiquity. Deception is a form of fleeting power that is never sustainable. Plato said, "Everything that deceives may be said to enchant."[1] Historically, the con artist type has little desire to make an "honest living," and a traveling circus was one great way to use their manipulative skills to earn money. Back in our fairy tale, in *The Wonderful Wizard of Oz*, Oscar Zoroaster Phadrig Isaac Norman Henkle Emmannuel Ambroise Diggs was such a man. Born in the no-nonsense town of Omaha, Nebraska, with a tongue twister of a name, as a showman he needed one catchy name for his magic show. But abbreviating his name to O.Z.P.I.N.H.E.A.D. only invited snickers, so Oscar Zoroaster suddenly became "The Great and Powerful Oz," someone perceived as invincible.

In the story of Oz, illusionists traveled from town to town in hot air balloons. When Oscar Zoroaster inadvertently landed in the faraway Land of Oz, fortune smiled upon this circus showman. Mistaking Oscar for a great sorcerer, the inhabitants of Oz made him the supreme ruler and built the Emerald City in his honor. Oscar received his wand not from merit but because *people wanted a wizard*. The citizens *projected* a collective illusion and vision onto Oscar to suit the wants and desires of the community. How could any illusionist with sticky fingers turn down such a seductive offer?

Munchkins idealize wizards like children idealize parents. The weak project powers not possessed onto others to feel safe and secure—even if the other person may not actually possess that power. Adolescents abhor hypocrisy and rail against parents and authority figures struggling with integrity issues. Dorothy and her companions went through a similar disappointing realization when Toto revealed Oscar as *not* a Great and All-Powerful Wizard.

Initially Oscar Zoroaster had a win/win situation: the citizens believed they had found a wizard, and Oscar got a comfy job with great benefits. Happy with his exalted position but frightened of being discovered as a fraud, Oscar protected his identity by becoming a recluse who never let his servants or anyone else see him. He also privately hired Glinda the Good to teach him conjuring skills and sorcery secrets to keep up the charade. Living as a recluse, he tried to prevent the wicked witches from discovering his true identity. Skilled in the art of smoke and mirrors, Oscar created the great and all-powerful shapeshifter persona to give the people what they wanted—a wizard, a lord, a guru, a supreme protective power. Maintaining his reputation with his subjects became Oscar's priority because he risked losing everything if revealed as a fraud.

Something inside dies when we believe our lies. Illusion begets delusion—like that old adage that one lie leads to another. When Oscar became the wizard that others wanted him to be, a web of deception imprisoned him. As a self-imposed recluse, he hid behind curtains of fear and manipulated Dorothy and her companions to do his dirty work. "Liquidating" the Wicked Witch of the West secured his livelihood. Portraying the archetype of a corrupt politician, the wizard may have started off with a hint of noble intentions. In the process of securing power, the showman surrendered his integrity.

Oscar accidentally gained power, but, like the classic cliché, he sold his soul to get it. This story offers a timeless example about the illusion of power, where principles become negotiable if the end justifies the means. However, just like Dorothy and the rest of humanity, Oscar also already had everything he needed all along.

Wizards do not frequent my office very often, but if Oscar did, I would help him figure out what happened or was missing that started the delusion that he must have an alter ego to feel whole. A discussion about his higher, emotional, and reptilian brains would ensue to examine if maintaining his "Great and All-Powerful Wizard of Oz" persona originated from a primary love template or a personal paradigm based upon previous trauma. Every unexamined monkey recycling an infant, child, or adolescent stress response, which refuses to accept and/or appreciate who Oscar really was, would be examined. Compliments would be given to Oscar for having the courage to admit his mistakes and make amends when he helped Dorothy reach her destiny. By abdicating his throne and promoting the Scarecrow, Oscar unified his kingdom and his decisions enriched the whole. Honesty, generosity, and wisdom flourished after he was humbled.

Idealistically, leaders serve others rather than manipulating the citizenry to serve the ruler and/or that ruler's personal noble cause. When Toto unveiled his deception, Oscar took responsibility for his actions and offered sage advice to Dorothy and her companions before abdicating his title of Supreme Ruler of Oz. Oscar acted like the wizard everyone thought he was when his self-imposed enchantments shattered. Admitting his flaws freed up the wizard within that he *really* was. Oscar redeemed himself when he valiantly renounced his throne to the *Scarecrow*, bravely fired up his balloon to bring Dorothy home, and offered her companions the following eternal wisdom, ". . . And remember my sentimental friend that a heart is not judged by how much you love, but by how much you are loved by others."[2]

SACRED ANTAGONISTS AND INCORRUPTIBILITY

"Oh—You're a very bad man!"
"Oh, no my dear. I'm a very good man. I'm just a very bad Wizard."[3]

Sacred antagonists serve a useful purpose because adversity tests our mettle and can make us incorruptible. Fairy tales are powerful teachers because complex concepts are simplified so that the paradoxes of life can be easily comprehended. Bad wizards, wicked witches, and mysterious illusions will enchant and release screeching flying monkeys in our head. Impulsive thinking to satisfy primal desires and/or sacrificing scruples to manipulate others will corrupt. Pretending to be Great and All-Powerful, those illusions will shrink into a simple humbug and hide behind the curtain like Oscar, when we access our sovereignty and become incorruptible. Before Toto opened the curtain, Oscar was a living example of how delusion even enchants the illusionist.

And similarly, returning to Kansas on her own was inconceivable to Dorothy until her illusion of powerlessness was revealed. Trial and tribulation strengthen our ability to transform perceptions of reality and accept the paradoxes designed to make us whole. Loving others from the bottom of our heart expresses a particular form of love that originates from our soul, which resides in a state of perpetual wholeness. When we retain our ability to be love throughout our life, like Dorothy modeled during her ordeal, we become the divine architect of our own experience.

Possessing commendable boundaries and high self-esteem, Dorothy modeled love and empathy for her companions. She removed rust from the Tin Man, restuffed the Scarecrow, and soothed the fears of the Cowardly Lion but maintained equanimity. Loving without expectation and not judging her adversaries reminded her companions of their own worthiness, divine essence, and lovability. In turn, those beloved characters loved her, dedicated themselves to their personal dream, and helped Dorothy fulfill hers.

Dorothy Gale embodied Plato and Plotinus's forms and liberated herself from the illusion that a wizard, holy man, guru, or healer was required to unshackle her. Initially swept up by a Kansas twister, her homesick heart proved to be incorruptible. The form of illusion, working through Dorothy's traveling companions, the Wizard, the wicked witches, and others, offered experiences for Dorothy to endure along the yellow brick road. She dealt with her "orphan" illusion that she did not belong and opened doors for others to renounce the illusions blocking their destinies. Mastering illusion requires wrestling matches with flying monkeys. When Dorothy realized her destiny was always within reach, her awareness became an empowerment transmission. The wisdom garnered from Dorothy's leadership was transmitted to others through example as opposed to advice offered from a wizard accustomed to smoke and mirrors.

Illusion provides humanity with the perfect storylines to prepare us to become sovereign and access divinity to reach our destiny. Life provides myriads of mirrors for us to see our reflection to create the inner unity necessary to experience wholeness externally. When the Wizard was corrupted, he provided Dorothy and her companions the challenges that eventually liberated each character from their shadows. The discoveries these beloved characters realized are no different than our collective destiny. We wrestle with illusions suited to fit our most treasured fears, and those illusions guide us toward empowerment. When we can retain our equanimity and incorruptibility in the midst of the fiery smoke and terrifying mirrors employed by the form of illusion, the promise of wholeness gets stronger.

In the 1939 film, do you remember when the Wizard instructed Dorothy and her companions to obtain the broomstick of the Wicked Witch in one climactic scene? In the original book, Oscar initially revealed himself as a disembodied green head to Dorothy Gale, a fairy princess to the Scarecrow, a giant beast with horns to the Tin Man, and a ball of flame burning in the air to the Cowardly Lion. Each of them was presented with a personalized terrifying image tailored to trigger that character's individual weakness. Often delivered in a terrifying manner, illusion has an underlying earnest intention to empower.

Viktor Frankl described a similar process that occurred in his life during a forced march as a prisoner during World War II. Instead of the suffering and inhumanity, he focused his attention upon his wife and her beautiful smile to transcend the terrible conditions of the Holocaust. Like the real-life example from Viktor, Dorothy Gale was a model of sovereignty, the embodiment of divinity and incorruptibility throughout her fairy tale ordeal in Oz. When she realized that the Wizard was phony, Frank Baum described her private thoughts about Oscar in the following way: "Dorothy said nothing. Oz had not kept the promise he made her, but he had done his best. So she forgave him. As he said, he was a good man, even if he was a bad Wizard."[4]

WE ALREADY HAVE WHAT WE NEED

Plotinus said, "But when he [the sage] is experiencing pleasures, health, and lack of pain, he will not consider them an addition to his happiness, nor, when he is in the opposite condition, will he consider them a negation or diminution of it. If one condition does not add anything to a subject, how could the opposite condition take anything away from it?"[5] The Wizard and the Wicked Witch of the West demonstrated that happiness is not sustainable when we rely on someone or something outside of ourselves to provide it. The Holy Grail metaphor symbolizes an exalted goal I believe is a metaphor for the secret of enduring happiness. Love and joy are the natural states of our soul, which is essentially who and what we are. The form of illusion provides mental mirages and seductive solutions from outside sources, which fail to sustain due to their temporal nature. A timeless entity, joy will endure when we let go of our addiction to quick fixes. Perfectionism and self-criticism originating from primary templates and personal paradigms need loving solutions. Civilizations, sages, and philosophers have always attempted to define the purpose for existence, and those definitions consistently evolve. When Aristotle talked about happiness as a lifelong process of fulfilling one's purpose, he may have had similar definitions about the nature of happiness in mind. Even if he defined happiness differently, his concept about fulfilling our purpose remains as salient today as it was in ancient Greece.

Impulsive pleasures are very addictive, and many of us behave like petulant children chasing after butterflies. However, love and joy are by-products of an internal journey. Henosis is often realized momentarily when our personality and divinity dance together in a unified field of love. Due to human nature, we experience wholeness on occasion and can re-experience it repeatedly. The forms help us to become incorruptible and eventually experience a unified state of self-empowerment. Dorothy, the Wizard, you and I—*we were empowered the very moment our souls came into being*. When Dorothy Gale and her companions were inspired by Glinda's words of encouragement, insurmountable mountains became molehills. Their illusion about needing wizards and external sources of power vanished. Like most of us, the characters in this story experienced the power of each form at one time or another without logically knowing how forms work or what was happening.

We need both friends *and* antagonists pulling our curtains so we can notice our illusions, transcend the shadows, and fulfill our destiny. Walking through all the beauty and ugliness while expressing the forms helped Dorothy and her companions return to where they came from, a place of oneness and wholeness. The Wicked Witch was Dorothy's sacred antagonist. Many of us would not seek solutions without the motivation suffering imposes. Sovereign and incorruptible by the end of the shared adventure, each character in Oz realized that each already possessed everything they needed all along—in real life we also possess all that we need to return home.

HENOSIS IS OUR HOME

> When there enters into a glow from the Divine, the soul gathers strength, spreads true wings, and, however distracted by its proximate environment, speeds its buoyant way to something greater. . . .
> Its very nature bears it upwards, lifted by the Giver of that love. . . .
> Surely we need not wonder that It possesses the power to draw the soul to Itself, calling it back from every wandering to rest before It.
> From it came everything; nothing is mightier.—Plotinus[6]

In this quote written approximately two thousand years ago, Plotinus suggested true empowerment occurs when we move beyond the distractions of our proximate environment and access the glow of the divine mirrored by our soul. Approximately six hundred years earlier, Plato suggested that people were born shackled prisoners in a cave of shadows, transfixed by flickering illusions dancing on walls posing as reality. Prisoners liberated themselves by exploring the sunlit world above . . . free to think and be their divine selves. Goodness was Plato's word for the glow Plotinus referenced. If humanity embodied the *Forms* located within divinity, we would experience henosis as our soul spreads its wings.

A thousand years ago the French poet Chretien de Troyes wrote *Perceval, the Story of the Grail*, which described the same journey as a quest to find the metaphorical Holy Grail. Adapted into English, the story evolved into the classic story of *King Arthur and the Knights of the Round Table*. During a forced march during the Holocaust in World War II, Viktor Frankl overcame his circumstances, became incorruptible, and experienced wholeness that Chretien de Troyes called the Holy Grail. In *The Matrix* film series, the Wachowski siblings reintroduced Plato's Allegory of the Cave concept when Neo took the *red pill* and went down the rabbit hole (Plato's prisoner left his cave and saw the light). He eventually mastered every illusion within the Matrix.

When a story endures and is retold to each generation, immortal wisdom lies within. *The Wonderful Wizard of Oz* is another such story whose imagery is completely embedded in our society despite being penned over a century ago. Many of the characters in Baum's enlightened tale provide important role models and maps to return home.

When challenged, heroes and heroines take action for righteous causes that reveal their core principles, underlying beliefs, and enlightened motivations. Empowerment occurs through our total commitment to evolve as circumstances change, and every one of these timeless stories demonstrates this necessary skill brilliantly. Exploring our known and unknown attitudes about the efficacy of pain and the purpose of punishment is another important crossroad along the way to our ultimate destination: liberation from suffering. Suffering and its parasitic mirrors will suck the life out of our dreams, if we continue as many of our ancestors have, by embracing pain as our primary teacher.

The major milestone to our reunification goal is finding out how to access our wisdom within and to discover what makes us loving and joyful—rather than using pain and suffering as our only teacher of what *not* to do. Physical existence provides an opportunity for each of us to unify body, heart, mind, and soul to fulfill our potential. It takes courage to leave victim/perpetrator paradigms and primary love templates of retaliation, retribution, and redemption frequented by terrorists, martyrs, and most of humanity. Consider forgiveness, self-responsibility, and the form of incorruptibility, which dignifies everyone.

Too many of us have accepted dogma or scripture that promotes human unworthiness. The form of incorruptibility tests and retests our sense of worthiness and challenges our will and resolve until our principles become unbreakable. Inner peace, mindfulness, and love, paradoxically, can harden equanimity into incorruptible steel. I believe that when enough people access incorruptible blueprints of our inherent worthiness, we will collectively transform the victim/perpetrator paradigms and primary love templates plaguing our world today. Terrorism and victimhood have nothing to do with an enlightened solution. If you are tempted to "teach someone a lesson," a lesson is waiting for you. Consult your soul; ask for divine guidance, wisdom, willpower, and the strength of character to act appropriately to bridge the troubling gaps.

In the future, if you were victimized, how would you answer the following questions to become more invincible and immune to illusion?

- How can I maintain my scruples, integrity, and humanity while sensing another's angst, suffering, or fear?
- During my ordeal, will I love others and myself fully?
- Can I respond with grace and dignity without retaliating?
- Will I surrender, embrace mystery, and transform misery during tragedy?
- By demonstrating cruelty, what gift is my antagonist offering me?
- When hatred is pointed at me, how might I respond mindfully?

Wholeness is a voluntary state of being, not one imposed by others. Terrorists hope to improve the world by taking control and making others suffer to change their circumstances. The victim/perpetrator paradigm misses the mark because perpetrating violence and retaliation creates more victims, which is the same behavior the perpetrators condemn in their adversary. Incorporating principles and values while nothing seems to be working and maintaining equanimity in our chaotic world is extremely hard to do. Can mankind stop killing and controlling others for security reasons? If tempted or provoked to "teach lessons," we must strive to fully embrace our soul's wisdom to respond appropriately and embody the form of incorruptibility.

Love is stronger than any force in the universe, especially hatred. Incorruptibility is an enlightened form, usually appearing at the end of the yellow brick road because it incorporates each of the previous forms. Many philosophers before me have suggested the world will eventually change one heart at a time. I have included their quotes in this book because I agree with them. Forty years as a psychotherapist and transformational teacher has taught me how long it takes to release our individual and familial templates. I can only wonder how long it will take for humanity to become whole globally. In his famous book *Hind Swaraj* (1909), Mahatma Gandhi challenged his fellow countrymen when he declared that British rule existed in India due to their implicit cooperation. Paradigms collapse without cooperation was his conclusion. My wish is that humanity will one day stop cooperating with the victim/perpetrator paradigm and instead try to become incorruptible to illusion. When we can truly live as one people . . . on one planet . . . re-accessing the promise of wholeness, perhaps we can eventually experience what Plotinus dreamt long ago when he said:

> A pleasant life is theirs in heaven; they have the Truth for mother, nurse, real being, and nutriment; they see all things, not the things that are born and die, but those which have real being; and they see themselves in others. For them all things are transparent, and there is nothing dark or impenetrable, but everyone is manifest to everyone internally, and all things are manifest; for light is manifest to light. For everyone has all things in himself and sees all things in another; so that all things are everywhere and all is all and each is all, and the glory is infinite. Each of them is great, since the small also is great.
>
> In heaven the sun is all the stars, and again each and all are the sun. One thing in each is prominent above the rest; but it also shows forth all. There a pure movement reigns; for that which produces the movement, not being a stranger to it, does not trouble it. Rest is also perfect there, because no principle of agitation mingles with it.[7]

THERE'S NO PLACE LIKE HOME

Plato, Aristotle, and Plotinus recognized that *we are all one* and reminded us a long time ago to work together and remember our origins.

More and more we hear that we are all one, but unity remains an elusive quarry for most of humanity. We need to take the time to notice, learn, and listen with our heart and soul rather than using logic alone to arrive at what I believe is the ultimate goal of humanity—the promise of wholeness.

Each form is part of a continuum that arises and vanishes throughout our lives in a brilliant check and balance system. Forms are building blocks and foundational bricks, not necessarily accumulated or placed in any precise order. Wholeness, as a form, grows as we mature and evolves as we develop a heightened state of incorruptibility. Similarly to the infinity symbol from the original snake eating its tail named *ouroboros* in Greek antiquity, the forms have no tangible beginning or ending. Each form contains principles and values that fortify our foundation and pave the yellow brick road as we become immune to illusion.

The promise of wholeness *is* a paradox like the eye of hurricane, which remains stable even with chaos surrounding it. The forms are variables affecting each moment, so we can in essence return home and then remember how we got there. The form of wholeness is the full actualization of the realized wisdom that our soul came to earth to express while encased in the complicated dynamics of human nature. Plato and Plotinus likened the sun to how the divine emanates light and love. The things we believe are divine qualities are reminders of the purest forms of light. The epic challenge of a person is how to truly become one with all the good and bad, while remaining incorruptible and surrendering to unexpected outcomes. The promise of wholeness is precious, sacred, and worth the trouble . . . because we use it to create heaven on earth.

Let's review how the forms assist us:

- Illusion reveals our lies and every delusion we bury in our unconscious.
- Love is what we are and what we take with us when we die.
- Cherish is a grammar school primer containing the essence of love.
- Grace is being present in a state of awe and loving innocence.
- Equanimity combines, balances, and harmonizes the forms through mindfulness.

- Empathy is oneness with awareness of which illusions belong to whom.
- Incorruptibility incorporates principles, values, and each form in all situations.

Contemplate this summary of the forms and then read the form meditation about wholeness. Initially you may comprehend its meaning, but it is far more important to simply let these words penetrate your being. Plato understood a form to be a conscious form of light, a living entity that humanity could use for inspiration. Hold the intention to become one with the creative, continuous flow of intuitive love and wisdom within henosis.

For now, just read the following meditation and let the ideas open up your awareness. Try reading this form aloud to own the message. I also suggest taking a break after reading this and any other form meditation. Breathe in any remembered experience of feeling whole; then attempt to strengthen this form through intention with the Camel Wave Meditation in appendix A. The Wise and Loving Inner Voice Meditation in appendix B is useful to discern which internal voice within our brain provides useful directions or merely delusions. Explore the freedom of letting the ideas, the feelings, and the thoughts that the forms trigger simmer and then move onto the next section.

When you feel the need, you can return to the form meditation for wholeness and reread it over and over.

FORM MEDITATION: WHOLENESS

The continuity of life as divine being living in a physical body is the most perplexing problem I will encounter on earth. I ask myself, how can I be divine when I feel so stupid, thoughtless, and careless at times? How does wholeness work when humans endure such suffering? When I am at my best, I love myself and treat others as I would want them to treat me. I am thrilled if I occasionally find the wherewithal to express this form of love, which some call the "Golden Rule," while under duress or during a stress response. If I feel lost and alone, it takes a prodigious amount of courage to love others without any reciprocation as an expression of the principles and values within the form of incorruptibility.

I know that my soul came here to master all the forms (illusion, love, cherish, grace, equanimity, empathy, incorruptibility, and wholeness). When I took physical form, I left the divine to discover if I could become whole as a sovereign, incorruptible human being. Earth is my adopted home, where I test my ability to cherish without the reflection of divine love mirrored back to me in a boundless sea of illusion. I know now the form of illusion challenges and strengthens my principles, values, and incorruptibility so I can eventually forgo every dysfunctional template and paradigm recycling suffering.

Henosis is the unifying presence of the loving frequency of the divine that happens to be embedded within every atom of existence. By becoming one with all that is (including my pain and the suffering of other people) and incorporating the form of equanimity and empathy, I can revisit the state of oneness within the form of wholeness and feel the fullness of my divinity. Experiencing oneness within diversity is an attribute of the forms of love and cherish. My sense of wholeness feels as if it bursts from my heart, but actually its source truly originates from my soul and flows throughout my physical body. When this heightened form of love is infused into my thoughts, words, and deeds, the form of grace may suddenly appear like a beautiful butterfly.

"Pay it forward" is a popular phrase for the phenomenon of actively loving others without expecting or anticipating reciprocation, which is the essence of wholeness. Expressing this innate instinct and my inherent loving nature when I feel alone or abandoned I know is an expression of my divinity. This quality of the soul sustains others and myself during our stay on earth particularly during dark nights.

Experiencing equanimity and expressing love so elegantly no matter the difficulty requires a significant amount of bravery. This omniscient awareness is accessed from the perspective of my soul, which is eternally and fully connected to the oneness of the divine. I can feel whole momentarily, but it may disappear like a butterfly. Love cannot be contained or forced, and there are no special secrets that keep my connection regardless of the circumstances. I try to maintain this elegant form for extended periods because loving without expectation helps me accept my next obstacle preventing a longer stay.

World events are troubling sometimes, and people behave badly within the victim/perpetrator paradigm around the globe. My suffering and the suffering my loved ones experience are far from blissful. I do see the suffering of others, and my heart cares for them. I am aware that others' agony may stick to me if I fail to maintain appropriate boundaries as a daily practice. I do not need to walk down every painful path or suffer endlessly when others miss their mark. Therefore, I am free to experience all and let some emotions go—except the love. When I feel whole, illusion has no hold on me and love becomes an irresistible force bursting from my heart and soul. The principles and values I weave into my soul comfort me so completely to where death is preferable to abandoning the forms of love and wholeness within me.

When I renounce my illusions, fear fades, anger wanes, and love grows. If I let go and practice each form, love fills my voids. Then I am able to openly discuss, encourage, and welcome divergent attitudes, alternative solutions, or different ways of being. Every aspect of creation is valuable and an integral aspect of divinity. When I access oneness with expanded awareness, I sometimes experience the pain of another as my own. The form of empathy protects me when I make accurate assessments and apply appropriate solutions. I am aware that everyone is a divine creator, and this gives me comfort. I know the negative events enter my life for mysterious reasons, sometimes through no fault of my own. While I do not pretend to be immune to suffering, I remain tranquil in a state of equanimity and incorruptibility. When wholeness visits me like a butterfly, an inner peace descends upon me like a gentle rain that soothes my heart and soul. Equanimity blossoms and helps me feel a passionate sense of awe, innocence, and instinct to love others similarly.

A Greek proverb says, "A society grows great when old men plant trees whose shade they know they shall never sit in." When I stand strong like a sturdy tree and embody my principles and values even when nothing is working, I become incorruptible. Ignoring my natural instinct to love causes pain, isolation, and feelings of abandonment. Inviting the sun and wind into my being daily helps me embrace life's beauty. Good deeds are like pebbles thrown into a pond; the ripples of love radiate endlessly until they return to me. Henosis opens my heart, lets me recognize life's joys, and fuels my fondest dreams. By relishing everyone and everything around me, life's bounty is attracted to me. My pillar of light shining within reminds others of the promise of wholeness. I marvel when others gather round and want to be near me. When I accept others without conditions, I find my heart bursting from the love *directed toward me. The love and joy I experience creates mirrors of the same, attracting more love to me like ants under a picnic tree. Wholeness is the alpha and omega of life that opens the doors to the secrets of the universe and the mysteries of life after life because it's woven into the fabric of my soul.*

CONCLUDING REMARKS AND HOPES

The most difficult thing in life is to know yourself.—Thales of Miletus[1]

Thales of Miletus (624–546 BCE), the father of Greek philosophy, ignored the popular mythologies of his day and attempted to find the first principle or the universal essence within all of nature, matter, and human existence. Since ancient times, questions like these have perplexed humanity: Why are we here? What's out there? And what causes what? *The Promise of Wholeness* honors the organizing principle throughout the universe, which Plotinus determined was unity, and being Greek, "henosis" was the word he chose. Philosophy, literature, and psychology seek first principles and recognize our creative responsibilities. Eastern and Western wisdom traditions about love, illusion, and being human were invaluable resources as I wrote this book.

When I first read translations of Plato and Plotinus's philosophy, in particular their use of the words "Intellect" and "Beauty" confused me. Words are powerful symbols representing concepts from a frozen moment of time, so I researched what those words meant in ancient times and how those words evolved. Contemporary translations did not completely mesh with how the ancients used these terms—the Greeks intentionally capitalized words to indicate their significance and potent meaning. When I had this realization, everything Plato and Plotinus had said suddenly made sense; I discovered that Intellect in ancient Greece meant *all known wisdom* and Beauty described *all realized love.*

Plotinus thought humanity and every aspect of nature have the same divine essence within linking us all together. Previously, in chapter 2, I mentioned that the Greeks used the word *ova-la*, which means *essence, nature, or that which belongs to itself.* In ancient Greek ontology, *ova-la* interpenetrated all matter and explained how divinity existed within diversity. According to Plotinus, our spiritual goal was to become incorruptible through purification and embodying principles to express our divinity lying dormant within us. Ugliness or evil was seen as merely a false form like mud on a stainless statue. Reunification occurs when we see the universality of humanity (divine *ova-la*), which exists within everything in the external world as well as within ourselves. Empathic connection to our positive and negative experiences teaches our body, heart, mind, and soul to become incorruptible and achieve our henosis goal.

Plotinus studied human nature and described divinity with every tool at his disposal. After observing humanity's relationship with the physical world, every philosopher ends up talking about the principles and values that lead to inner peace, love, and wholeness. People learn from both wisdom and pain, which motivates humans to master the illusions recycling suffering and seek loving solutions. Knowing what to do differently next time after making a mistake is the goal. Knowledge accrues from actual experience. Failure motivates innovation. Creating strategies intended for the *highest good* of everyone, you included, and then surrendering to what happens is an enduring principle.

Empathic people naturally experience what others feel without hesitation. *Vonrov* is a Greek word describing how a mind interprets its experience. Until they learned about their empathic nature, my daughter Allison and client Ruth suffered from too much *pathos* and criticized themselves unmercifully for absorbing others' emotions. Once these women followed the suggestions offered in this book to cleanse the heart and create healthy catharsis, they could interpret their emotional swings with much more wisdom. Enchantments make us fall, but addressing our flaws helps us get back on our feet and working together benefits us all. Friendships based upon mutual respect, shared goals, and a mutual love for one another are potent tools to overcome obstacles.

As this book comes to a close, I hope your mind and heart were opened to new possibilities and strategies to help you become whole.

My intent while writing this book was to provide information and suggestions to help readers resolve their human paradoxes as they become incorruptible to illusion and return to henosis. I hope you take every idea offered in the book for a test drive. Keep what works and discard the rest. I learned a long time ago that one size really doesn't fit all, unless it is the promise of wholeness.

Clients often ask me if treating so many people in the midst of suffering is draining. I do get tired some days, but what really excites me and energizes my soul is passing on some hard-fought gem of wisdom or strategy to relieve another's agony. I hated being bullied in my youth, but every ounce of pain was worth the trouble when I see the excited faces of my clients who take my advice and stop their internal bullies once and for all. Being empathic, I experience a great deal of joy witnessing success and passing love forward.

Developing the emotional maturity to embody each form as best you can leads to enduring wholeness and happiness. Becoming incorruptible to illusion and seeking enlightenment are not simple tasks. Stand on the shoulders of the great philosophers and add to the collective wisdom of humanity. Please pass along what you learn and pay love forward to inspire others. And help others remember what Dorothy discovered in Oz—we have had the power all along to become whole and return home.

APPENDIX A

Camel Wave Meditation and Follow-Through Instructions

The Camel Wave Meditation incorporates aspects of the Tibetan Co-coon and Tummo breathing patterns, full-body wave movements, and intentional use of the forms explored in this book. This meditation can help remove primary love templates and victim/perpetrator paradigms and reveal our illusions. In the Tibetan language, *tummo*, pronounced *dumo* in English, literally means "inner fire." Breathing in the divine stokes our own inner fire to burn off illusion . . . thus strengthening our incorruptibility.

Your body is a sovereign vessel of light that occasionally needs to be recharged and realigned with divinity. The meditation itself has three aspects: breath, movement, and intention. When your spine undulates in a wave motion while breathing and with focus and passion, your body, heart, and mind quickly align with purpose. Inhaling the ideals infused within a form with a sincere desire to awaken similar qualities within is a powerful practice. Releasing the illusions that recycle your suffering restores your potential to transcend and/or transmute any obstacle.

This meditation gets its name from the camel pose in yoga, and similarly our heart will push forward in the middle of a wave motion when you trace the hump of a camel by undulating your body. In this meditation, your chest arches whether you start at your sacrum and continue to your head or reverse the motion. Practice breathing with intention and then undulate your spine in rhythm. Continue until both feel natural; then you are ready to complete Camel Wave Meditation.

By simply inhaling a form into your being, you can access its wisdom and then exhale a desire to incorporate that form into your daily life. This activity unifies your physical/spiritual nature and activates divine support. When your breathing, spinal movements, and intentions synchronize and work together in unison, those in effect become spiritual dental floss intent upon Roto-Rooting illusion. Heartfelt passion, focused intention, and the Camel Wave Meditation have a quantum-like effect to help you become more incorruptible. Problems are illuminated, debris clears, and solutions appear spontaneously with laser-like accuracy.

THE CAMEL WAVE MEDITATION

Notes: Choose a form you would like to focus on and reread the text quietly or out loud. Then go to a quiet, private area and get comfortable. You may choose to do this meditation while lying or sitting down with your head above your hips. You can lie face down with a pillow under your chest or turn over on your back with your knees cocked for leverage if those positions feel more comfortable. I suggest you lie on either side if that works easiest for you.

General Instructions

Begin with undulating your spine and arching your chest forward and backward in a natural wave-like motion. Do this wave motion from the base of your spine (sacrum) and let the wave travel to your head or vice versa. Tilt your pelvis and push your chest (heart) out as you inhale. Drop your shoulders and let your chest return during your exhalation. Undulate your back in a wave motion similar to traveling over the hump of a camel. Breathe naturally and develop your own rhythm. Continue until you feel comfortable with your wave motion. As you undulate, imagine the form cleansing your spine and every nerve center along the way all the way down to the base of your spine like spiritual dental floss.

Choose a form and slowly inhale those ideals into your body; then exhale your intention to incorporate these qualities into your life.

On inhaling, set your intention to **receive** the essential qualities of that form. Continue the Camel Wave motion by undulating your spine, and let awareness of the physical effort fade into the background until your breathing and movements eventually go into automatic pilot. As you inhale, focus upon the form you selected and internally whisper its name for inspiration.

On exhaling, hold your intention to **embody** the qualities of your selected form in your life. For example, you could internally whisper a Suggested Form Phrase (see below) or words or phrases you prefer as you exhale. Shortening the phrase to one word makes everything easier. Purposeful intention and soulful passion are more important than rote behavior.

Some meditations invite you to be empty, but the Camel Wave Meditation incorporates many activities. When the mind focuses on forms and movements, memories, insights, and/or emotions will emerge, so as those come, go with the flow of the wave and process this new information with awareness. Stay present and remain in the moment to witness what wants to happen so you can grow, heal, and evolve. Return to your breath, movement, and intention when gaps appear and the original energies feel complete.

Suggested Intentions and Form Phrases

Notes: Your full attention will be required to notice subtle changes in your body, track memories you may unearth, and/or release buried emotions and immature decisions surfacing while using the Camel Wave. It is difficult to conceptually capture the quintessential essence of a form during an inhalation; therefore I have included a suggestion for an intention for each form. While you breathe and undulate your spine, shorten these to two to four-word phrases to capture the essence of the form and whisper those words as you exhale.

Here are some suggested phrases and intentions:

Table 10.1.   Camel Wave

INHALE	EXHALE	SUGGESTED INTENTION
Illusion	Reveal my illusions	Reveal my illusions so I can transform and transcend them.
Love	Be love	Show me where and how I can become more loving.
Cherish	Be cherishing	I cherish self and others.
Grace	Embody grace	Presence, awe, and loving intentions.
Equanimity	Be balanced	I wish to be balanced in my physical, emotional, mental, and spiritual life.
Empathy	Boundary awareness	Assist my emotional awareness and show me where I absorb another's suffering.
Incorruptibility	Maintain my principles	Embody my principles until I reach a state of incorruptibility.
Wholeness	Become whole	Embody inner peace, mindfulness, and love.

Combining Breath with the Forms to Heal Specific Physical, Emotional, or Mental Problems

Inhale the selected form; then exhale your intention to surrender to whatever it takes to resolve your issue physically, emotionally, and/or mentally. Duplicate the general instructions for the Camel Wave Meditation but also place the specific problem you need help with in your heart. If you can feel the problem, go to the place where it exists energetically or physically and put your focus on this location. Inhale the form you selected and move it into your heart or the place of discomfort. You may spontaneously change forms.

Be aware of these points:

- Memories, insights, physical releases, and/or emotional material may occur. Unconscious beliefs, emotional trauma, and addictive illusions sometimes take time to emerge so maintain your focus, undulate your spine, and let your breath act like ocean waves eroding a beach, clearing emotional debris and/or revealing what wants to transform.

- Unconscious primary love templates and personal paradigms may emerge, which originated when we were so young there are no words and/or concrete memories to retrieve. Empathic individuals can absorb problems from others like Velcro, and this meditation is good at clearing accumulated emotional debris. Continue the undulating wave motion and breathing rhythm until any emotional energy releases to remove any unconscious template or paradigm blocking your path.
- Make note of inner guidance you receive and decide which behavioral, emotional, and mental adjustments need to change to incorporate this form.

HOUR-BY-HOUR AND DAY-BY-DAY MONITORING

Incorporate the inner guidance you receive into practice and check in hour by hour or day by day to determine if any new suggestions actually work in the long term. If any suggestion misses the mark, remember any distinguishing characteristics of that internal voice and redo the Camel Wave Meditation with the intention to get better information. The Wise and Loving Inner Voice Meditation can be used to sort out which inner voice holds wisdom or illusion and works well with this meditation.

APPENDIX B

Wise and Loving Inner Voice Meditation

Crows, monkeys, and people have two voices, one is conversational and the other warns its clan about impending danger. Have you ever thought you were listening to loving inner guidance or sage advice and later discovered you were snookered by an inner voice mired in illusion pitching some harebrained delusion? Untreated trauma, unconscious templates, and dysfunctional personal paradigms have belief systems, logic patterns, and vocal signatures you can learn to recognize. Infant, child, and adolescent stress responses can activate screeching monkeys and cawing crows sensing danger.

The Wise and Loving Inner Voice Meditation provides a reliable method to examine and evaluate every interior voice within your mind. Their logic patterns and vocal signatures can be recognized. Wise and loving solutions endure over time. Screeching monkeys and cawing crows fixate on danger and may not be connected to your heart and soul. However, we all have access to an inner voice that suddenly appears like a hummingbird and offers sage advice and enduring love. Discerning conversational eternal wisdom from internal voices that promote illusion is the goal of this meditation.

Noticing how we recycle our dysfunctional templates, paradigms, and dramas infected with illusion is imperative for maturation. Your evolution into the higher realms of consciousness and personal sovereignty requires access to your wise and loving inner voice that knows how to embody all the forms. An essential aspect of this meditation is noticing and recognizing when illusion grabs the microphone in your head. Memorizing the distinguishing vocal characteristics of your internal hummingbird is a valuable asset.

You can access your enlightened inner voice and evolve intentionally when you ask the question "What is the most loving thing I can do?" and follow the guidance received regularly. Intention and passion can flip the ignition switch, engage the engines of creation, and access accurate vocal discernment. Misguided mental strategies create suffering and become your destiny if you lack the intellectual curiosity or the emotional maturity to distinguish your hummingbird's conversational whisper from cawing crows and screeching monkeys. Intention, passion, and consistent action toward your goals awaken matching supportive energy from the universe. You can enter the quantum field when your body, heart, and soul align their collective wisdom and love with your inner hummingbird voice helping you reach your goal.

The Wise and Loving Inner Voice Meditation helps:

- identify the logic patterns and vocal signatures of your inner voices;
- provide a format to distinguish loving wisdom from debilitating illusions;
- unify our physical, emotional, mental, and spiritual natures; and
- access positive intention to revise missteps and take corrective action.

This meditation uses repetition and practice, which create reliable outcomes, to help sort out your internal voice that possesses loving wisdom versus the inner voices mired in illusion. It may be useful to reread any of the forms that speak to you and do the Camel Wave Meditation to find the most mature inner hummingbird voice within your higher brain that can access the wisdom and love of your soul.

STEPS TO THE WISE AND LOVING INNER VOICE MEDITATION

1. Ask yourself with heartfelt desire, what is the most loving thing I can do?

   Center yourself and hold the intention to connect to your loving and wise inner voice that embodies the forms outlined in this book. The ultimate goal is to connect to your hummingbird voice, which whispers guidance from your soul to meet a personal need, want, or private desire, while remaining in alignment with all of divinity, as opposed to listening to the cawing crows and screeching monkeys of the unexamined, unconscious mind mired in illusion.

2. Determine a course of action.

   Listen carefully for inner guidance from the hummingbird within and notice its logic, tonal, and distinguishing qualities before following through with its recommendations. Remember your hummingbird converses and nurtures your heart and soul, but listen also to those voices fixated on danger and suffering.

3. During the activity chosen, revisit your inquiry to ask, does this behavior still feel loving now?

   Halfway through the activity, check in physically, emotionally, and mentally to see if you concur that the course taken feels like loving, sage advice. If your need, want, or desire is being addressed appropriately, complete the activity, but check in regularly to see if your original strategy feels wise and loving over time.

4. Check again repeatedly after completing the activity.

   Review and reassess your results an hour later, the next day, or sometime during the following week. Ask yourself, "Does this behavior still feel like loving, sage advice now?" You can even check a month or a year later to determine if the behavior you chose still feels loving and wise.

   If the answer is yes all the way through, you have accessed your wisest inner voice and aligned your physical body, emotions, and actions (three-legged stool) to loving wisdom. Consistent feedback from the external world lets you know if you chose a long-term loving strategy and actually accessed the hummingbird within whispering your soul's wisdom.

5. Failing leads to success.

   Become Sherlock Holmes and identify as many details as you can about the inner voices that may be deceiving you. Whenever an activity or strategy doesn't feel loving anymore, it means that the Wise and Loving Inner Voice Meditation ferreted out an immature inner crow or monkey struggling with illusion. Memorize the behavioral strategies, emotional qualities, and mental perspectives of each inner voice for future reference.

6. Get back on your feet in the following ways:

   - Forgive yourself for missteps.
   - Let go of any punishment paradigms.
   - Re-access your positive intention.
   - Decide what you want to do differently.
   - Repeat the meditation again.

Intentions possess royal qualities and provide a divine spark to start the engines of creation. If you don't like what you created, the Wise and Loving Voice Meditation helps you reboot your positive intention and chart a new course of action. Cawing crows and screeching monkeys warn us about danger until they get noticed. We want love, wisdom, and enlightened solutions to suffering, but sometimes our personalities are shackled by ignorance and immaturity. The Wise and Loving Inner Voice Meditation reminds us to re-access the positive intention when we make mistakes until we find our hummingbird inner voice. Letting go of punishing ourselves for a misstep is a powerful practice and an integral aspect of this meditation. All we need to do is dust ourselves off, open our mind to another possibility, and listen again for our wise and loving inner voice.

This exercise is a powerful practice that distinguishes hummingbird wisdom from illusion. When we ignore the templates, paradigms, and stress responses duality offers, we can forgive ourselves or an adversary's mistakes by accessing the need, want, or desire behind our intention to take advantage of enlightened perspectives and enduring solutions.

NOTES

PROLOGUE

1. Plato, *Theaetetus*, translated by Harold Fowler (Cambridge, MA: Harvard University Press, 1921), 155d.

2. *Ontology* is a Greek word, combining *onto* (which means being, that which is or I am; verb), and *logia* (logical discourse); thus, the study of that which comes to be.

3. William Ralph Inge, *The Philosophy of Plotinus, Volume II*, Gifford Lectures at St. Andrews, 1917–1918 (Eugene, OR: Wipf and Stock Publishers, 2003), 106.

4. Plato, *The Republic*, V, trans. Desmond Lee (New York: Penguin Books, 1955), 457c.

I. ANCIENT PERSPECTIVES ABOUT WHOLENESS

1. Please note that, throughout the book, I refer to *The Wonderful Wizard of Oz* in reference to the original book published by the George M. Hill Company in 1900. Mentions of *The Wizard of Oz* refer to the 1939 MGM film, which varies greatly from the original story penned by L. Frank Baum.

2. Plotinus, *The Six Enneads*, trans. Stephen MacKenna and B. S. Page, accessed at http://classics.mit.edu/Plotinus/enneads.html, V.1.2.

3. William Ralph Inge, *The Philosophy of Plotinus* (London: Forgotten Books, 2012), 7.

4. Plotinus, *The Six Enneads*, IV.8.1.

5. Ibid., VI.5.1.

6. Plato, *The Republic*, V, 473c.

7. Porphyry, "Life of Plotinus," *Theosophy* 25, no. 3 (January 1937): 101–110, accessed at http://www.wisdomworld.org/setting/plotinus.html.

8. For the purposes of this book, I use the term "delusion" defined as mistaken belief that endures despite compelling evidence to the contrary, rather than a psychotic hallucination that is bizarre or grandiose and/or may contain an implausible delusion associated with a severe mental health disorder.

9. Plotinus, *The Six Enneads*, I.6.9.

10. Most famous of the secret religious rites of ancient Greece (*Encyclopedia Britannica*, accessed at http://www.britannica.com/topic/Eleusinian-Mysteries).

11. Jalal al-Din Rumi, "A Community of the Spirit," in *The Essential Rumi*, trans. Coleman Barks (New York: HarperOne, 2004), 3.

12. Plato, *The Republic*, VII (paraphrase of conclusion).

13. Plato, *Apology, Crito, and Phaedo of Socrates*, trans. Henry Clay (Philadelphia, PA: David McKay Publisher, 1897), 32a.

14. Inge, *The Philosophy of Plotinus*, 208.

15. Ibid., 123.

16. Swami Krishnananda, *Studies in Comparative Philosophy* (Rishkesh, India: The Divine Life Society, 1999), 26.

2. ILLUSION AND THE PARADOX OF BEING HUMAN

1. Aristotle, *Nicomachean Ethics*, vol. 19, trans. H. Rackman (Cambridge, MA: Harvard University Press, 1934), 1098a16.

2. Yogananda, "Self-Realization Fellowship Glossary," http://www.yogananda-srf.org/glossary/Glossary_R_%E2%80%93_S.aspx#.VEQeyldV0g4.

3. A. H. Armstrong, *Plotinus*, volumes I–VII (Cambridge, MA: Harvard University Press, 1984), V.9.10

4. Plotinus, *The Six Enneads*, III.2.15.

5. Dr. Seuss, *How the Grinch Stole Christmas* (New York: Random House, 1957), 30. Animated television special version from December 18, 1966, accessed at http://ninjamonkeyspy.livejournal.com/585154.html.

6. Elizabeth Beard, "Public Penance, Public Salvation: An Exploration of the Black Death's Influence on the Flagellant Movement," 2013, accessed at http://history.ucsc.edu/under-graduate/undergraduate-research/electronic-journal/journal-pdfs/1415_Beard.pdf.

7. Giacomo Rizzolatti et al., "Premotor Cortex and the Recognition of Motor Actions," *Cognitive Brain Research* 3, no. 2 (1996): 131–141.

8. Albert Einstein, paraphrase of energy equivalence from his theory of special relativity, 1905.

9. Laozi, *Tao Te Ching*, trans. Feng Gia-Fu (New York Vintage Books, 1972), chapter 27.

10. Plotinus, *The Six Enneads*, I.4.4.

11. Aristotle, *Nicomachean Ethics*, II, 1109a27.

12. Plato, *Apology*, 39d.

13. Plato, *The Republic*, 566e.

14. Alphonse Marie Louis de Prat de Lamartine, *France and England: A Vision of the Future* (London: H. G. Clarke & Co., 1848), 24.

15. John Dalberg-Acton, 1st Baron Acton, letter to Bishop Creighton (1887), accessed at https://en.wikipedia.org/wiki/ John_Dalberg-Acton,_1st_Baron_Acton.

16. Plato, *Theaetetus*, 176a–177a.

17. Inge, *The Philosophy of Plotinus*, 213.

18. Confucius, "The Doctrine of the Mean," accessed at https://en.wikiquote.org/wiki/Confucius.

19. Plotinus, I.2.1, in Grace H. Turnbull, *The Essence of Plotinus* (New York: Oxford University Press, 1948), 22.

20. Paul Pearsall, *The Heart's Code* (New York: Broadway Books, 1998), 62–63.

21. Plotinus, *The Six Enneads*, VI.5.2.

22. Pierre Hadot, *Plotinus or The Simplicity of Vision*, trans. Michael Chase (Chicago: University of Chicago Press, 1976), 54.

23. Plotinus, *The Six Enneads*, I.1.1.

24. Turnbull, *The Essence of Plotinus*, 22.

25. John of the Cross, *The Dark Night of the Soul*, trans. E. Allison Peers (Mineola, NY: Dover Publications, 2003).

26. Edwin Wallace, *Aristotle's Psychology* (Cambridge: Cambridge University Press, 1882), 61.

27. Armstrong, *Plotinus*, I.2.6.

3. MERGING HUMANNESS WITH LOVE

1. Plato, *Symposium*, fourth speech of Aristophanes, 193 (sourced from Professor Brandon Cook, http://www.uky.edu/look/Phi%20260-Symposium.pdf).

2. Inge, *Philosophy of Plotinus*, 225.

3. Rumi, *Rumi Daylight: A Daybook of Spiritual Guidance*, trans. C. A. Helminski (Boston: Shambhala, 1990).

4. Armstrong, *Plotinus*, IV.8.4.

4. THE CHERISHED HUMAN

1. Plato, *The Republic*, VI, 508e–509c.

2. Rumi, "There's Nothing Ahead," *The Essential Rumi*, 205.

3. Plotinus, *The Six Enneads*, IV.3.2.

4. *The Matrix*, directed by the Wachowski Brothers (Burbank, CA: Warner Brothers, 1999).

5. Laozi, *Tao Te Ching*, chapter 57.

6. Armstrong, *Plotinus*, IV.3.11, VI.4.2.

5. GRACE

1. Plato, *Phaedrus*, trans. Paul Woodruff (Indianapolis, IN: Hackett Publishing Company, 1995), 235c.

2. L. Frank Baum, *The Marvelous Land of Oz* (Chicago: Reilly & Britton, 1904), 103.

3. John Burnet, *Early Greek Philosophy*, 3rd edition (London: A & C Black, Ltd., 1920).

4. Laozi, *Tao Te Ching*, chapter 16.

5. Plotinus, *The Six Enneads*, V.5.12.

6. Ibid., I.6.8.

7. Ibid., VI.6.18

8. Plato, *Apology*, 17.

6. MINDFULNESS, SOULFULNESS, AND EQUANIMITY

1. Hadot, *Plotinus or the Simplicity of Vision*, VI.4.14, 28.

2. *Legend of Bagger Vance*, directed by Robert Redford (Universal City, CA: Dreamwork Pictures, 2000), script accessed at http://www.script-o-rama.com/movie_scripts/l/legend-of-bagger- vance-script.html.

3. Steven Covey, *The Seven Habits of Highly Effective People: Powerful Lessons in Personal Change* (New York: Simon and Schuster, 1989), 12.

4. Anne Frank, *The Diary of a Young Girl* (New York: Doubleday, 1996), 192.

5. Armstrong, *Plotinus*, IV.4.17.

6. Plotinus, *The Six Enneads*, III.1.10.7.

7. Ibid., II.3.15.

8. *Legend of Bagger Vance*.

9. Hadot, *Plotinus or The Simplicity of Vision*, V.8.11, 34.

10. Helen Schucman, *A Course in Miracles* (New York: Viking, 1996), chapter 16, IV, 6.

7. THE BRAIN

1. *The Wizard of Oz* (1939, film).

2. Baum, *The Wonderful Wizard of Oz*, 21.

3. I. McGilchrist, "Reciprocal Organization of the Cerebral Hemispheres," *Dialogues in Clinical Neuroscience* 12, no. 4 (December 2010): 503–515.

4. D. Hecht, "Cerebral Lateralization of Pro- and Anti-Social Tendencies," *Experimental Neurobiology* 23, no. 1 (March 2014): 1–27.

5. McGilchrist, "Reciprocal Organization of the Cerebral Hemispheres."

6. Ibid.

7. I. McGilchrist, *The Master and His Emissary: The Divided Brain and the Making of the Western World* (New Haven, CT: Yale University Press, 2009).

8. Plotinus, *The Six Enneads*, III.8.4.

9. S. W. Porges, *The Polyvagal Theory: Neurophysiological Foundation of Emotions, Attachment, Communication, and Self- Regulation* (New York: Norton, 2011).

10. Richard Maurice Bucke, *Cosmic Consciousness: A Study in the Evolution of the Human Mind* (Eastford, CT: Martino Publishing, 2010), 78–81.

11. Aristotle, *Metaphysics*, a paraphrase of the first two sections/chapters of Book I.

12. M. R. Longo, A. Kosobud, and B. I. Bertenthal, "Automatic Imitation of Biomechanically Possible and Impossible Actions: Effects of Priming Movements versus Goals," *Journal of Experimental Psychology: Human Perception and Performance* 34, no. 2 (April 2008): 489–501.

13. Baum, *The Wonderful Wizard of Oz*, 84.

14. M. Anisfeld, "Only Tongue Protruding Modeling Is Matched by Neonates," *Developmental Review* 16, no. 2 (1996): 149–161.

15. Terje Falck-Ytter, Gustaf Gredebäck, and Claes von Hofsten, "Infants Predict Other People's Action Goals," *Nature Neuroscience* 9 (2006): 878–879.

16. This visualization combines well with the Wise and Loving Inner Voice Meditation in appendix B to discern a practical strategy with each of your monkeys.

17. This phenomenon is covered more deeply in chapter 8, "The Empathy Paradox."

18. Laozi, *Tao Te Ching*, chapter 61.

8. THE EMPATHY PARADOX

1. Robert Vischer (reprint and translation from the original German), "On the Optical Sense of Form: A Contribution to Aesthetics," *Empathy, Form, and Space: Problems in German Aesthetics, 1873–1893* (Texts and Documents Series) (Santa Monica, CA: Getty Center for the History of Art, 1993), 89–123.

2. E. B. Titchener, "Introspection and Empathy," in *Dialogues in Philosophy, Mental and Neuro Sciences, from Lectures on the Experimental Psychology of the Thought Processes* (1909): 7:25–30.

3. R. Hurlemann et al., "Oxytocin Enhances Amygdala-Dependent, Socially Reinforced Learning and Emotional Empathy in Humans," *Journal of Neuroscience* 30, no. 14 (April 7, 2010): 4999–5007.

4. W. Ickes, *Empathic Accuracy* (New York: Guilford Press, 1992), 2.

5. Karla McLaren, *The Art of Empathy: A Complete Guide to Life's Most Essential Skill* (Boulder, CO: Sounds True, 2013), 27.

6. Anne Katherine, *Where to Draw the Line: How to Set Healthy Boundaries Every Day* (New York: Fireside Publishing, 2000), 16–25.

7. Aristotle, *Aristotle on Rhetoric: A Theory of Civic Discourse*, trans. George Alexander Kennedy (New York: Oxford University Press, 1991), 119.

8. McGilchrist, "Reciprocal Organization of the Cerebral Hemispheres."

9. Sharon Stanley, *Relational and Body-Centered Practices for Healing Trauma: Lifting the Burdens of the Past* (New York: Routledge, 2016), 18.

10. Hecht, "Cerebral Lateralization of Pro- and Anti- Social Tendencies," 1–27.

11. Porges, *Polyvagal Theory*, 52–59.

12. D. Kalsched, *Trauma and the Soul: A Psycho-spiritual Approach to Human Development and Its Interruption* (London: Routledge, 2013), 6–10.

13. Plotinus, *The Six Enneads*, V.5.8.

14. Maryann Mott, "Did Animals Sense Tsunami Was Coming?" *National Geographic News*, accessed at http://www.dormanhigh.org/UserFiles/dorman_h/Documents/English/Denise%20Madonna/Did%20Animals%20Sense%20Tsunami%20Was%20Coming.pdf.

15. Plotinus, *The Six Enneads*, I.6.8.16.

16. Ibid., V.8.9.

17. Miles Menander Dawson, *Analects: The Ethics of Confucius* (New York: Bibliolife, 1915), 59.

18. Michael E. Kerr, "Eight Concepts," accessed at http://www.thebowencenter.org/theory/eight-concepts.

19. Previous trauma, unresolved issues, and primary love templates also provide triggers, and this assessment does not address these circumstances. The psychological strategies to resolve previous trauma and victim/perpetrator paradigms require further self-examination than the suggested solutions for somatic empathy–related problems.

20. Caitlin Matthews, *Psychic Shield: The Personal Handbook of Psychic Protection* (Berkeley, CA: Ulysses Press, 2006), 40–41.

21. Adapted from the original Integrated Awareness affirmation by Consuela Newton, 1996.

22. Ruth incorporated the Somatic Empathy Solutions into a daily practice.

23. Nischala Joy Devi, *The Healing Path of Yoga* (Berkeley, CA: Ten Speed Press, 2010), 13–14.

24. Laozi, *Tao Te Ching*, chapter 8.

9. HUMAN INCORRUPTIBILITY

1. Armstrong, *Plotinus*, I.2.4.

2. Baum, *The Wonderful Wizard of Oz*, 72–73.

3. *The Wizard of Oz* (1939, film).

4. Baum, *The Wonderful Wizard of Oz*, 27.

5. Plotinus, *The Six Enneads*, VI.4.16.

6. Laozi, *Tao Te Ching*, chapter 54.

7. Neil Douglas-Klotz, *The Hidden Gospel: Decoding the Spiritual Message of the Aramaic Jesus* (Wheaton, IL: Quest Books, 1999), 131–133.

8. Accessed at https://www.va.gov/opa/publications/factsheets/Suicide_Prevention_FactSheetNew_VA_Stats_07-06-16_1400.pdf.

9. Viktor E. Frankl, *Man's Search for Meaning* (Boston: Beacon Press, 1959), 88.

10. Ibid., 87.

11. Ibid., 137.

12. Ibid., 56–57.

13. Frankl gave many speeches around the world about man's search for meaning after the war. Perhaps his experience of infinite glory is why he likely told his audiences, "What is to give light must endure burning."

14. Thucydides, *History of the Peloponnesian War*, trans. J. M. Dent (New York: E.P. Dutton, 1910), chapter 17.

15. Walter Wink, *Engaging the Powers* (Minneapolis: Fortress Press, 1992), 175–184.

16. Walter Wink, *The Powers That Be: Theology for a New Millennium* (New York: Doubleday, 1998), 99–100.

17. Shelley Tougas, *Birmingham 1963: How a Photograph Rallied Civil Rights Support* (North Mankato, MN: Compass Point Books, 2010), 12.

18. Barry Eichengreen, *The European Economy since 1945: Coordinated Capitalism and Beyond* (Princeton, NJ: Princeton University Press, 2007), 57.

19. Rumi, "A Great Wagon," *The Essential Rumi*, 36.

20. Plotinus, VI.9.10. In Turnbull, *The Essence of Plotinus*, 221.

10. THE PROMISE OF WHOLENESS

1. Plato, *The Republic*, II, 413c.

2. *The Wizard of Oz* (1939, film).

3. Ibid.

4. Baum, *The Wonderful Wizard of Oz*, 99.

5. Hadot, *Plotinus or The Simplicity of Vision*, I.4.15, 81.

6. Porphyry, *Life of Plotinus* (*The Six Enneads* 38:6:22–23). In Turnbull, *The Essence of Plotinus*, 199.

7. Inge, *Philosophy of Plotinus*, volume II, 86.

CONCLUDING REMARKS AND HOPES

1. Henry Southgate, *Many Thoughts of Many Minds* (London: Griffin, Bohn, and Co., 1862), 338.

BIBLIOGRAPHY

ANCIENT PHILOSOPHY AND COMMENTARY

Armstrong, A. H. *Plotinus*, volumes I–VII. Cambridge, MA: Harvard University Press, 1966–1988.

Aristotle. *Aristotle on Rhetoric: A Theory of Civic Discourse*. Translated by George Alexander Kennedy. New York: Oxford University Press, 1991.

———. *De Anima* (On the Soul). Translated by Hugh Lawson-Tancred. London: Penguin Classics, Reissue Edition, 1987.

———. *Metaphysics*. Translated by Hugh Lawson-Tancred. London: Penguin Classics, New Edition, 1999.

———. *Nicomachean Ethics*, vol. 19. Translated by H. Rackman. Cambridge, MA: Harvard University Press, 1934.

Bucke, Richard Maurice. *Cosmic Consciousness: A Study in the Evolution of the Human Mind*. Eastford, CT: Martino Publishing, 2010.

Burnet, John. *Early Greek Philosophy*. 3rd Edition. London: A & C Black Ltd., 1920.

Confucius. "The Doctrine of the Mean." Accessed at https://en.wikiquote.org/wiki/Confucius.

Dawson, Miles Menander. *Analects: The Ethics of Confucius*. New York: Bibliolife, 1915.

Hadot, Pierre. *Plotinus or The Simplicity of Vision*. Translated by Michael Chase. Chicago: University of Chicago Press, 1976.

Hines, Brian. *Return to the One: Plotinus's Guide to God-Realization*. Salem, OR: Adrasteia Publishing, 2004.

Inge, William Ralph. *The Philosophy of Plotinus*. London: Forgotten Books, 2012.

———. *The Philosophy of Plotinus*, volume II. Gifford Lectures at St. Andrews, 1917–1918. Eugene, OR: Wipf and Stock Publishers, 2003.

Laozi. *Tao Te Ching*. Translated by Feng Gia Fu. New York: Vintage Books, 1972.

Plato. *Apology, Crito, and Phaedo of Socrates*. Translated by Henry Cary. Philadelphia, PA: David McKay Publisher, 1897.

———. *Phaedrus*. Translated by Paul Woodruff. Indianapolis, IN: Hackett Publishing Company, 1995.

———. *The Republic*. Translated by Desmond Lee. New York: Penguin Books, 1955.

———. *Symposium*. New York: Penguin Books, 2003.

———. *Theaetetus*. Translated by Harold Fowler. Cambridge, MA: Harvard University Press, 1921.

Plotinus. *The Six Enneads*. Translated by Stephen MacKenna and B. S. Page. Accessed at http://classics.mit.edu/Plotinus/enneads.html.

Porphyry. "Life of Plotinus." *Theosophy* 25, no. 3 (January 1937): 101–110. Accessed at http://www.wisdomworld.org/setting/plotinus.html.

Southgate, Henry. *Many Thoughts of Many Minds*. London: Griffin, Bohn, and Co., 1862.

Thucydides. *The Peloponnesian War*. Translated by J. M. Dent. New York: E.P. Dutton, 1910.

Turnbull, Grace H. (compiler). *The Essence of Plotinus. Extracts from the "Six Enneads" with Porphyry's "Life of Plotinus."* Translated by Stephen McKenna. New York: Oxford University Press, 1948.

Wallace, Edwin. *Aristotle's Psychology*. Cambridge: Cambridge University Press, 1882.

MODERN PSYCHOLOGY

Anisfeld, M. "Only Tongue Protruding Modeling Is Matched by Neonates." *Developmental Review* 16, no. 2 (1996): 149–161.

Beard, Elizabeth. "Public Penance, Public Salvation: An Exploration of the Black Death's Influence on the Flagellant Movement." 2013. Accessed at http://history.ucsc.edu/undergraduate-research/eletronic-journal/journal-pdfs/1415_Beard.pdf.

Covey, Steven. *The Seven Habits of Highly Effective People: Powerful Lessons in Personal Change*. New York: Simon and Schuster, 1989.

Dalberg-Acton, John, 1st Baron Acton. Letter to Bishop Creighton (1887). Accessed at https://en.wikipedia.org/wiki/John_Dalberg-Acton,_1st_Baron_Acton.

Devi, Nischala Joy. *The Healing Path of Yoga*. Berkeley, CA: Ten Speed Press, 2010.

Douglas-Klotz, Neil. *The Hidden Gospel: Decoding the Spiritual Message of the Aramaic Jesus*. Wheaton, IL: Quest Books, 1999.

Eichengreen, Barry. *The European Economy since 1945: Coordinated Capitalism and Beyond*. Princeton, NJ: Princeton University Press, 2007.

Eliot, Lise. *Pink Brain, Blue Brain: How Small Differences Grow into Troublesome Gaps and What We Do About It*. New York: Mariner Books, 2010.

Falck-Ytter, Terie, Gustaf Gredebäck, and Claes von Hofsten. "Infants Predict Other People's Action Goals." *Nature Neuroscience* 9 (2006): 878–879.

Frank, Anne. *The Diary of a Young Girl*. New York: Doubleday, 1996.

Frankl, Viktor E. *Man's Search for Meaning*. Boston: Beacon Press, 1959.

Harbour, Dorothy. *Energy Vampires: A Practical Guide for Psychic Self-Protection*. Rochester, VT: Destiny Books, 2002.

Hecht, D. "Cerebral Lateralization of Pro- and Anti-Social Tendencies." *Experimental Neurobiology* 23, no. 1 (March 2014): 1–27.

Hicks, Esther, and Jerry Hicks. *Ask and It Is Given: Learning to Manifest Your Desires*. Carlsbad, CA: Hay House, 2004.

Hurlemann, R., et al. "Oxytocin Enhances Amygdala-Dependent, Socially Reinforced Learning and Emotional Empathy in Humans." *Journal of Neuroscience* 30, no. 14 (April 7, 2010): 4999–5007.

Ickes, W. *Empathic Accuracy*. New York: Guilford Press, 1992.

John of the Cross. *The Dark Night of the Soul*. Translated by E. Allison Peers. Mineola, NY: Dover Publications, 2003.

Katherine, Anne. *Where to Draw the Line: How to Set Healthy Boundaries Every Day*. New York: Fireside Publishing, 2000.

Kalsched, Donald. *Trauma and the Soul: A Psycho-spiritual Approach to Human Development and Its Interruption*. London: Routledge, 2013.

Kerr, Michael E. "Eight Concepts." Accessed at http://www.thebowencenter.org/theory/eight-concepts.

Krishnananda, Swami. *Studies in Comparative Philosophy*. Rishkesh, India: The Divine Life Society, 1999.

Lamartine, Alphonse Marie Louis de Prat. *France and England: A Vision of the Future.* London: H. G. Clarke & Co., 1848.

Longo, M. R., A. Kosobud, and B. I. Bertenthal. "Automatic Imitation of Biomechanically Possible and Impossible Actions: Effects of Priming Movements versus Goals." *Journal of Experimental Psychology: Human Perception and Performance* 34, no. 2 (April 2008): 489–501.

Matthews, Caitlin. *Psychic Shield: The Personal Handbook of Psychic Protection.* Berkeley, CA: Ulysses Press, 2006.

McGilchrist, I. *The Master and His Emissary: The Divided Brain and the Making of the Western World.* New Haven, CT: Yale University Press, 2009.

———. "Reciprocal Organization of the Cerebral Hemispheres." *Dialogues in Clinical Neuroscience* 12, no. 4 (December 2010): 503–515.

McLaren, Karla, *The Art of Empathy: A Complete Guide to Life's Most Essential Skill.* Boulder, CO: Sounds True, 2013.

——— *Energetic Boundaries: Practical Protection and Renewal Skills for Healers, Therapists and Sensitive People.* Boulder, CO: Sounds True, 2003.

Mott, Maryann. "Did Animals Sense Tsunami Was Coming?" *National Geographic News*, accessed at http://www.dormanhigh.org/UserFiles/dorman_h/Documents/English/Denise%20Madonna/Did%20Animals%20Sense%20 Tsunami%20Was%20Coming.pdf.

Orloff, Judith. *The Empath's Survival Guide: Life Strategies for Sensitive People.* Boulder, CO: Sounds True, 2017.

Parness, AlixSandra. *Activate Joy: Live Your Life Beyond Limitations.* Pompton Plains, NJ: New Page Books, 2012.

Pearsall, Paul. *The Heart's Code.* New York: Broadway Books, 1998.

Porges, S. W. *The Polyvagal Theory: Neurophysiological Foundation of Emotions, Attachment, Communication, and Self-Regulation.* New York: Norton, 2011.

Rizzolatti, Giacomo, et al., "Premotor Cortex and the Recognition of Motor Actions." *Cognitive Brain Research* 3, no. 2 (March 1996): 131–141.

Roach, G. M. *The Diamond Cutter: The Buddha on Managing Your Business and Your Life.* New York: Doubleday Books, 2000.

Rumi, Jalal al-Din. *The Essential Rumi.* Translated by Coleman Barks. New York: Harper One, 2004.

———. *Rumi Daylight: A Daybook of Spiritual Guidance.* Translated by C. A. Helminski. Boston: Shambhala, 1990.

Schucman, Helen. *A Course in Miracles.* New York: Viking, 1996.

Slate, Joe H. *Psychic Vampires: Protection from Energy Predators and Parasites.* St. Paul, MN: Llewellyn Publications, 2004.

Stanley, Sharon. *Relational and Body-Centered Practices for Healing Trauma: Lifting the Burdens from the Past.* New York: Routledge Publishing, 2016.

Titchener, E. B. "Introspection and Empathy." In *Dialogues in Philosophy, Mental and Neuro Sciences, from Lectures on the Experimental Psychology of the Thought Processes.* New York: The MacMillan Company, 1909.

Tougas, Shelley. *Birmingham 1963: How a Photograph Rallied Civil Rights Support.* North Mankato, MN: Compass Point Books, 2010.

Van Der Kolk, Bessel. *The Body Keeps Score: Integration of Mind, Brain, and Body in the Healing of Trauma.* New York: Penguin Books, 2014.

Vischer, Robert (reprint and translation from the original German). "On the Optical Sense of Form: A Contribution to Aesthetics." *Empathy, Form, and Space: Problems in German Aesthetics, 1873–1893* (Texts and Documents Series). Santa Monica, CA: Getty Center for the History of Art, 1993.

Wink, Walter. *Engaging the Powers.* Minneapolis: Fortress Press, 1992.

———. *The Powers That Be: Theology for a New Millennium.* New York: Doubleday, 1998.

Yogananda. "Self-Realization Fellowship Glossary." http://www.yogananda-srf.org/glossary/Glossary_R_%E2%80%93_S.aspx#.VEQeyldV0g4.

FAIRY TALES AND FILMS

Avatar. Film. Directed by James Cameron. Los Angeles: Twentieth Century Fox, 2009.

Baum, Frank L. *The Marvelous Land of Oz*. Chicago: Reilly & Britton, 1904.

———. *The Wonderful Wizard of Oz*. Chicago: George M. Hill, 1900.

Dr. Seuss. *How the Grinch Stole Christmas*. New York: Random House, 1957.

Groundhog Day. Film. Directed by Harold Ramis. Culver City, CA: Columbia Pictures, 1993.

Legend of Bagger Vance. Film. Directed by Robert Redford. Universal City, CA: Dreamwork Pictures, 2000. Script accessed at http://www.script-o-rama.com/movie_scripts/l/legend-of-bagger-vance-script.html.

The Matrix. Film. Directed by the Wachowski Brothers. Burbank, CA: Warner Brothers, 1999.

The Wizard of Oz. Film. Directed by Victor Fleming. Los Angeles: Metro-Goldwyn-Mayer, 1939.

INDEX

ABOUT THE AUTHOR

Eric Ehrke, LCSW, LMFT, is a determined pathfinder who understands the tangled overgrowth of illusion. Relieving suffering and restoring wounded hearts is his passion. During his forty-plus years of psychotherapy practice, Ehrke recognized early on that modern psychological wisdom, ancient philosophical principles, and complementary mind/body/spirit approaches universally lead humanity toward the promise of wholeness. Inspired, he has merged traditional knowledge with practical applications to create effective approaches to transform pain, transcend circumstances, and increase our capacity for love.

An active teacher and seasoned clinician, he has studied the eternal principles from the ancient philosophers and what makes mind/body/spirit healing modalities work. Additionally, he explores the metaphors within the classic fairy tales and the traditional behavioral, emotive, and cognitive psychological theories that effectively explain our current understanding of the human experience. After testing his original discoveries in the field of psychology and within the mind/body/spirit communities, Ehrke has added many new teachings, including the Primary Love Template and his Somatic Empathy Theory, and new critical exercises and stress responses.

He received his undergraduate degree in psychology and his master's degree in clinical social work at Ohio State University. Also a graduate of the Family Institute of Northwestern University, Ehrke is a member of the National Association of Social Workers, American Association for Marriage and Family Therapists, and Collaborative Family Law Counsel of Wisconsin. He is a Prepare/Enrich Pre-Marriage Assessment Facilitator and served as a student/faculty of the Inner Focus School of Soul Directed Advanced Energy Healing for twelve years.

Ehrke works at the Ommani Center, which is an intentional, integrated medical community in Pewaukee, Wisconsin. Married for thirty years, he lives in Wisconsin with his wife, a technology project manager, and close to his daughter, son-in-law, and granddaughter; a second daughter lives in Chicago, Illinois.

It is said that wisdom and pain are humanity's primary teachers. After personally exploring suffering in great detail, Ehrke offers this book as an alternative solution. He considers *The Promise of Wholeness* a living, breathing entity, and over time, new insights, tools, and wholeness strategies will unfold. Please visit his blog and website often to stay in touch and to learn more navigational insights on your own journey to wholeness. His website is http://ericehrke.com.